INSPIRED

INSPIRED

STORIES OF SPORTING GREATNESS

SIR STEVE REDGRAVE

with Sue Mott

headline

First published in 2009
by HEADLINE PUBLISHING GROUP

1

Cataloguing in Publication Data is available from the British Library

Hardback ISBN 978 0 7553 1964 0

Typeset in Baskerville by Ellipsis Books Limited, Glasgow

Printed and bound in Great Britain by
Clays Ltd, St Ives plc

Headline's policy is to use papers that are natural, renewable and
recyclable products and made from wood grown in sustainable forests.
The logging and manufacturing processes are expected to conform to
the environmental regulations of the country of origin.

HEADLINE PUBLISHING GROUP
An Hachette UK Company
338 Euston Road
London NW1 3BH

www.headline.co.uk
www.hachette.co.uk

To Francis Smith, Mike Spracklen and Jurgen Grobler
who helped, guided and inspired me to be the best I could be
and without whom it would never have happened.

CONTENTS

ACKNOWLEDGEMENTS

I WOULD LIKE TO thank all those friends, athletes and champions who gave up their time to talk about their experiences for this book. Even the ones that were rude about me. It was great to hear from Bobby Charlton, Seb Coe, Nicole Cooke, James Cracknell, Robin Dixon (now Lord Glentoran), Tim Foster, Cathy Freeman, Katherine Grainger, Tanni Grey-Thompson, Jurgen Grobler, Lewis Hamilton, Matt Hampson, A. P. McCoy, Matt Pinsent, Oscar Pistorius, Francis Smith, and Shane Warne and I am very grateful.

Also thanks to my PA Melanie Clift, for all the help and the sandwiches, to Michael Pask, Vicky Bryant and Sarah Wooldridge at IMG for their support and encouragement, to Rhea Halford and David Wilson at Headline for their insight and guidance, and to Sue Mott for her shorthand and persistence.

Finally, a heartfelt thanks to my family, Ann, Natalie, Sophie and Zak for their understanding and tolerance – especially when it comes to golf.

INTRODUCTION

To be honest, I can't tell you what inspired me. Not with absolute conviction. I can say that it might have been the Olympians I watched and admired on television when I was growing up. It might have been the discovery that I was good at a sport that hadn't previously crossed my mind. It might have been the support of a close and happy family. It might very well have been down to my stubborn nature for which I seem to have become renowned.

It is impossible to completely break up human motivation into its constituent parts. All I know is that by the time I reached Sydney in 2000, I was truly fired up and inspired to give everything for one last assault on an Olympic gold medal.

I lived for winning as an athlete. It was my obsession and my goal but looking back now from a vantage point of nearly ten years I can clearly see that my determination to win was backed up by other attributes I had either stored in my DNA or gained along the way.

Realising this has made me think about the qualities that successful athletes share. Physically, mentally, emotionally we're all different, but show me an athlete without a deeply-ingrained competitive drive and I will show you a loser.

But there's more to it than the pure blind urge to beat an opponent, whether that opponent be Joe Frazier, a racehorse or – as I have painful cause to know – a golf course. Competitiveness without work ethic, confidence and dedication is just another bad golfer beating up his clubs.

For this book I ransacked my memory of those moments in my life that I felt were formative to my career. Some things are painful to remember: the illnesses, the injuries, my mounting sense of panic in Atlanta, the death in front of my eyes of my best friend. Other things were wonderful: the partnerships and friendships you make through sport, the sense of elation and relief with every Olympic victory, the tragicomedy of suffering that is a rower's training routine and the masochistic pleasure I used to draw from it.

Through it all my family have been incredibly supportive. First my parents and my sisters inherited the short straw, then my wife and children had to put up with me as I went through the turbulent ups-and-downs familiar to every sportsman and woman. An athlete chasing his Olympic dream once is not necessarily a joy to live with. Let alone five successive times over two decades.

But there they all were – my family – in Sydney. My eldest sister, Christine, was not going to be there, but four days before the final her partner said to her: 'Look, why don't you go. If you don't, you might regret not witnessing the whole thing first hand.' So she did come and we were all there together to celebrate the victory, three generations of Redgraves, all of whom had been put through the wringer by one man over the years – me. Perhaps in some small way the champagne made up for the rest of it.

I'm not unique in this. For every athlete I have admired and drawn inspiration from, there will be a family acting as back-up. You can aspire alone, but you need a team to achieve. Family, coaches, supporters all play their massive part in the gathering of sporting trophies. The gold medals I won at the Olympics are in my care, but a piece of them belongs to other people who helped me along the way. Especially to my coaches: Francis Smith when I was a schoolboy, Mike Spracklen when I graduated to the British team and Jurgen Grobler with whom I won three of my five medals.

In writing this book I talked to good friends and acquaintances in different sporting fields to understand what inspires them. It was both a pleasure and slightly worrying to see how much we had in common. Many are fellow obsessives who give themselves ten out of ten for competitiveness. All of us are endowed with strong self-belief which, I hope, is not the same as arrogance. All of us have been prepared to graft for our ambition.

I started to build a picture of what it takes to achieve not just in sport but in life. For a start, you get nowhere without preparation. Success in rowing entirely depends on half-killing yourself every day of your career. I admit rowers take endurance to an extreme, but in no sport do you succeed without working very, very hard towards your goal.

Tiger Woods isn't a great golfer because he was born with a gift. He was born with a gift *and then he practised*. Jonny Wilkinson isn't a great kicker because the skill was innate. He's a great kicker because *he practised kicking for up to five hours a day*. These high-achieving global superstars are not randomly decided. They are exalted because they put the work in. I firmly believe that nothing worthwhile can be gained without effort. You might have one day's fluke without it, but a lifetime's failure.

Self-confidence, belief, mental toughness are different ways to describe the same thing. I wasn't an extrovert kid. You wouldn't have picked me out of the schoolroom as the boy most likely to succeed. I was shy and retiring, I guess. I had dyslexia. I was in the remedial English class. If anything. I had cause to suffer self-doubt. But being good at rowing – later very good at rowing – gave me confidence. It was something I could do, so it was something I liked doing. The more regattas I won, the more I thought I could win. It became a self-fulfilling prophecy.

Others took an entirely different route to belief. Muhammad Ali for one, born with as much confidence and charisma as any man on the planet. I loved watching him fight when I was young. To me he was a compelling and wonderful figure, perhaps my favourite sportsman when I was growing up. Obviously I didn't treat him as a role model. No one could accuse me of being a self-publicist or telling the world 'I'm the greatest', but in a quiet way I acknowledge that self-belief is essential to any kind of enterprise, in life, in business, in sport.

Unless you lead a charmed life, it all goes wrong occasionally. There cannot be a single sports person who hasn't suffered some kind of downturn in their career. It can be minor; it can be a major calamity. It is not the event that defines you, it is your response to that event.

Lance Armstrong's fight against cancer remains one of the landmarks of human, let alone sporting, comebacks. I thought my career was dead and buried when I was diagnosed with diabetes three years before the Sydney Olympics. For some reason, my doctor didn't think so. With medical help, my team-mates' understanding, my family's unswerving support, I kept going. There were times when the quest bordered on lunacy. But there were also times when it all came together. It is not the adversity itself which destroys us, but the urge to give in when the going gets tough.

Obsession helps. It blinds you to pain and the difficulties strewn in your path. It probably drives all the people around you mad, but the nice word for obsession – determination – is crucial in getting to the top.

Funnily enough, few athletes I know – if any – admit to being obsessed. We all think it's perfectly normal to divert every avenue of your life towards one huge, if temporary, goal. For some, training becomes an end in itself. For others it is winning, and then winning, and then winning again that provides the essential motivation.

Either way, look at the commitment of the national hunt jockey Tony McCoy to riding winners, the extraordinary focus of cyclist Nicole Cooke, my seemingly endless pursuit of the next gold medal, and you probably see a crazy person. Unless you are a fellow athlete. Then you just see someone pursuing their sport.

For some, it will be the bestowal of star quality, the X-factor that marks them as different from the crowd. Shane Warne has that in such massive dosage that he was the single most important factor, in my view, of Australia's cricketing domination for a decade.

As men, we couldn't be further apart in terms of personality. But as contributors to our sport, I would be proud to think I was trying to give as much back to rowing as it gave to me and as Shane gave to cricket. My support for Katherine Grainger and her bid for an Olympic gold medal, means almost as much to me now in retirement as rowing for a medal of my own once did. I would love to see her succeed. Not because it would change her as a human being but because the whole purpose of sport is to strive for something tantalisingly difficult. If it was easy, who would bother?

We're born survivors, the human race, and so we are programmed to reach out for attainments that hover just out of reach. If someone told me when I was nineteen that I would row at the next five Olympics, I would have dismissed them as insane. But each attainment made me believe that the next one might be possible. Even when the last attempt – in Sydney – became obscured by illness and poor performance, I didn't quite lose faith in myself. Nearly, but not quite.

I persevered. Not a glamorous trait, but probably the most important of them all. Sometimes your nerve will desert you, sometimes luck plays a vicious trick, sometimes your body fails to function efficiently and sometimes you're just dead on your feet and despairing. Then you pick yourself up, view the lengthening odds with disdain and bloody well get on with it. You know it's not easy, but it's a challenge.

Those that win for a living like a challenge.

1

PREPARATION

I<small>T'S PITCH DARK</small>, of course, when the alarm goes off. That shouldn't surprise me. I've been getting up in the dark for about twenty years. God, I hope it's not raining. I roll out of bed and listen. It's raining. It is 6.45 a.m.

I look around for my kit and start to step into it, but some of the stuff could be anywhere. All these years as an Olympic athlete haven't taught me to get ready the night before. I pull layers on, one after the other: T-shirt, long-sleeved shirt, rugby shirt, sweat shirt and a sleeveless quilted jacket, in that order. In about three hours most of those layers will be lying in water at the bottom of a rowing boat, stripped off, piece by piece, as I get over-heated. I pack my bag with the other kit I'll need today: gym kit (soon to be soaked in sweat, lying on the window sill of the changing room in the Leander Club), a second lot of rowing gear and finally civvies to go home in (and, I hope, lie on the couch in while I catch up on my rest). I am an Olympic rower. I train, eat and sleep. That's it. Ask anyone. Ask my wife.

Ann is stirring as I make my first breakfast. Maybe I'll hear a few sounds from the children, but they know better than to direct any noises at me. I make a cup of tea and a large bowl of Shreddies, and eat standing up in the kitchen. The TV is on, but I'm not paying attention. Ann might be saying something to me. I grunt in reply. I am not a morning person. I'm an athlete, with all the pain, repetition and boredom that goes with it, occasionally lightened once every four years when it comes to winning a gold medal. That's a slight exaggeration. Just don't ask me to make sense of what I do at this time in the morning.

Damn, I'm running late. Not as late as Tim, who is always, without fail, the last one to arrive. Just as our coach, Jurgen, is always, without fail, the first one to arrive, immaculate, organised and ready, usually with a loaded clipboard in his hand. I pick up my tea cup and take it to the car. I'll just have to drain it on the way. I'm on automatic pilot for the twenty-minute journey, listening with half an ear to Radio Five.

This is how pre-programmed I am: on those rare days when we don't train in the morning, I take my two daughters to school and instead of taking them to school I find myself on the by-pass to the Leander Club. They never stop me. They think it's hilarious. They just sit in the back of the car and snigger.

I arrive at Leander, park the car and note that Matt and James are already here. Tim, of course, is not. He's the hippy of the outfit, the laid-back, easy-going character for whom early starts were certainly not invented. I'm next worst. Then Matt. Then James, who I think would happily bivouac in the grounds of the club, killing wild animals with his bare hands for protein, as committed as a Royal Marine.

Finally, a little after 8 a.m., we're all there, going for a jog in the rain along the riverbank. 'Jog' is an inadequate description. It's more of a 400 metre shoe shuffle, especially since I insist on wearing my flip-flops. Jurgen puts up with it because he knows there's no alternative. I'm 6' 4" and 17 stone. I'm not a long-distance runner.

It's getting lighter, but only just, as we haul the boat on to our shoulders and carry it down to the water. The rain drips down our necks and splashes up from the dark, swirling water of the Thames. God knows how many times I've done this, pushing off from the bank in hail, sleet, snow, ice, cloud, wind, sun. I've known every meteorological condition on earth, except a typhoon, but it doesn't make any difference. I've still got to row twenty kilometres and every stroke of the blade cutting through the Thames has to count. Four men in a boat, united in one quest. Four men in a boat, too bloody tired to speak to one another yet. Which suits me fine.

We row at a low, steady pace, holding our heart rate at about 120–140 beats per minute (bpm). I've been over 200 bpm, when normal people would be close to black out and even we get the taste of blood in our mouths. It's a popular belief that this happens to us every Olympic final, but it doesn't. We've trained four years for that moment. It's much more likely that we push our bodies into horrible overload at the first competitive race of the season. When you finish racing, the adrenaline subsides and you find every muscle screaming in pain.

It's nothing like that today. This is about endurance. It's rhythmic, repetitive and bloody boring. My mind's wandering. I'm thinking about going to the supermarket or something ridiculous. Then I'm thinking about a speech I have to make soon for my sponsor. I mentally shake myself out of it. I'm supposed to be thinking about nothing except the endless quest for the perfect rowing technique. 'Concentrate,' I tell myself silently.

Because this training method that Jurgen brought over from East Germany works. It's at the heart of our medal quest. It is the base-work on which we build our belief. We can hear his occasional instruction from the bank, as he cycles along the tow path, which he has marked, with typical Teutonic meticulousness, every 250 metres with a pink-painted wooden post. The pink isn't to interject a note of frivolity – it's the famed colour of the Leander Club.

'For this 1000 metres, quicker catches,' says James. That's it for conversation. Four strokes unite – or try to. We focus our minds together, making sure the oars enter the water smoothly, quickly, in perfect synchronicity. We're Olympic oarsmen, halfway to the next – my last – Games and we're going to win. Not try to. We will.

At last we're back at the dock, hauling the boat out of the water. The rain still drips steadily. I hate days like this. I hate them more than the icy days when the hairs in your nose freeze and icicles form at the back of your neck – at least the exertion warms you up. But on days like this it's just depressing. My only consolation is that at least I'm not an Olympic swimmer. All they've got is chlorine and submersion in water for hours and hours, watching a black line go by. However tedious training can be, at least we're outdoors, and we've got the seasons, and the riverbank and swans. I quite like swans, at least more than the Canada Geese that land in flocks on the water and poo all over the landing stage.

James is moaning. There's something wrong with the boat. 'The rig isn't right . . . It's not going fast enough . . . How can we expect to win a gold medal if . . .' There is nothing odd about this. James always comes off the water moaning and he's always the first to speak. We mount the boat on the trestle so it can be examined for all these faults that James has discovered.

He's dyed his hair again. 'Idiot,' I think. 'God, what's the point?' but I don't say anything. They think I'm the old man of this boat. Maybe I am, but my theory is this: why would you want to hand a rival team any excuse to think you're a wally? You want them to be scared of you. You want them to believe they can't beat you. You don't want them to think, 'That guy looks a prat. We're not going to get beaten by some guy with dyed bright red hair.' You don't want to give the opposition an excuse for pulling harder.

There was this annoying German guy. He always motivated me at the major events. We'd be doing a warm-up jog – OK, shuffle – before a race and he'd wave at us trying to wind us up,

13

going, 'Ooh, hallo. How are you?' We'd grunt, 'Fine, thank you very much,' but inwardly I'd be saying, 'I can't wait to get on the water and beat the hell out of you, mate.'

By now Tim is talking. He's the antidote to James. He felt good out there, he's taken positives from our row, he's refusing to be dampened by the mood of his rowing mate, which is some feat in this steady downpour. He's always like this – light to James's dark, cheer to James's gloom. Matt and I, the old hands, are less extreme.

We take our various shades of optimism and pessimism into the club for breakfast. We need fuelling, preferably with a vast bowl of porridge, and half a loaf and jam. As Olympic oarsman we have to eat between 6,000 and 7,000 calories a day, and we take this seriously, some more than others. Matt has a fry up. We all drink out of jugs. They don't even bother with cups at the club canteen. Tim says that some of his rowing pals at London University don't bother with plates either. One used to eat out of a dog bowl and another used a flower pot.

We're actually talking to each other now. It's the first sign of human communication. It's not exactly cerebral, but it's civil. Soon we might even attempt banter, especially if my football club, Chelsea, have lost. Actually, at the moment, we're swapping stickers for our World Cup Panini football albums. There's a race on to see who fills theirs first. I'm going to win this, because I've got a secret weapon. I've written to Panini for the remaining stickers. 'What are you smiling about?' asks James. 'Nothing,' I say.

There is absolutely no smiling for the next hour, just grimaces of pain as we do seventeen exercises with heavy weights and fifteen, twenty or thirty repetitions. I hate the exercises. Bench pulls, sit ups, press ups, dorsal raises, more bench pulls, squat jumps, lateral pulls, leg curls, side bends, step ups . . . I hate them all. All the other rowing nations do this, but we're the only ones who work like this. I've seen how the Australians do it. It's all very deliberate and focussed, but our approach is about intensity and speed. It's on another level.

No one speaks. No one can speak. I'm doing deep knee bends with a weight-carrying bar across my shoulders. No short cuts. Full squat, bum to heels. Thirty repetitions. It kills your knees, it kills your back. I've pinched a nerve in my neck. The pain is intense, but I've just got to get on with it.

It's an hour of torture, but we never short-change it. Our gym kit is stinking and soaked in sweat. We change and go for lunch. More calories. Pasta and pudding. Matt and I never skimp on pudding. I can see Tim frowning. He thinks Matt's too heavy. He thinks I'm too heavy, but not as heavy as Matt. There is friction between these two. They're two really nice guys and it's not obvious, but it's just there. I don't know why. Maybe it dates back to 1988 when they rowed in the junior championships. Tim was the star in those days. He was known as the better performer, but then Matt started rowing with me in 1989 and went on to win the Olympic gold in 1992. Maybe that's part of it. Maybe not. I don't ever ask. As long as the boat goes fast, that's all that matters.

Then it's back on the water for the third session of the day. This is the 12 kilometre technical row. Down to Hambleden Lock, back up to the club and once around Temple Island, the start of the famous Henley Royal Regatta course. Don't ask me about the folly on the island that I've rowed past about a thousand times. It's not an architectural wonder to me, it's a signpost. I like it best when the signpost reads 'Nearly over'.

Tim, our best technical rower, tends to lead these sessions. It's still endurance-based, but more analytical, and we scrutinise every stroke and every improvement to every stroke we can make. 'Roll-ups,' says Tim and we start from backstops, push the oars down, slide forward, put the blades in the water, but don't pull. We're concentrating hard. I've forgotten it's still raining. Somewhere I'm registering the still sodden conditions out there, but when you've been doing it for six hours a day, seven days a week, forty-nine weeks a year, for about twenty-two years, it's like water off a mad oarsman's back. It hurts, but it's what you do. It's what you have to do.

JOHN NABER

Sport isn't always about the most talented. Talent is a God-given raw material, but it's what happens next that counts. In my case, I worked at it. I had the body and the aptitude for rowing at the start, but for the next twenty-five years I worked like a bull, pig-headedly, stubbornly, relentlessly. Basically, I didn't let it drop. The gains, the improvements, were noticeable. How small did the gain have to be? Virtually imperceptible, as long as it was a gain. And you did it again and again, and again, and again, over hours, weeks, days, months, years, decades. The ramparts were built on the foundations of tiny, but appreciable, improvements.

That may explain my fondness for the story of a college kid from Evanston, Illinois, whom you've probably never heard of. He went to the Munich Olympics as a 'domestique', a training partner who doesn't compete in the finals, for Mark Spitz. This sixteen-year-old kid, a college backstroke champion, had been recruited to help his much more glamorous colleague win seven gold medals in one Games. He did the job. He swam for the medley relay team that qualified for the final, but having done the donkey work he was ejected in favour of the more famous names in the final. He didn't complain. He simply made a vow. Next time it would be different.

The story of John Naber is one I often use in motivational speaking. It's about finding a way to make the impossible possible. I like that idea. If someone had said to me before the Los Angeles Olympics in 1984 that I was going to win a gold medal in five successive Olympic Games, I'd have thought they were out of their mind. It was, I would have said, completely impossible – but somehow it happened. The story of John Naber explains why.

Not many people remember the name Naber. Spitz still adorns the record books, even though Michael Phelps has over-taken his tally with eight gold medals in Beijing, but Naber's vow to himself and its outcome is as inspirational as anything I have come across in sport.

His vow was this: that in the next Olympics, in Montreal, he would not only swim as an individual as opposed to a disposable member of a team, but he would also compete in his favourite event, the 100 metres backstroke and, furthermore, he would win. He did his homework, this college kid. He went back through the record books and calculated, by looking at the improvements in times from Olympics to Olympics, that he could achieve his ambition with a time of 55.5 seconds. The only flaw in this was that his personal best time was 59.5 seconds, a full four seconds slower, which in swimming terms might as well have been an eternity.

At this point Naber did what I did after the Seoul Olympics in 1988: he came close to giving it all up. In my case it was because of rowing overload. I'd been doing virtually nothing else for ten years. In Naber's case it was from pure disenchantment with the numbers. How the hell was he going to make up a margin like four seconds in four years?

Maybe it was the simplicity of the maths that made him think again, but he then looked at it in an entirely different way. He had four years to make up four seconds, but try breaking that down and it sounded a whole lot better. He had a whole year to improve by just one second. One year – one second. Deal.

Then he broke it down again. He trained for ten months a year, so he would only need to improve by one tenth of a second over the space of a month. There are roughly thirty days in a month, so he would only need to improve by one three-hundredths of a second every day. He trained for four hours every day, so he only needed to improve by one twelve-hundredth of a second every hour.

The blink of a human eye takes five twelve-hundredths of a

second. All he had to do was improve by a fifth of an eyeblink in every hour's training and he would be fast enough to win the gold medal in Montreal. How hard was that? Premature retirement was shelved. He climbed back into the pool and kicked on. The chlorine dream revived.

It was then he realised the hard part. That fraction of an eyeblink was easy – once. A doddle – twice. No sweat – ten times, maybe twenty times. But he had to make that minuscule, yet measurable, improvement every hour of every day of every training month of every year for four solid years. Could he do it? Could he summon the pitiless dedication and endless hours in the pool required to achieve his goal?

He made the Montreal Olympics and the final of the men's 100 metres backstroke, where he faced the East German, Olympic and world champion, Roland Matthes, who had been undefeated for seven years from 1967–74. The start gun sounded. Exactly 55.49 seconds later Naber was hailed the new Olympic champion and world record holder. Matthes, who had suffered an appendectomy six weeks before, came third, nearly two seconds slower.

Naber went on to win four gold medals in Montreal and must go down in sporting history as the finest example of human refusal to be deterred by an apparently insurmountable goal. History has all but forgotten him, but not me. As a fellow stubborn operator, he has my all-time admiration.

TIGER WOODS

The first and so far only time I met Tiger Woods was hardly guaranteed to boost my self-esteem. It was on a makeshift tee in Hyde Park in 2000, not long after the Sydney Olympics, where Matt and I had been invited to join him from the audience as he gave a public demonstration of his prowess with the golf club. I remember standing there, praying, 'Please, please, please don't ask me to hit a shot.' Can you imagine how awful it would be? Like giving Lewis Hamilton a lift.

In the event, Matt distracted him by letting him borrow his gold medal (he wasn't having mine) and we were spared the ritual humiliation. I am not saying I'm bad at golf. My handicap is 14. It has been as low as 13.7, if I'm being specific, but I still get nervous at pro-am tournaments. One misguided lash and you could kill someone. Rowing is a good deal safer. Unless you happen to be a duck.

Tiger is, if not the greatest golfer of all time, one of them. I'm probably not in the top million. I know why. I'm lazy. Training at one sport has been enough for me. When it comes to golf it is pleasure, sometimes a grim pleasure, but there's no way I'm going to expend precious energy when I'm just about good enough to beat Matt. Sometimes.

We like golf. Occasionally we liked it so much we might neglect to mention either to Ann or Jurgen that we were just off for a quick round. We didn't have much else to do as light relief. Dangerous sports were banned, and when Matt had once tried to take me up in a helicopter we had discovered that between us we exceeded the maximum payload and were grounded. Golf was the sensible, civilised response to our leisure requirements.

Our preparation would be pretty basic: grab clubs, drive to course, put ball on first tee, agree to play for a fiver (as things stand at the moment, Matt owes me about £1,000,005) and hope for the best. Tiger is a little more scientific.

He was trained to play golf from birth, although you have to be careful to separate truth from myth when it comes to the precocious skills of baby Tiger. So prodigious has his talent proved to be that legend insists he was going round courses under par before he was out of nappies. That can't be true, can it? However, he did appear on an American TV show at the age of two, putting against Bob Hope, and won his first tournament at the age of four, beating an extremely crushed ten-year-old. As child prodigies go, he was a sporting Mozart.

The preparation, there can be no doubt, had been laid down by his late father, Earl. The former Vietnam War Green Beret dedicated his life to raising an exceptional American citizen and chose golf as the vehicle. There was a reason for this. He was forty-three when Tiger was born. He had been forty-two when he discovered golf and the mesmeric effect golf has on certain humans was still in full operation by the time Tiger came along.

Earl played jazz to baby Tiger when he was just five days old to sow the seeds of musical appreciation. In just the same way he would sit Tiger in his high chair in the garage and let his little son watch with curious fascination as he hit golf ball after ball into a specially strung-up net. Far from being bored by the enterprise, the youngster was raring to have a go.

By eleven months, according to Earl, Tiger had a serviceable golf swing. By the time he could speak he was practising every day. When he was four he beat the local pro over nine holes. He was freakish in his understanding and execution. His dad was by his side every day.

This is not the way most sportspeople prepare for their career. It is certainly not the way I prepared. I had no idea I'd ever sit in a rowing boat until I was nearly fourteen. I loved the Marlow regatta, but only because the fair came to town. And as for my dad grooming me for the sport – it didn't happen like that at all.

The only so-called sport we did together was fishing. I throught it was boring and, as I discovered later, he hated it, too. We both secretly thought it was one huge waste of time, but went through with it out of some misplaced idea of male bonding. I don't know how much bonding actually happened while I went off to play in a field. Dad took anything I happened to catch off the line and that was the last I saw of it. I hate fish.

If anything, Dad prepared me best by letting me get on with my sport. A quiet man, a loner by nature, he was always self-employed, mainly in the building business. He and my mum never pressurised me to get a job, so I could train like a professional even when rowing was still amateur. I did occasionally enter the work market as a teenager, sometimes as a self-taught landscape gardener (more rocks than flowers) and sometimes on one of Dad's building sites. He used to call me 'the Foreman' though, because I stood around with my hands in my pockets, not actually doing anything useful.

I didn't come up the Tiger way then, but I understand fully

one aspect of Earl's design. When he said, 'Son, you get out of it what you put into it – no short cuts,' he was telling no more than the truth. Tiger, it seems, never shirked practice. As a toddler, his mum made him learn his multiplication tables over and over until she was satisfied, and only then would he be allowed to phone his father at work to arrange their practice session later in the afternoon. I would imagine I was sitting around watching children's TV or, more likely, climbing up some dangerous bit of scaffolding when Tiger was already halfway to his first Amateur Championship.

When he was a little older, he and his father developed a putting game. They would keep placing the ball three feet from the hole and see how many consecutive putts they could make without missing. The idea was to keep going until one player missed, then the other would have his turn. Tiger started. Straight in the hole. He moved the ball back to three feet away again. Same thing. Straight in the hole. When he had done this seventy times in succession, Earl decided it was time for a drink. Game over.

Earl used to joke he'd 'created a monster'. He may have been right. Few sportsmen in the world possess Tiger's mental toughness. That was no accident either. Two tours of Vietnam, under fire, had given Earl an appreciation of strength of mind in battle. He claimed he used the prisoner-of-war interrogation techniques he'd learned to foster mental rigour in his son. Basically, he gave him a hard time.

'I pulled every nasty, dirty, rambunctious, obnoxious trick on my son week after week after week. I dropped a bag of clubs at the impact of his swing, I imitated a crow's voice while he was stroking a putt. When he was about ready to hit a shot, I would toss a ball right in front of him, I would jingle the change in my pocket . . . in other words, I played with his mind. And don't forget, he was not permitted to say a word.'

Funnily enough, I understand that training. I learned to play golf with some rowing mates following the World Championships in Nottingham in 1986. The emphasis was on banter and ridicule, with the result that I feel quite at home if there's noise and distraction going on. It's the deathly silence at the start of a pro-am, when all eyes are trained on you and no one dares to breathe, that I find horribly intimidating.

Tiger also, I note, has a 'deliberate hook'. Even as a youngster, he developed the ability to hit a one iron over the perimeter fence of a driving range, make the ball turn from right to left, come back over the fence and land in the middle of the range. I can do something along those lines. In my case, it is called the 'accidental hook' and it has a close ally in my 'accidental slice'. Not to belittle myself completely, I also have a 'deliberate gentle fade', but I would be the first to admit it is hardly reliable and has a big problem negotiating trees.

I would have to give Tiger the edge if we were doing a head-to-head comparison. Earl didn't just create 'a monster', he created a winning monster. If Tiger had the strength of mind and purpose to win the US Open in June 2008, his fourteenth Major, with a double stress fracture in his left tibia and a ruptured anterior cruciate ligament in his left knee, it may have been because his dad had prepared him years ago for the task.

Earl said of golf, 'At a professional level, the game is ninety per cent mental,' and in fact you can say that of any sport. A fit physical specimen will make it to the start line, but only the mentally tough become champions. Not everyone will be coaxed to stardom by a dad who learned about toughness as a target for Vietcong sniper fire, but as preparation goes it's pretty thorough.

DICK FOSBURY

As an athlete I'm not built for the high jump. I'm not fat, but I'm dense. It would take a lot more than a ten-step run-up to fire my bulky frame seven feet into the air. Maybe a cannon would do it? However, I have nothing but admiration for the men and women, all built like the beanpoles I use gardening, who can leap higher than their own body height.

The greatest of them all, in my estimation, was the one-man revolution, Dick Fosbury. Now preparation doesn't get greater than this. As a sixteen-year-old kid in 1963, he was just a track-and-field athlete who was pretty average at the high jump and had a personal best of 5' 4". So he took the sport to pieces, turned it upside down and rebuilt it to win the Olympics in Mexico City five years later. That's not just preparation, that's engineering.

The 'Fosbury flop' is now enshrined as the jump of choice at the Olympics, for all that it was derided and maligned when first invented. How many athletes can say that? No one rows a 'Redgrave'. I may have won five gold medals, I may have enhanced the reputation of a sport that had been easy to ignore, but we sat in a boat and rowed backwards at the start of my career and we sat in a boat and rowed backwards at the end of it as well. My life changed, the sport changed (we became more professional and we won more), but the essential technical nature of the sport remained the same.

The crazy thing is that Fosbury didn't even have the Olympics in his sights when he started experimenting with the jump. An engineering student at Oregon State University, he simply realised that the traditional 'straddle jump' (taking off on the inside foot, swinging the outside foot up and over the bar, travelling face down) had its limitations. He began working on a version of the old 'scissor method' (jumping upright, kicking one leg and then the other over the bar), and evolution happened faster than Darwin ever envisaged. By racing up to the bar at great speed and taking off from his right (outside) foot, then twisting his body to travel over the bar head first, face-up and backwards, Fosbury converted his horizontal running speed to vertical take-off and perfected the 'flop'. In two years, his personal best rocketed from 5' 4" to 6' 7".

It's fascinating that Fosbury could 'evolve' like that, without the added spur of an Olympic medal to aim for: 'I adapted an antiquated style and modernised it to something that was efficient. I didn't know anyone else in the world would be able to use it and I never imagined it would revolutionise the event. I didn't train to make the Olympic team. I simply trained for the moment. I never even imagined I would be an Olympic athlete. It just seemed to evolve.'

There was a setback – war. The same war in which Earl Woods was engaged. Having succeeded so well in his high-jump career,

Fosbury was flunking his engineering degree. He was thrown out of university, which left him available for the draft and he was duly called up for Vietnam. With exquisite irony, he was then turned down by the military after X-rays revealed he had a bad back. You have to wonder what his recruiting sergeant must have thought when, a year later in 1968, he watched, incredulously with the rest of the world, as Fosbury and his flop broke the World and Olympic records to win the gold medal in Mexico. He literally raised the bar. In his case to 7' 4 ¼". By 1980, thirteen of the sixteen Olympic finalists were using the Fosbury flop. The world record – a Fosbury flop – now stands at over 8 feet.

Not many athletes have the ingenuity to reinvent their sport in order to dominate it, but some have had the depravity to reinvent themselves and this was the era in which the taking of anabolic steroids began to debauch the concept of fair sport. But Fosbury didn't cheat and he didn't use chemical agents or chemistry. For him it was an issue of human bio-mechanics – how to get his body over a bar in the most efficient and effective manner. His solution changed his sport for ever, but at the time it was controversial. Being radical, different and American, there were those who immediately wanted to ban his invention, but history has made a different judgement. At every Olympics at which I've participated the Fosbury flop has been the chosen style of the jumpers, with only the occasional dissident. The man was a genius and the fact that he retired after the Mexican Games, aged twenty-one, to concentrate on the rest of his life shows he had a lot more common sense than I did.

LEWIS HAMILTON

First a word about cars. Cars have been heavily involved in both the best and worst surprises I've ever had in my life. I should add that I hate surprises.

The best happened moments after landing at Heathrow Airport in 2000, fresh from the celebrations in Sydney. I'd returned with a gold medal from my four previous Olympics to find a few family members waiting for me and perhaps an airport cleaner showing mild-to-nil interest. This time it was different. There were crowds of cheering people to support the successful GB team.

As we left the terminal the first thing I saw was a brand new, gleaming, silver Jaguar XJR. 'Mmmm,' I thought, 'that might be a "welcome home" drive from my sponsor,' but it was better than that. Ann pressed the keys into my hands. 'That's from me to you,' she said. I was stunned. It had always been a dream of mine to drive such a fabulous car. Somewhere I still own a glass jar half full of pennies which was supposed to be the start of my fund to buy one. Jeremy Clarkson had been driving one on *Top Gear* and when Ann saw me going dreamy-eyed, she'd asked, 'Is that the kind of car you want?' I'd nodded and consigned the thought to the bin. Now here it was, all silver, all powerful, all mine.

It was only when I was halfway home that another thought came to me. 'Hang on, we've got a joint bank account, so actually I've bought half this car,' but it seemed churlish to say so and, in the event, Jaguar never sent us the bill. They let me keep the car. That was my best ever surprise. And I became a Jaguar Ambassador.

My worst, ironically, also involves Jeremy Clarkson. I've been asked about the occasion many times, because, as well as being my worst ever surprise, it was also aired on national TV.

I remember the morning well. I had to be up at 5 a.m. to be driven to London for an appearance on breakfast TV. I was talking about Sporting Giants, the campaign to identify tall, strong men and women for sports where size matters, like rowing and volleyball. Then I was going to have a meeting at the London Mayor's office followed by a visit to IMG, my current agent. It was going to be a long day. Meanwhile, back in Marlow, the *Top Gear* team, including Clarkson, was descending on my house to commit the sacrilege of a makeover on my garden in the name of Sport Relief.

I have to say at this point that our house is pretty sacred. If I allow anyone to take photographs there, I make sure they do so with an anonymous background. *Hello!* magazine were allowed in just after Atlanta, but that was very shortly after we had moved in and so it was more of a building site. But that's it. Ann is similar to me. She is a very low-key person, who keeps herself to herself. There is no way she would open up our house for public viewing – or so I'd imagined.

However, I hadn't taken into account my daughter, Natalie, who was *Top Gear*-mad. Nor the appeal of doing something for a very worthwhile charity. Nor the fact that I'd once dug a hole for a swimming pool behind the garage and then left it sitting there unattractively for a whole year. Maybe I should have seen Ann's revenge coming.

My assistant Melanie came along to IMG to pick me up and

take me home. While we were driving I had to take a conference call from the trustees of my charitable trust and it didn't go well. I was not in a good mood. When I came out of my preoccupied daze we were at the Maidenhead junction of the M4 and I noticed that Melanie was receiving a huge number of texts. This struck me as pretty weird. We were only fifteen minutes from home.

'Do you want me to get those, Mel,' I asked her. 'Oh no, it's all right. They're just from Adam,' she said hastily. 'Yeah, well, I've known your husband longer than you have,' I said, mystified by this sudden secretiveness. Oh my God, I think she's having an affair, I thought, uncharitably. 'I'll tell you about it tomorrow,' was all she said.

We turned the corner of my road. There was a low-loader standing there, with a digger. 'That's weird,' I thought. 'No one's having work done round here.' We came up my drive and I saw my father's car parked behind the trees. 'That's weird, too,' I thought. 'Why hasn't he parked at the house?' Then I saw caterpillar tracks across my grass. 'Oh, good old Dad,' was my immediate thought, 'he's come to fix the septic tank.' Then we came round another corner and my brain just could not comprehend the scene before my eyes.

There was a fire engine. There was a crane. There was a digger overturned in a ditch. There was a greenhouse, but I don't have a greenhouse. There was a shed. THE SHED WAS ON FIRE. Melanie pulled up the car and said, 'Just enjoy yourself.'

I looked at her incredulously. 'No, I bloody well won't,' I said.

I didn't know what to do with myself. I put down the briefcase I was carrying and just marched around in circles. Jeremy Clarkson tried to come up and speak to me, but I was distraught. It seemed that for some insane reason the people close to me had thought I would be amused by contributing to a joke episode of *Top–Ground–Gear–Force* in which the three petrolhead presenters turned their attention to a makeover of my garden. But, no, I was not amused.

By now my two youngest children, Zak and Sophie, were in tears. I let myself into the house to try and calm down. This did not immediately work because I was greeted by my mother, who told me not to be so stupid, and to get out there and enter into the spirit of the thing. It's not every day you tell your mother to just shut up.

Eventually two producers came in to try and make peace. James May and Richard Hammond, the other two presenters of *Top Gear*, came in, too, and they struck me as nice blokes, but Clarkson just climbed in his car and cleared off.

Matt phoned me when the piece was televised. He said, 'Did you know anything about it?' I told him no, I didn't. He said, 'I thought so. You're not that good an actor.' A week after the incident it was our twentieth wedding anniversary. Ann and I still weren't talking. No cards, no presents. Nothing. On both sides.

So, when it comes to cars and all things connected, I have a set of profoundly mixed feelings. Like Lewis Hamilton, I learned to drive pretty early. I remember sitting on my dad's knee at the controls of a dumper truck when I was really young. I graduated to a digger. It took me a while to drive something as mundane as a car. When I did, it was not always with precision. I remember once going through a junction and being hit side-on by a car. 'How did that happen?' I wondered before it dawned on me that I had just sailed through a red light. But I'm not a speed freak. I wouldn't be braking into bends at 150 mph. Lewis, on the other hand, was prepared for these things.

I've met Lewis three times. Twice at the BBC Sports Personality of the Year awards. The second time I was presenting him with a runner-up award. 'Don't worry,' I whispered, 'it won't be long before you win the main prize.' But it was pretty obvious he wasn't worried anyway. He was cool, unfazed and a nice guy. He had just become the youngest ever Formula One world champion. Perhaps that made finishing runner-up to Olympic cycling gold medallist, Chris Hoy, in the BBC viewers' poll a little more bearable.

Lewis is an undoubted superstar in the most glamorous and rewarded sport in the world, and yet the man you meet is still the boy who grew up on a council estate in Stevenage. He has changed his address and his bank balance, but not his view of himself. He once said, 'I don't feel like a superstar. I don't understand people who do have that mentality "I'm a superstar!" It's just a job. It's a fantastic job and people perceive you for some reason as a superstar, but at the end of the day I'm just Lewis. I've always been Lewis and it's important to stay like that.'

I don't feel like a superstar either. I just see myself as someone who stumbled across rowing, got a lot of fun out of it and won races. Just because you win races shouldn't change you as a person. Obviously, success means you have more opportunities and they will shape you as an individual, but I don't feel I've changed fundamentally in who or what I am.

I will admit this, though. When I won my first gold medal in Los Angeles, joining that iconic roll call of British Olympians, I did think – in my ignorance – that when I came back to Marlow Bottom I'd be mobbed in the streets. It didn't happen. We were rowers not footballers and the level of interest was pretty low. Footballers younger than I was then now earn huge amounts of money, ridiculous amounts, and if someone had given me millions in my youth I'm sure it would have changed my outlook on life. As it was I had to wait twenty years to be an overnight success.

So they pay differently, but Lewis and I were both pitched into sports that might have been quite surprised to see us initially. When I started out there weren't many rowers from the local comprehensive on the river. It was, by tradition and perception, a toff pursuit for public schoolboys in peculiar blazers on their way to high public office. I was a comprehensive kid with conspicuous dyslexia on my way to a good CSE in woodwork.

Lewis was even more unusual in his surroundings, being black (a rarity in high-grade motorsport) and not rich (a virtual impossibility in high-grade motorsport), but that is where a parent's preparation can take you. Call it pushiness, insight, devotion or management, there is absolutely no doubt that Lewis

Hamilton would not be where he is today were it not for the uncannily correct calls made by his dad.

However, unlike with Tiger Woods, it was not the father who decided on the sport, it was the child – in Lewis's case via a battery-powered remote controlled electric off-roader. He was six. He was an early convert. When I was six I very much doubt I noticed the river except as some dim backdrop.

I've seen the archive footage from *Blue Peter* of the very young Lewis demonstrating his skill with the car, answering the presenter's questions politely, but never taking his eyes off the vehicle as he moved the joysticks with absolute precision. The champion was already half-formed, but natural talent is only ever part of the equation.

His preparation for world domination – achieved just sixteen years later – is a textbook case of getting all the ducks in a row. From beating the older kids at remote control car racing – you can imagine how annoyed some of them must have been – he moved on to kart racing on his eighth birthday in January 1993. His father, with limited access to money, working as he did for British Rail, had cobbled together the cash to buy a second-hand kart, which he had stripped, repainted and presented as a Christmas present. Understanding that this was only half the job, Anthony Hamilton had also bought a box trailer and a generator, which he intended to hook up to his old Vauxhall Cavalier. This would be their equivalent of an F1 motor home for the next few years. To complete the picture, Anthony took on extra curricular jobs, among them erecting signs for estate agents at £15 a sign.

That is the essence of preparation. To see clearly what needs to be done and to do everything possible to achieve it. It paves the way for performance. No preparation, no performance.

The performances, however, came. Even as a nine-year-old Lewis was extraordinarily good. He had an overwhelming desire to be the best; he would not be distracted, he had unquestionable talent; he had an instinctive feel for driving; and he had an amazingly supportive family, including his step-mother, Linda, and, by now, a younger brother, Nicholas.

There is no mistaking the deep affection between the half-brothers. The impact of Nicholas's cerebral palsy on Lewis is visible all the time. It seems to ground him. He is aware that high-achieving is a relative term; that victories of many different kinds can be won, even if they don't all end in champagne-spraying. 'He's an inspiration, not only to me, but to a lot of other people. Whenever I think I have problems I just think how many problems in life he has. I mean, he can't do half the things that I can do and yet he's always happy. For sure, having him as a brother has had a major effect on the way I think.' When everyone's telling you that you're wonderful, it can be easy to become caught up in the hype, but families have a good habit of bringing you back down to earth. It's hard to think of yourself as an icon when you're dropping the kids at school or doing the weekly grocery shop.

Meanwhile, the Hamilton story kept getting better. He was such a prominent talent in karting that his father's lack of finances was eased by the arrival of sponsors, including Jensen Button's father, who provided him with free engines. Events seemed to fall into place, but I don't believe that. Yes, there are elements of fortune, but events only fell into place because Lewis was the real deal and Anthony was propelling him. An example of this is the famous story of Lewis approaching Ron Dennis at an awards dinner. By winning the main national Cadet Championship when he was ten, Lewis attended a motorsport awards ceremony in central London. Anthony and his son could easily have sat there, enjoying the occasion, the food and the high-octane atmosphere, and gone home happier for the experience, but Anthony had a plan. He pointed out Ron Dennis, the head of McLaren, to his boy. 'Go over and tell him you want to drive for McLaren one day,' Anthony told him and, Lewis being Lewis, cool and unabashed by most things, he did.

It was preparation. Pure, opportunistic, clever preparation. If Lewis had not had the talent, had not continued the steep learning curve towards brilliance, had not demonstrated the mentality of a future champion, he would not have been signed into the McLaren Mercedes Young Driver Support Programme less than three years later. If that initial introduction had never happened, though, who knows if the story would have been the same.

In 2007 Lewis became the first black driver on the F1 grid and lost the World Drivers' Championship – by a point. In 2008 he became the youngest ever world champion – by a point. Orderly as ever. From June 2007 when he won his first Grand Prix in Canada and gushed, 'This is the best feeling I've ever had. You cannot compare it to sex. But you know? I would say it is better than sex. It is!' to November 2008 when he won the world title in Brazil was a very short space of time, yet he was ready. Maybe he was born ready. He was, after all, named 'Lewis Carl' by his parents, in the expectation he might have something in common with Carl Lewis. It turned out he would be about 140 mph faster around the bends, but the ambition was certainly right.

Champions can't be made at birth, of course, otherwise we'd all call our boys Martin Johnson and wait for them to become captain of the England rugby team. There is more to it and the Hamiltons unfailingly prepared the path for success. But that way of doing things doesn't work for everyone. I enjoyed the days working with my dad, but mainly because he was so easy-going. He was never demanding, probably because he had been brought up so strictly by his own father. Having been hit so often himself (even though he says he deserved it), he made a promise he wouldn't ever strike his children and he didn't, although he must have wanted to sometimes.

I remember one incident clearly. I used to love burning things and, because we had eight acres of land around the house, there was always room for a bonfire. My first job, when I was about twelve or thirteen, was stacking shelves in the fruit and veg shop in Marlow Bottom. I remember what I was paid, because it was 20p an hour. It was a big occasion when I received a 5p pay rise. At the end of the day I'd collect up the rubbish, Dad would come down in his transit van and we'd take it home to burn in the garden.

As time went by more extravagant materials were added to the pyre, like the plastic tunnels Dad used to grow crops when he started his market garden business. It is probably not ecologically recommended to burn yards of plastic tunnelling and as the flames went higher so did thick plumes of dark acrid smoke. 'Don't go near it,' Dad warned. 'That smoke releases the same gases that they used in World War One.' That gave me an idea. Although I was sheltered from the clouds, I pretended to choke and splutter for a joke. Dad, who'd been wandering away, came roaring back to rescue me to find me grinning back at him. Even then he didn't give me a bollocking. I don't think he had the temperament to be another Earl Woods or Anthony Hamilton. Which is just as well, because he didn't know a thing about rowing.

2

BELIEF

I'M AT THE WORLD CHAMPIONSHIPS in Copenhagen in 1987. Andy Holmes and I are competing in a rare and perhaps over-ambitious double. We are strong favourites in the coxless pairs, but we are also competing in the coxed event, with Pat Sweeney. It is a dummy run for the Olympics next year in Seoul, where we will be attempting the same feat. Some people think we're insane doubling up like this – then again, some people think rowers are insane, full stop – but we (I) like the idea of the challenge.

It's my fault. I'm the one who looked at the timetable and said, 'Let's go for it.' It's never been possible before because, traditionally, the finals of both events have been held on the same day in World Championships. The women's finals were always on Saturday, the men's on Sunday, but the governing body had a rethink. The men always pull a bigger crowd, so in search of a clever way to build a bigger audience over two successive days, they decided to split the sexes. Now the finals of men's and women's events are shared over the weekend and we can chase a new challenge.

There wasn't much argument when I 'explained' what I wanted. Andy, as usual, went with the flow and Penny Chuter, the Director of Coaching, found us a cox in Sweeney, who had spent some time coxing the women's eight and had been working in California. He couldn't join us immediately, but we found a very acceptable substitute at our training camp in Amsterdam. We settled a 50 kilo toolbox in the cox seat and it worked a treat.

When Pat took over the effect on our steering was dramatic – and I don't mean dramatically good. On our first outing we just about stayed in our lane, but he had us weaving from side to side like a drunk. Andy and I exchanged looks when it was over, thinking exactly the same thing. 'We're favourites to win an Olympic gold and we've just got this muppet on board. Bring back the toolbox.'

But that was last year. Now we've ironed out the problems and Sweeney is still on board, navigating a straighter line and, at last, an improvement on a box of spanners. We have just come from our training camp, in Amsterdam again, and appear to be in stupendous form. On one training run on the lake we unofficially broke the world record in the coxless pairs and almost broke the record in the coxed. We're flying. We're on fire. We feel great.

We could win gold in both events here and really frighten the opposition a year out from Seoul. That's the plan anyway, but that's always my plan – to intimidate the entire fleet of rivals before we start.

So far, so good. We have won heats in both events. There are less than twelve boats entered in the coxed pairs, so we are straight through to the final to face the Italian Abbagnale brothers, but we have to compete in the semi-finals for the coxless event and that's where things begin to unravel. Sport does this to you all the time. For reasons beyond science or calculation, things just start to go wrong.

Our semi-final does not feel entirely right. I am not sure how or why. The alarm bells aren't deafening, I am not unduly worried, but there is a slight buzz of concern in the back of my mind. The pressure of competition always adds an extra burden of weight. Sometimes we carry it well, like that toolbox in Amsterdam, but sometimes the strain is inexplicably tougher. And so we lose. We finish our semi-final third. It isn't disastrous, for the simple reason that everyone out there thinks we were just saving ourselves for the assault on two finals. They think it was a tactical row. Good. Let them think it. I might even persuade myself that's the reason, but I am not honestly sure.

So that was the build up to this moment, when we are competing in the first of those two finals, the coxless pairs, and our nearest rivals, the Romanians, are rowing in the next lane. They are decent the Romanians, but we are better. We also have the psychological edge. One of the Romanian camp is so awed by our size and strength that he nudges a friend of mine at a regatta, looking up at me, saying: 'How heavy is he?' My mate adds a few kilograms for graphic effect. 'Oh, he's so strong,' sighs the Romanian, already sinking to the depths of resignation. Perfect. Let them think I'm some kind of freakish physical specimen.

However . . . the specimen is having a bad day and our plan is unravelling fast. Andy and I have taken a lead, as we normally do at the start, and we're leading at the halfway point. This is where we would expect to push on and break any crew strong enough to have lived with us so far. This time it's different.

The Romanians are coming back at us. They're edging in front and I realise I'm dead. I'm absolutely dead. We've got another half of the race to row, another 1,000 metres, and I have nothing left to give. My legs, my back, my lungs have all retired for the day. Andy, blissfully unaware of this in the bow seat, shouts, 'OK, let's go' and I have nowhere to go except, possibly, over the side.

Somewhere buried in my brain, a small thought is forming: 'OK, you have to give it your best shot. Try or die.' I do a deal with myself. I'll row as hard as I can for ten strokes and that's it. If we're not in front, I'm giving up. Then I will have to stop before I actually die.

One . . . two . . . three . . . ten. That is all I have. Our boat spurts into a slender lead again as this superhuman effort translates (very temporarily) to speed. The Romanians watch us go and I can almost hear their thought process across the churning water. They are thinking, 'You know what, we've given it a great go. We've challenged the mighty Olympic and world champions. We have fought closely, but these are the favourites, all season. We are the reigning Under-23 world champions. We have done enough. OK guys, we can't beat the greatest coxless pair on the planet. Don't be silly. Let's give up and be happy with what we've got. In fact, hooray for what we've got.'

They don't stop physically, they are going through the motions, but mentally they have given up the race and grasped the silver medal, because we are Steve Redgrave and Andy Holmes. We are the physical freaks. Our reputation, pure and simple, is winning this world title. It sure as hell isn't my body.

In a minute, as the new world champion, I am going to have to carry this boat out of the water. I don't think I am going to be able to lift it one inch. I am mentally and physically exhausted. But I will. I'll put a mask of nonchalance on my face and somehow drag the thing out, as though I have endless reserves of energy and absolute faith in my strength. What a lie, but what a valuable lie. If you can spread your self-belief into the minds of your rivals, so that they believe you are invincible, too, some races are won on the start line. I am world champion today because the Romanians believed I would be. They believed it and, funnily enough, I am.

*

Barcelona 1992. The eve of the Olympic final. This is Matt's first Olympics and we're sitting around a table – him, me and our coach, Jurgen – going through the race plan and the tactics for the last time before bed. We're going through the motions really. We know what to do. We've been through it tens, if not hundreds, of times before, but it's all about reinforcing the message that our one sole purpose is winning the Olympic gold.

However, unbeknown to me, Matt is waiting for a deeper message. He is waiting for the magic formula that will somehow guarantee the victory to be revealed to him. He knows it will be coming, he just doesn't know when. He knows where it will be coming from, too. Jurgen Grobler, from the old German Democratic Republic, our coach for the last eighteen months, has been coaching rowers to win gold medals since 1972. He is a genius, a guru, a conjuror of precious metal. Now it's our turn. This is what Matt, aged twenty-one, is thinking, but tonight is not the night of magic messages. Jurgen just says, 'OK boys. Get some rest. See you in the morning.' That is definitely not 'it', Matt is thinking as we walk back to our room in the Olympic Village.

Matt reads for a while and then drops into a deep sleep. I've always found this extremely annoying. He keeps me awake with the light on while he relaxes with a book and then crashes out without a care in the world while I'm still struggling to fall asleep. But it doesn't bother me too much tonight. I have other thoughts to occupy me and eventually sleep comes.

We wake the next morning without the need of an alarm. The sleepy daze that normally characterises our first few hours is banished. We're focussed on the task in hand. There is no need for words. We have an Olympic final to contest.

We have one last on-shore debrief and Matt is still waiting for his message. He waits in vain. Jurgen is being his usual clear, specific, Germanic self. He has our boat on a trestle to give it a last minute polish and check. This is rather more prosaic than Matt was expecting. There is certainly no unlocking of mysteries going on.

OK, Matt's thinking, Jurgen's tantalisingly saving it to the final countdown. Of course, he is. Just as we come together an hour before the race begins for a nerve-easing jog by the lake, that's when Jurgen will finally reveal the magic formula. It makes sense. We perform our traditional shoe shuffle and return, Matt in a high state of anticipation, but Jurgen continues to say nothing.

It is now thirty-five minutes to race time and we carry the boat to the boating pontoons. Matt is impatience itself. Surely now, in these highly charged precious seconds before we go out to battle, Jurgen will reveal the key to lifelong Olympian success, known only to the chosen initiates? We lower the boat into the water. Jurgen reaches down to help push the boat away. It is now or never. He clears his throat and addresses us with his final portentous pre-race words – 'Ja, boys. Have a good race. I think you'll win.' What? Matt is inwardly screaming. That's it? That is it? This guy's won twenty-six gold medals and all he's got to say is, 'Have a good race. I think you'll win.' Funnily enough, we do.

*

Sydney 2000. The Olympic final, 250 metres into the race, 1,750 metres to go. I'm a 38-year old diabetic who suffers from colitis with a recent history of erratic training and my last ergo result was pathetic. My team-mates are, variously, a long-haired blond with two discs missing from his spine, a temperamental workaholic with a recent girlfriend problem and an Oxford-educated tank with a tendency to overeat. Our last competition brought us crushing defeat, my body strength is receding along with my hairline, I'm being tagged a liability, the Italians and Aussies are tough rivals, rowing is agony at the best of times, let alone when competing under the pressure of winning a fifth successive gold medal for yourself and your country, and yet . . . I am filled, at this moment, with the absolute conviction that we are going to win. Funnily enough, we do.

MUHAMMAD ALI

When we came off the water having just won the gold medal in Sydney, still dripping with sweat, the BBC was waiting to interview us. 'When did you know you'd won the race, Steve?' 'After 250 metres.' 'D'you mean with 250 metres to go,' Steve Rider corrected me, clearly thinking I'd be crazy to imagine the race won after only an eighth of the distance. 'No, I mean after 250 metres,' I said. I wasn't joking.

The trouble with self-belief is that it can look dangerously similar to madness. The outcome decides your level of sanity in the eyes of the world. If you go for the 'almost impossible' and succeed you are hailed a patriotic hero. If you aim for the 'almost impossible' and fail people shake their heads and call you a nut. Our win over Italy by 0.38 seconds made me a sane man.

I know that some people also thought I was arrogant. That's another peril of self-belief. It might have appeared arrogant in that exchange with Steve Rider, but it was only the truth. I genuinely felt that at the time, mainly because the belief doesn't spring from nowhere. It arrives because you work like a dog for years and years and years. I'd built stubborn faith in myself with decades of hard graft and experience. If that couldn't buy you 0.38 seconds when you needed them, then nothing else in the world would do it.

If the back-up isn't there, the rest is hot air and ego. I've seen that plenty of times; athletes who talk themselves up with great conviction and then burst like a balloon when they lose. Reality is hard to avoid in sport. You can con the people, you can con yourself, but you can't con the finishing line.

Self-belief – or the will to win, mental toughness, whatever you want to call it – is probably the most crucial factor in sporting success. The bodies are roughly equal, the training is similar, the techniques can be copied, what separates the achievers is nothing as tangible as split times or kilograms. It is the iron in the mind not the supplements that wins medals. Poignantly, given the sad disabilities now suffered by a once-colossal athlete, no one embodies this invisible power of self-belief more than Muhammad Ali.

I have never thrown a punch since some scuffle in the school playground – although I got fairly close the day Jeremy Clarkson wreaked havoc with my garden. My experience of boxing is pretty limited. The only time I ever did climb through the ropes was to be introduced to the crowd at a black tie boxing dinner. I was wearing pink Leander socks at the time, which became horribly and clearly visible as I clambered into the ring. The air was torn between hilarity and abuse. Put it this way, I've never worn pink Leander socks again.

That was bad enough and the thought of standing opposite some hostile hulk in boxing gloves, in the certainty of imminent assault by a sledgehammer-like blow, is not my idea of fun. Ali did that, but he did so much more. He turned sport into theatre, entertainment, comedy, tragedy and the towering influence in his life was his own all-powerful, undaunted self-belief.

As someone who even now doesn't really enjoy public speaking – I'd prefer to be my quiet self than get up in front of an audience – the ability of Ali to do the talking anywhere, anytime, complete with poems, amazes me. His supreme confidence in everything he did is so striking. Many times, struggling with the thought of making a speech, I've thought: 'God, wouldn't it be great to be like him.'

I suspect he was born an extrovert, but he certainly sharpened up the act as he grew older. The story goes that he was impressed by the self-glorifying pronouncements of a professional wrestler called 'Gorgeous' George Wagner, who could whip up a furious storm of ticket-selling attention with his loud-mouth, high-decibel bragging. It was good for show business and while Cassius Clay, as he was then, was an athlete, he had the looks and the temperament of a Hollywood star. He put it all together and his sport was transformed.

His outrageous pronouncements of self-appreciation still make me laugh. The Louisville Lip was in a class of his own: 'I am the astronaut of boxing. Joe Louis and Demsey were just jet pilots. I'm in a world of my own'; 'It's hard to be humble when you're as great as I am'; 'I'll beat him so bad he'll need a shoehorn to put his hat on'; and the unanswerable – 'I am the greatest.'

I wasn't like him in terms of volume. No one ever called me the 'Marlow Mouth' and I didn't stand up before our race in

Sydney and shout, 'I am the greatest,' but perhaps it was somewhere in my thoughts as we approached the first 250 metres of the gold medal race. Otherwise how do you account for the way I felt? We hadn't established an unassailable lead, the opposing crews were still with us and yet I was *sure*.

In Ali's case, it was part of an act, but at the core was the truth. Ali's monumental self-belief was at the heart of his barely credible story. He was twenty-two when he fought Sonny Liston, the malevolent, mafia-backed heavyweight champion of the world, for whom dark alleys had been invented. People laughed. A reporter from the *New York Times* was told to check out the distance from the ring to the hospital. That's where Ali would be soon enough, they reckoned. Instead, he was on his way to becoming the greatest sportsman of the twentieth century.

He said he'd beat George Foreman, the huge, hammer-hitting champion, in their 'Rumble in the Jungle' in Zaire. People were genuinely fearful for his safety. He won. Few expected him to beat Joe Frazier ever again, after his undefeated professional record was taken away by Frazier at Madison Square Garden in 1971. The fight was so huge that Frank Sinatra only gained entry by masquerading as a *Life* photographer. It was worth the ringside seat. In a brutal encounter, Ali was knocked down by a fifteenth round left hook – 'the punch that blew out all the candles on the cake'. Ali just rebaked the cake and beat Frazier, not once but twice.

His belief in himself was exemplified in Zaire when an hour before the fight against Foreman he looked at his quivering, terrified entourage and tried to encourage them to relax. He grinned at them. 'This ain't nothing but another day in the dramatic life of Muhammad Ali,' he told them. 'Do I look scared? I fear Allah and thunderstorms and bad plane rides, but this is like another day in the gym.'

I don't suppose he was ever as nerveless as he seemed. None of us are. Many times before a major race I've wished I was a thousand miles away from a rowing lake, but at least no one was going to climb in our boat and punch me in the face. This was about to happen to Ali in Kinshasa. Everybody knew it. Foreman's professional record was forty wins, no losses. He made a habit of not hanging around. His eight most recent bouts had been brought to abrupt ends in the first or the second rounds. His victims included Joe Frazier and Ken Norton. No one but Ali thought Ali had a chance.

They were even more convinced when Ali's tactics turned out to be lying on the ropes and letting Foreman lay into him with monstrous punches, only protecting himself with his forearms and elbows. From ringside it looked like assisted suicide, but slowly, surely, the champion's energy was draining and then Ali went on the offensive. Foreman himself was amazed. 'I went out and hit Muhammad with the hardest shot to the body I ever delivered to any opponent. Anybody else in the world would have crumbled. Muhammad cringed. I could see it hurt. And then he looked at me; he had that look in his eyes, like he was saying "I'm not gonna let you hurt me."'

That was self-belief, the stubbornness of mind that acknowledges the physical pain, but discounts it for a higher purpose. God knows, rowing hurts. Not like a left hook, but at least that's over quickly. The pain of rowing is the scream of lungs, legs, back and muscles. That's just one stroke. Multiply that by 240 strokes in a 2,000 metre race. I understand pain, but Ali ignored the pain in the interests of regaining his title, stripped from him after refusing the draft to join the US Army and make himself available for Vietnam. He was determined to achieve the destiny he had set for himself and he did so with typical melodrama.

In Ali's fight with Foreman we saw an exhibition of self-belief that looked almost superhuman. It wasn't. I knew how to fake that, too. It was a combination of stubbornness, pride, revenge and the imprint of years of work. I never underestimate work and neither did Ali. 'It's not braggin' if you can back it up,' he once said.

Having been assured that he was 'The Greatest' again in the eyes of the world – he already knew it himself – he relaxed. A reporter, visiting his residence in the President's Kinshasa compound on the morning after the fight, found him on the veranda doing conjuring tricks – with rope, aptly enough – for a crowd of excitable children. 'And it was hard to tell who was having a better time, Ali or the children.'

I like that image, because it's so down to earth and normal. We sometimes elevate athletes into gods, as though human qualities alone aren't enough to win the great sporting titles of the world. I don't agree. It is men and women who win titles, not superhumans, and they win them with human qualities. It might be amazing that these qualities all converge on one moment, but it's not a visitation from outer space. I think in every respect I am an ordinary man who did an extraordinary thing. Even Ali, 'The Greatest', was a man. He just happened to be a man with colossal levels of conviction.

His mother said he was such a self-confident boy that when she tried to spank his little brother, Rudolph, he'd tell her off, saying, 'Don't you spank my baby.' When he started boxing at twelve he was all speed and spindly legs, but onlookers talked of an aura about him. He won the Olympic light-heavyweight title in Rome at the age of eighteen. Four years later he was facing Sonny Liston in Miami, an event that most thought would double as Ali's execution.

That didn't bother the challenger, an attitude of mind he went so far as to reveal with his extraordinary behaviour at the weigh-in. He seemed out of control. He shrieked at Liston, 'I can beat you anytime, chump! You're scared, chump. You ain't no giant! I'm gonna eat you alive,' while being held back by five men. He was apparently bent on slugging Liston right there and then.

Yet when he came out for the fight, in his terry towelling robe with 'The Lip' embroidered on the back, he was coolness and calmness itself. He made a playful, low bow to Sugar Ray Robinson sitting in the crowd. People were astonished at his self-possession and by the start of the seventh round they were astonished even further out of their wits. Liston remained on his stool in the corner. The new heavyweight champion of the world was Cassius Clay, just as he knew he would be.

A visitor to his modest training base in low-rent Miami had noticed a doodle in light blue ink on the mattress in Ali's bedroom. It was a signature. 'Cassius Clay,' it said, in flowery writing, and, 'Cassius Clay is next champ. Champion of the world. Liston is finished. The next champ: Cassius Clay.' Modern psychologists would call it visualisation. Ali just knew it as fact.

It went on too long. That's the trouble with self-belief. It's not supplied with a tap, you can't turn it off, and it follows that people hard-wired to believe in themselves go on believing long after the body can cope. Their head is dealing in miracles, while the body is subject to reality. Ali was thirty-nine when he fought Trevor Berbick. Inevitably he lost, but he still summoned the old rhetoric before the fight. 'They say I'm washed up. They say I'm too old, that I'm finished, that I can't talk no more, that I've got brain damage, that I have bad kidneys, that I'm broke, that I'm sad. Oooooh man, I've got so many critics to whup.' Some would accuse him of trading in empty hype, but I wouldn't be surprised if he was expecting, hoping for, just one more miracle.

Ali fought way beyond a time that was sensible, but I understand why. It wasn't just that he needed the money or a sop to his ego, it was because he sincerely believed in his powers. Experience had taught him so. I'm the right man to know how he felt. When I began to realise I was pretty good at rowing, my ambition was an Olympic gold medal. Simple as that. One gold medal was my goal. I achieved that in Los Angeles, ahead of schedule. Why didn't I stop then? My ambition had been satisfied. Why not live the rest of my life in that happy knowledge and then get a real job?

The answer is simple: I thought I could do better and win another one. And I did, with Andy Holmes in Seoul. Why didn't I stop then, especially when I developed colitis in 1991? Two gold medals was already beyond my initial expectations. I remember my sister's boyfriend saying to me before Barcelona, 'Why don't you retire? Why on earth are you putting your head on the block again when you've already achieved two gold medals?' I tried to explain it was because those two medals had gone now. In the present I had another challenge: to be a better rower and win a gold medal to prove it. It didn't matter that it was number three, it mattered that I had another goal.

By the fourth in Atlanta in 1996 even I'd had enough. That was when I came out with my one and only famous quote. After Matt and I had won our gold medal we were interviewed by the BBC. It was just after the race – always a dangerous time when the brain is not fully in gear – and the question arose of whether we were going to Sydney. At that moment, we were not. 'Anyone sees me go anywhere near a boat, you've got my permission to shoot me,' I said and immediately entered the sports quotes book market. That makes my one to Ali's one thousand.

Of course, I did go on to Sydney at the age of thirty-eight, only one year younger than Ali when he had his last fight. As it turned out, I was correct and Ali was delusional, but if we had lost I would have been utterly condemned and just as apparently delusional as him. Self-belief puts you on a knife edge all your life. Anyone who believes in miracles can look like a madman, but if you don't you will never achieve your dreams.

I have never met Ali to talk to, but I have been close. He was sitting one seat away from me at the BBC Sports Personality of the Year awards in 1999, when he received his Sportsman of the Century award. The only problem was the person in between us was the heavyweight champion, Lennox Lewis, who formed a pretty daunting obstacle. Afterwards Ali was absolutely mobbed. I'm not the type to push myself forward, so I just admired him from afar.

I had seen him once before, though. It was the opening ceremony of the Olympics in Atlanta in 1996. I was carrying the flag for Great Britain and the climax of the evening was Muhammad Ali igniting the Olympic flame. There was such a nervous hush in the arena as this revered figure came forward, the torch visibly shaking in his hands from the ravages of his illness, and I for one wasn't sure whether he would be able to perform his role. He seemed so diminished from the great warrior I remembered and it made me feel sad, yet he did light the flame and, as the crowd roared, the sadness was replaced by a different feeling altogether. The power of the man – call it charisma, nostalgia, whatever it may be – was tangible. I didn't come away sad. I came away with the thought that I'd just witnessed something magical.

CATHY FREEMAN

Cathy Freeman was there that night in Atlanta, too. She sat with her mother in the stadium, a novice to the Olympics, young and awed, wondering how she would run in her event, the 400 metres. The ceremony went on late into the night and she had to leave before the end, even before Muhammad Ali lit the flame. Cathy simply could not have known or even imagined that four years later she would be the one standing there, Olympic torch in hand, waiting to perform the same rite in front of a worldwide audience of billions. In her mind, in Atlanta, she was just a little Aboriginal Australian girl racing in her first Olympics.

Four years later she was the focal point of the planet. As someone who also felt the weight of expectation in Sydney, I very much doubt that any other athlete on earth has experienced what Cathy went through on the night of the 400 metres Olympic final. I was there, in the same country, at the same Games, but it was only afterwards, when my mind refocussed on world events rather than just 'me, team, boat, gold', that I came to appreciate how much she had accomplished, how brave she had been and how strong.

Self-belief is one thing, but the weight of expectation pulls in another direction entirely. Confidence lightens you, but pressure makes you heavier. The pressure on Freeman at the Sydney Olympics in 2000 was of a force that flew off the scale. She was representing her country and her people, which were two different things. She had the hopes of not one, but two, nations on her shoulders. Two nations, furthermore, who had been warring politically for decades and who saw in Cathy Freeman their one genuine hope of unity. It was as if the Australian people had decided that if Cathy could win gold in the Olympics, the painful past that Aboriginals had endured and the guilt the Australians still carried could somehow all be resolved. That was a lot of weight to run a lap with.

Then she had her rival, Marie Jose Perec, the double Olympic champion to deal with. The Frenchwoman had swept to the 200/400 metres double victory in Atlanta, achieving the feat twenty minutes before Michael Johnson. She won the 400 metres final with an imperious display of long-legged supremacy and in an Olympic record time of 48.25 seconds – the fastest time recorded in ten years. Cathy was second in 48.63 and so had begun the forty-eight-month countdown to Sydney.

There had been many scheduled competition dates between Freeman and Perec in the lead up to the Games, but always the Olympic champion seemed to pull out at the last minute. In some athletes this is a means of preserving mystery, in others a desperate smoke-screen behind which to hide injury. In Perec it might just have been a whim, but it was another burden, another worry, that Freeman carried with her.

There was also the personal baggage. Between Atlanta and Sydney Cathy had split with her coach and boyfriend, and married a sports clothing executive. I can't say the love life of other athletes interests me that much, but I can see that emotional trauma can affect an athlete in all kinds of difficult ways. I had it myself, in a different form, worrying in Barcelona about my colitis and in Sydney about the effects of diabetes.

By the time Sydney arrived, I think the pressures on Cathy were almost intolerable. All attention was on her, all hopes were on her, all demands were on her and yet here was a young woman who had never won gold before. At least when the pressure cranked up for our four in Sydney I knew what winning a gold medal entailed. If all else failed, I could say to myself, 'I know what to do. I've done it before. I can do it again.' Cathy had no idea, no golden track record, and yet it was as though her life, her country and her ancestry all depended upon it.

Then, just when you thought the burden couldn't get any heavier, the organising committee had asked her to light the Olympic cauldron at the opening ceremony and she had unhesitatingly agreed. I am not sure I would have been that generous. I might have preferred to be selfish and rested, rather than standing under a fountain in the dead of night, with a head cold, on live TV, broadcasting to billions, beneath a piece of machinery that wasn't working, while a disembodied voice in my earpiece was shouting expletives. Cathy said she nearly laughed at that moment. All I can say is she is a better man than I am.

She agreed to do one major press conference before her event and even that ended up revolving round a dramatic issue. Perec had pulled out of the Olympics and was last seen at Sydney Airport apparently making her escape. Cathy fielded a string of questions about her absent rival, and was probably both relieved and unsettled by her departure.

The juggling act between two cultures continued. Some sections of the Aboriginal community wanted her to boycott the Games, while the mainstream Australian government was keen for her to attend official functions, which left her contending with divided loyalties. Few athletes have walked on to the running track in an Olympic Stadium with greater attempts going on all around them to politicise the simple act of running.

This is when the strength of her belief would have been tested. She might have looked slight, but she had the spirit of an army. After all the traumas leading up to her first heat she still knew that as long as her body stayed strong the gold medal was hers.

'This was my arrogance coming out. It is a side of me that I never display in public. I have a Jekyll and Hyde personality – one minute I'm the shy girl from Mackay, the next I'm this arrogantly confident woman who is invincible. To be the best in the world you have to be arrogant. I know I've got it.

'On the track I feel it. What is it? Tiger Woods has it on the golf course. Michael Jordan had it on the basketball court . . . When I was fit I knew none of these girls could beat me. I'd always thought Perec and I were at another level, and now that she was gone I knew I was going to be the Olympic champion.'

Even so, there were so many things that could have derailed her and the medal wasn't around her neck yet. It is very dangerous for an athlete to presume the job has been done before the start gun sounds. Visualisation is good, presumption bad.

I still struggle to understand how Cathy held herself together in those days and hours, counting down to the final, but the more you know her the more you can see that her habit of floating away in her head must have saved her. She herself has said, 'I can't explain how I do it, but I have an unbelievable ability to shut everything out.' To bring herself back to the moment, she had the endearing habit of tugging both eyelids to make sure she was focusing on reality and the race.

I was amazed when I read that she slept peacefully the night before the final. Rowers sleep for England, thanks to our usual state of exhaustion, but I don't remember being particularly restful the night before the final of the coxless fours. Cathy really does have an on/off button. What she did on the day leading up to the race is a classic example of how not to get involved with anything that knocks your equilibrium.

She ate breakfast, she played Scrabble, she methodically attached her number – 1110 – to her bag, uniform and running suit. That suit. Just to add to all the mental pressures bearing down on her, she had decided to run the final in a skin-hugging, all-in-one body suit, complete with a hood, in green and gold. That says something about her confidence. There is no way I would have rowed an Olympic final in anything other than our usual Lycra gear. Why give opponents more reason to beat you? In a hood? Not a chance. But Cathy didn't mind. She said she'd have run in a pink tutu if she had believed it enhanced her performance. Belief, again. I doubt she ran any better in the suit, but if it gave her one extra ounce of confidence going into the race it was worth it.

As the afternoon wore on and the race time approached Cathy said less and less, and understood less and less of what was said to her. She entered a world of her own. Donna Fraser, the British 400-metre runner and a good friend, chatted as they warmed up together. None of Donna's words even registered. 'I was in another place,' Cathy said later. Carl Lewis told her afterwards that he'd spoken to her on her way into the stadium, but she doesn't even remember.

On the start line she had the sensation of a dull noise at the back of her head. She had no idea what it was. Everything beyond the immediate necessity of the race ahead had been minimised. She was drawing on all her inner resources. The outer world no longer existed. This is how she explained it: 'Running for me is always more than just physical and mental; it is also emotional and spiritual. You can draw energy from the universe, the stars and the sun, everything around you. You can draw energy from what has happened in your life, the tragedies and successes. When you combine it all at the right moment it moves you, propels you forward. It's like your blood is boiling, like there are ants in your blood. You're overwhelmed by this sense of confidence – it's like you're floating. I don't know where it comes from and you can't practise having it. All I know is that just minutes away from the gold medal race I had that feeling.'

When Cathy won her gold medal she looked stunned, bemused, doubled over in bewilderment. The dull noise in her head turned out to be the roar of the crowd, but she had been too locked away in her own world to understand where it came from. It took her a while to struggle out of her mental hideaway – the place she had gone to escape the expectation – and join in the wild celebrations.

I have so much respect for what she did that night. When people expect as much of you as they did of me in Barcelona, Atlanta and, finally and especially, Sydney, all you can do is equal those expectations. You can never exceed them. They expect you to win – you win – that's it, mission accomplished. You rarely saw me celebrating at the finish of the race. Partly I was too exhausted to lift an arm or an eyelid, but partly it was because the major emotion was relief. Not elation, that came later, just undiluted relief. Job done.

It occurred to me once to ask Cathy how she stayed as together as she did. I was intrigued and she told me, 'I still do look back on my gold medal and think, "Wow!" I think I always will. Nine years on and I'm still getting my head around the "special" conditions I performed under. I've finally grown to understand that Sydney 2000 was a definitive moment, not only for Australia as a nation, and as an indigenous nation, but more so for me on a very personal level. One thing is for sure, what helped me cope with the pressure was my inner peace, which I believe I owe to an appreciation of where I came from – my ancestors, my memories and my sense of self.'

To be honest, I don't really know what that means. I think it means that – like me – she did what she had to do. Under all that pressure, the one thing that kept her from crumbling, from letting all the expectation get to her, was her innate belief in her ability and the knowledge that she would win.

BRIAN CLOUGH

How can I understand someone like Brian Clough? I shut up and get on with it. Clough lived life with a megaphone. The classic example is the speech he reportedly made to the players of Leeds United when he was appointed manager of the most powerful team in British football in 1974. International players, virtually to a man, he stood in front of them and let each player know exactly what he thought of them. He told Peter Lorimer, nicknamed 'Thunderfoot' for his prodigious long-range shots, that he dived and rolled around and played injured when he wasn't. He told Billy Bremner, the captain of Scotland, that he cheated and tried to intimidate referees. He told Eddie Gray, a wonderfully gifted winger who unfortunately was suffering from injury, 'You, Gray, if you'd been a racehorse you'd have been put down months ago.' It's even been said he called them all cheats. and said none of their medals had been won fairly.

My sporting career would be better condensed into a silent movie. When Matt Pinsent and I were put together I don't remember making a speech of welcome. We just climbed into a boat and rowed. When Jurgen Grobler, the most successful rowing coach in East Germany, was appointed to run the British team I deliberately didn't say much. I thought I'd wait and see how he did. He did OK. I'm trying to remember the speech I gave at my wedding. I can vaguely recall it, but what I mainly remember is a photographer who kept getting in the bloody way.

Clough's confrontational attitude is miles away from mine. He lived to speak, shock, and galvanise. He believed in himself, like I did, but he told everyone how much he believed in himself, which is something I didn't do.

It makes me smile just to recall the kind of sayings he made famous. My favourite was his reply when asked how he handled a player who disagreed with his methods: 'I'd ask him how he thinks it should be done, have a chat about it for twenty minutes and then decide I was right.' That appeals to me. That's more or less how I like to do things, although twenty minutes seems a bit excessive.

His working life was as dramatic as his delivery. Horrible injury cut short his career as a player. He became a young and highly successful manager of Hartlepool with his long-time side-kick Peter Taylor, later winning the First Division championship – the highest echelon of British football – with a bunch of unfancied players at Derby County. Then he resigned in haste after an argument. Clough failed ignominiously at Brighton, suffered the Leeds debacle, then resumed his partnership with Taylor at Nottingham Forest, where the magic act produced two of the most unexpected results in the history of football.

Being a Chelsea supporter I didn't always appreciate Clough's special quality and, anyway, his Derby County team were a little before my time, but even I know that Clough had the gift of producing teams, cheaply assembled, formidably motivated and vastly over-achieving.

The history of the European Cup is one long celebration of superstars funded by treasure chests of money. The list of winners reads like a *Who's Who* of world football. The seventies appeared to be no different. Champions from 1970 on were: Feyenoord, Ajax, Ajax, Ajax, Bayern Munich, Bayern Munich, Bayern Munich, Liverpool, Liverpool . . . *Nottingham Forest,* followed by, even more incredibly . . . *Nottingham Forest.*

Anyone born after Clough's era had ended would be tempted to think history had been hacked into by some mad revisionist from the Midlands. How could some cash-strapped little provincial outpost beside the River Trent ever have aspired to the aristocratic heights of Johann Cruyff's Ajax or Franz Beckenbauer's Bayern? Answer: because Clough was their manager. He believed and he instilled belief.

The 1984 Olympic coxed four in which I won a gold medal was dubbed 'The Unlikely Lads' by the press. We featured a Cambridge-educated doctor, a temporary hod-carrier with a

French degree, an aggressively competitive teacher and me, the unemployed ex-comprehensive boy with my now famous CSE in woodwork. Except in the small world of rowing we were completely anonymous allsorts. Clough's Nottingham Forest was similar. There were few out-and-out glory boys, but they worked for each other. Maybe they were too terrified not to, with Clough on the touchline, yelling 'That's crap!'

However, sometimes a team just clicks, like ours did in Los Angeles and like Clough's Forest did. They personified the unglamorous, especially centre-half Kenny Burns with his toothless grin, yet they won the European Cup, not once but twice. Only belief could have carried them all the way to successive finals and that belief was all the doing of Clough. In a way, it was an act of faith. He had such bullish charisma that his players seemed to follow him like American congregations follow evangelical preachers.

I've heard the theory that he was a driven man because his playing career had been cut dead by a cruciate ligament injury sustained in a collision with a Bury goalkeeper when playing for Sunderland on Boxing Day 1962. I don't dispute that might be the case, but I suspect his belief was already there. His kind of personality didn't arrive on the treatment table. It was a genetic inheritance or it developed from having to fight for his place among eight siblings growing up in working-class Middlesborough.

Journalists have occasionally tried to paint me as a man driven by the shame of his academic past to haul myself to Olympian heights, but it just doesn't work for me. Yes, I am dyslexic and, yes, I was routinely pulled out of French to take extra lessons in English at school. I disliked reading. I still do. I'm not comfortable with it and I would accept that I do have a slight sense of insecurity about it.

As President of the Amateur Rowing Association I often attend dinners and have to make a presentation. I remember one where I was given an envelope containing what I thought was the name of the winner. I didn't think anything of it, but when the moment came to rip the envelope open and make the presentation, I found a citation I had to read out. Until very recently I would have frozen. I would have panicked. When I'm reading something out loud I need prior warning. I have to work through it, word by word, beforehand, to make sure I can manage without stumbling. On this occasion I had no choice. I read it out, but not without a few mistakes.

However, I can still tell you, without a shadow of a doubt, that I did not become an international oarsman because I only achieved a CSE in woodwork. That is not the equation. I became an international oarsman because I discovered it by accident and was good at it. Who doesn't want to do what they're good at?

Clough was good at managing football teams. His dodgy knee made him more determined, but the self-belief was already there. It had to be. Few managers have as public and catastrophic a time of it as he had at Leeds United. In a short space of time he went from heroically winning Division One with unfancied Derby County to a misguided resignation, unremitting failure at Brighton and then forty-four days of arrogant confrontation at

Leeds United, before being brutally sacked. That would be humiliation enough to most men, but he bounced back with second division Nottingham Forest, even more unfancied than Derby, and announced, 'There's only one thing in the club's favour now. It's got me.'

For all the downsides, the accusations of taking bungs, the hubris, rants, punches and controversies, the alcoholism that so affected his health and the stomach cancer that claimed his life at 69, he was dead right about that. He arrived at Nottingham in January 1975 and resigned in 1993. In that time the little club won promotion to Division One, the League Championship, four League Cups, reached a FA Cup Final, went undefeated in forty-two games in the late seventies and transformed a set of unlikely lads into the Kings of Europe.

When he died, the Matt cartoon in the *Daily Telegraph* imagined what Brian Clough's epitaph might be. It read, 'The Greatest Manager Of All Time . . . Even If I Do Say So Myself'. It's perfect. I've been wondering what mine would be. Given my chosen sport and my no-nonsense personality, it would probably just say, 'Pushed Off.'

DALEY THOMPSON

Daley Thompson and I overlapped. When I was winning my first gold medal in Los Angeles, he was winning his second. He stood on the podium and whistled the national anthem. He knew some people would consider this disrespectful, but he didn't care. He had just become the first athlete to hold Olympic, Commonwealth, European and World titles at the same time, setting a world record of 8,847 points in the decathlon which would stand for eight years. Why shouldn't he whistle if he wanted to?

He wore T-shirts, too, that asked leading questions. 'Is the world's second greatest athlete gay?' was one of them, a barbed remark made in the direction of Carl Lewis, who had won four gold medals to Daley's one in America, but was still considered by the British decathlete to be of sub-Thompson quality.

I should have been in Moscow, too, where he won his first Olympic gold, but Margaret Thatcher orchestrated a boycott after Soviet troops invaded Afghanistan. Rowing sent a cut-down team and I was thrown over the side. No one ever did fully explain to me why a man in a vest rowing on a lake in Moscow could have a powerful effect on a Soviet tank commander rolling into Kabul, but our sport still fell into line. Athletics obviously had greater autonomy. It was the Olympics of the great Coe–Ovett rivalry and Thompson, energetic son of a Nigerian father and Scottish mother, with a trademark handlebar moustache, made the most of the outing.

His most significant rival, Guido Kratschmer of West Germany, had obeyed the political edict to boycott, but all Thompson could do was beat the guys who were there, which he did with considerable ease. The Soviet crowd gave him a standing ovation when he wrapped up the title, which, considering he was beating two Russians into silver and bronze position, says much about his popularity.

He probably enjoyed that. If you're talking about athletes whose self-belief shades into arrogance, I think he comes into that category. It was a fundamental part of his competitiveness. It is how he psyched out opponents. I remember being impressed by the way he would never roll around on the ground after the final event in the decathlon, the killer 1,500 metres. Instead, he would be careful to stroll away, casually, unconcerned, even if he was dying with exhaustion inside. That's how I liked to behave, too. Never let the opposition know you're hurting.

I also remember being very impressed by the fact that he even trained – and let it be known that he trained – on Christmas Day. His main rival in Los Angeles was Jurgen Hingsen, known as the German Hercules, who had been world record holder several times in the preceding years. The West German, unwisely, had claimed prior to the event that he would come away from LA with the gold medal. Daley's response was typical. 'There's only two ways he'll do that. He'll have to steal mine or win another event.' I have little doubt that Daley out-psyched Hingsen at that Olympics. To pile on the pressure, he won the first two events, the 100 metres and the long jump (with a leap that would have seen him finish fifth in the event proper), and set a personal best in the shot put. Hingsen won the high jump, but aggravated a knee injury.

Perhaps due to the injury, Seb Coe found him crouching down near the tunnel area at some point in the competition. A close friend of Daley, and not above a little piece of patriotic mischief, Seb found the opportunity too much to resist. He looked over to where Daley was standing and back at the suffering German athlete. 'He's an animal, isn't he?' said Seb, with pseudo sympathy. Hingsen said nothing. He just sighed and hung his head.

When, after enduring the formality of winning it, Daley finally received his medal, Princess Anne offered a word of congratulation. He was asked later what she had said. 'She said I was a good-looking guy,' Daley claimed. Perhaps she did. I can only add that she didn't say that to me in Sydney.

3

Overcoming Adversity

Cape Town, training camp, autumn 1997 – that's it then. The end. I knew it would have to finish sometime, but not like this, not so cruelly, not lying in some anonymous motel room feeling more alone than I've ever felt in my life. The rest of the guys have gone sight-seeing, but I don't have the energy. All I can do is lie here on the bed, exhausted, looking out of the window at the car park – I haven't even got a room with a sea view – knowing this is the last day of my rowing career.

Steve Redgrave, four-time Olympic gold medallist, seven times world champion, has reached the end of the line. I can't do it any more. I have to face the fact that my body just doesn't perform the way it once did. The diabetes is too hard to control after all. I'm too drained. I've tried, I've really tried, to the point of numbness, but if I can't perform in training I don't deserve my place in the boat. There is no point being emotional about it. It's a fact. I'm not good enough any more.

I hadn't expected to be the same athlete, but I didn't expect it to be such a miserable grind. We've come out here to the sunshine to kick-start our season and day after day my performance just seems to be getting worse. It's intense. We're doing three or four sessions of training every day – cycling, weights, rowing, touch rugby – and in all of them I'm off the pace. Worse, I am really suffering. By the time I finish one thing, everyone else has moved on to the next. They have lunch while I'm still completing the long-distance cycle; they have moved on to the weights while I eat by myself. I'm feeling a growing sense of hopelessness and isolation. I'm fighting it, I'm trying not to show it, but the sense that I'm failing is with me all the time.

I found myself out today. I admit I'm not exactly king of the mountains when it comes to cycling, but I've never been so left behind as I was on our training ride around the Cape this morning. Usually I'm competitive enough to stay in the peloton, especially if I slipstream behind Matt – the joke is that lorries could slipstream behind Matt he forms such a massive buffer. Then I use my power to sprint for the line. Often enough, I win.

Today winning wasn't an option. There was only survival. I knew I'd suffer, but not that badly. My last ergo test, measuring my muscle work rate, was horrendous. Normally, I sit there at the start wondering whether I'll be able to complete the 20 kilometre session. This time I sat there and wondered if I'd be able to complete *a stroke*. *A single stroke*. It was so mentally and physically painful. I wanted to stop. For a full hour and twenty minutes I desperately wanted to stop. I survived by completing just one stroke at a time. 'If you did that one, Steve, you can do just one more.' I said that to myself hundreds of times. One plus one plus one . . . stretching into what felt like infinity. My time was a full ten minutes slower than usual. I am performing like an average – no, *below* average – club oarsman.

I don't know if the others have noticed how bad it is. Obviously, they can see I'm struggling, but I doubt they know the extent of my depression. I am good at covering up. Unemotional. Anyway, they'll be concentrating on themselves. There are sixteen of us here and four seats in the top boat up for grabs. This may be a team sport, but it is also a ruthless competition among individuals. They're not looking at me, they're hoping that Jurgen is looking at them.

Tim Foster: It is sad to see him struggle, but it is almost an embarrassment, so I don't say anything. Steve being Steve he doesn't want it to be a public thing. James and I have furtive conversations when he's not around. 'How can we help him?' we say to one another. In the end, we decide there isn't much we can do, but I still have incredible respect for him. He does absolutely every piece of training to the bitter end. He never cuts corners. He never makes excuses. He still wears his famous external armour of invincibility, no matter how cracked up his body may be.

About a month previously I'd been diagnosed with type two diabetes. I realised it was serious and I'd expected to feel different, to perform more poorly than usual, but this deterioration is beyond my worst imagining. And today on the bike was the most disillusioning experience I've ever had.

I started off feeling fine and then, suddenly, my energy left me completely. It was like switching off a light. One minute on, next off. Nothing in between. Normally, as you become fatigued your strength slowly dwindles away, but this experience was nothing like that. It was sudden and brutal. My legs went from pedalling to just hanging. There was no strength in them to cycle, there was only weight. I could push one pedal down through the sheer weight resting on it, then it would take all my willpower to do the same on the other side. It was like that ergo test all over again.

'I want to get off and just push,' my head was saying to me. 'Why am I doing this? . . . This is sheer hell . . . I'm not doing this any more . . . I can't do this any more . . . I'm going home.' I climbed slowly, torturously, with these thoughts invading my head and eventually joined the other guys at the mid-way resting point. I arrived looking and feeling like death-warmed-up, just as they were about to leave.

Matt Pinsent: We'd been resting for about twenty-five minutes when this forlorn figure came into view. I remember it so distinctly. We'd been standing around eating and drinking, saying over and over again, 'Where is he?', looking down the road where he should have arrived ages ago. Now here he was at last, looking awful. He wordlessly gave Jurgen his empty water bottle, stuck a filled one in his bicycle cage, grabbed a banana and pushed off again. He didn't even step off his bike.

I was desperately sorry for him. It was like one of those North Sea convoys in the Second World War. If one of the vessels was struck by a torpedo or generally struggling to keep up, the others didn't wait, didn't stop, didn't go back to search for survivors. There was safety only in numbers. We couldn't do anything for him. We couldn't go at his pace, he couldn't at ours. I'd never seen him struggling like this in all our time together. And then he got a puncture.

Jurgen was following in the van. He pulled up beside me and said, 'Throw the bike in the van, I'll take you back.' Any sane man would have grasped the lifeline. I grunted and refused. I was adamant. However long it took me, however much pain it caused, I wanted the grim satisfaction of knowing I'd completed my last ever training session. The Olympics in Sydney were no longer an option, a fifth successive gold medal was a dream I'd never fulfil, but it would have taken a personality transplant there and then on the sun-drenched tarmac of the coast road round Cape Town to persuade me to give up before I'd finished the task in hand. I have never warmed to the concept of surrender.

Jurgen knew better than to argue. A quiet, reflective man, he merely nodded and drove away. I don't think I even bothered to watch him go. I repaired the puncture and toiled on. By the time I finished the others had been back for an hour. They were making plans to go into town. I made plans to collapse on my bed. I didn't tell them about the other resolution I'd made: to pack my bags and take a cab to the airport, tonight, this very night, and leave my sport behind. I wasn't being dramatic. I wasn't being hysterical. I was being dispassionately scientific. I'd rowed with ulcerative colitis for six years. I could cope with one incurable illness, but two was too much. The onset of diabetes was too great a disability for me to overcome.

I'd been taught to inject myself with insulin, but it wasn't the needles that disturbed me, it was simply the effect of the condition. I was running on empty. The energy wasn't there and no matter how hard I tried it wasn't coming back. We had three years to train before the Sydney Olympics. If I couldn't train, I couldn't be an Olympic athlete. It was a simple, pragmatic equation. Jurgen would agree, so would Matt, so would James and Tim. They deserved their places in the boat. I didn't.

When my colitis was diagnosed just ten weeks before the Barcelona Olympics in 1992, Jurgen and Matt had held a meeting about replacing me if the illness significantly impaired my performance. It didn't, but I have never fully known why, although it was partly the medication that finally controlled the diarrhoea that had been plaguing me on and off for about six months. I thought it was just a bug at first. Then it was diagnosed as salmonella, before finally I was sent to hospital for a biopsy of my intestines which, thanks to where they send the tube up, was a painful experience in just about every way you can imagine.

At first the specialist refused to believe I could have ulcerative colitis, a debilitating disease of the intestines involving inflammation and internal bleeding, because of the high levels of work I'd been doing in training. But dismissing agony is what oarsmen do. None of us would get beyond the 500 metres line if we took much notice of pain.

Both before and after the Olympics the colitis was hard to manage and sometimes excruciating, but for a ten-week window which culminated in Barcelona I was fine. That's why I say it was only *partly* the medication that helped me to my third gold medal and Matt to his first. The other part was something I never fully understood, something along the lines of willpower. I don't know whether stories of women finding the superhuman strength to lift the ton-weight of cars to rescue their children are purely mythical. All I know is that I'm more prepared to believe them after the Barcelona Olympics.

That was my mind-set when the diabetes hit me. Deep down I'd believed in my body's power to overcome it, but now I'm lying here acknowledging that that belief is a lie.

I'm going to call Ann right now and tell her I'm leaving. I'm packing my bags and coming home. I'm sure she'll be quietly delighted, although she will have more sense and tact than to tell me so. She told me after Atlanta that she wanted me to give up. She wasn't adamant about it, but she wants a husband, someone who contributes to the family, someone who helps with the children, not some selfish bloke still not earning a living who leaves the house every morning to go out to play. I don't blame her.

I'll ring her now. I know what she'll say. It'll be, 'OK, come home now,' and she'll be secretly relieved. I dial the familiar number of home. I let it ring a few times. She's probably busy with the dog, or the children, or work or the house. Eventually, she answers. 'Ann, look, I can't do this any more.' 'Why, what's happened?'

I'm telling her about the bike ride today, the pitiful ergo test, the futility of carrying on this charade when my body has so clearly had enough. I'm waiting for the words I know will come next: '*OK, come home now.*' It takes me a few seconds to realise the words haven't come at all and it's a different set of words I'm hearing. I struggle momentarily to make sense of them: '*Don't worry. We'll get through this. We'll find an answer.*'

The room with the view of the car park starts to swim. It's not like me to feel this emotional, but I am realising I am not as alone as I thought. The sense of hopelessness starts to lift. Maybe we can get through this, maybe this is the lowest point of my life, but I can battle back through the diabetes, just as I did with colitis, with a combination of determination, bloody-mindedness and medical intervention. And maybe the smartest thing I ever did was to marry a doctor.

LANCE ARMSTRONG

It would be six gruelling, miserable weeks before I began to see a glimmer of hope in my training. Eventually we realised that the diabetes had made my colitis worse and the medication for my colitis made my diabetes worse. Nice one. Plus I was trying to get by on so many fewer calories, to help control the diabetes, my body was running out of energy. We tore up the treatment and started again. I'd eat just as much as I had before and boost the amount of insulin I used instead. Slowly, but visibly, the new procedure worked, but it was the most wretched time in my whole career.

Now I can put that in perspective. At the time it was impossible. My intestines were raw and bleeding internally, I was injecting myself with insulin to try and control my diabetes, my form was depressingly poor. One specialist suspected I might have Crohn's disease, a pre-cancerous condition of the gut, so I had another biopsy session in London – more tubes, discomfort, indignity. On the way home in the car, Ann had to pull over suddenly so I could throw up on the hard shoulder of the M4. You remember these things with awful clarity. I'm supposed to be an Olympian. On that day I was just a big, exhausted bloke vomiting by the edge of a motorway near Chiswick. However, as I said, I can now put that in perspective.

I was doubled up on the hard shoulder, Lance Armstrong was on his death bed. He wasn't told at the time of his cancer diagnosis, but one doctor treating him informed him later that he reckoned he had a three per cent chance of survival. He had stage four testicular cancer with lesions on his brain and twelve tumours in his lungs. He went through brain surgery and four cycles of chemotherapy so toxic that one of the fittest cyclists in the world was reduced to a grey-skinned shell, lying on his side in bed, curled up in blankets, fighting nausea, unable to do anything except keep himself alive. Barely.

He concluded later that some of his visitors, notably a team sponsor, thought they were looking at a dead person when they saw him. Apparently the same sponsor went away and immediately tried to radically reduce his contract. Sport can be a ruthless business. You could say that Armstrong took his revenge by winning the Tour de France seven times – for a different team.

I admit Armstrong is a controversial figure. I know there have been doping allegations surrounding him, which he has categorically denied. I accept that background, but here I'm talking about overcoming adversity and Armstrong's story is a powerful one about a man who refused to succumb to mortal illness.

He doesn't come over egotistical about it. He was and remains scientific. That's how I prefer to look at things. He says it was about good medicine, good luck and good health going into the ordeal. He is not saying he is special and he is not saying he provides a template. You don't have to be an elite sportsman to survive cancer. People without an ounce of positive thinking survive and others without an ounce of negative thinking die. People who can't cycle up the sheer side of a mountain survive cancer. It wasn't who he is that is so inspirational, but the manner of his fight.

At first, his personality did him harm. He refused to believe in the symptoms. He ignored them. Everything that felt wrong was attributable to another cause in his mind. I completely identify with that. Athletes, perhaps rowers and cyclists especially, learn to will discomfort, even agony, away. We expect to suffer and actually take a peculiar pride in suffering. It's a form of madness, but a necessary one that allows us to train to compete. Armstrong calls cycling a 'sport of self-abuse'. Rowing is not far behind, except we don't row vertically and there are fewer collisions.

He paid no attention when he didn't feel great in 1996. His

ht testicle was slightly swollen, he was unduly tired when he
n a race over twelve days in Carolina and he had a pounding
adache on his twenty-fifth birthday, which he put down to the
argaritas. He even dismissed coughing up blood as a sign of
ything serious. Finally, when the testicle was the size of an
ange, he consented to see a doctor. He had literally ridden
rough stages one, two and three of testicular cancer without
owing it. Here he was at stage four with his chance of recovery
sening by the minute.

Still he believed in his survival. What else was there to do? He
nt out to dinner the night before his brain surgery with friends
d family, hospital bracelet on his wrist and dots on his head
ere the incisions would be made into his skull. The surgery
ked his eyesight, motor skills, movement and, furthermore,
ath. Still he believed in his survival.

'To believe in the face of utter hopelessness, every article of
idence to the contrary, to ignore apparent catastrophe – what
er choice was there? We do it every day, I realised. We are so
ich stronger than we imagine, and belief is one of the most
iant and long-lived human characteristics ... To continue
ieving in yourself, believing in the doctors, believing in the
atment, believing in whatever I chose to believe in, that was
most important thing, I decided. It had to be.'

I agree with him. When it came to the decision about whether
hould row on to Sydney or give up, I had every reason to
nsider a surrender. I was ill, older, less fit and would never be
good an athlete again as the one I had been. Those days were
er. So I made my decision. I rowed on.

81

I'm not arrogant enough to think that a sportsman's self-belief is on a higher plane than that of the rest of the human race. I only know that it has to be well developed to thrive in sport. Maybe that helped me make my decision and maybe that helped Armstrong survive a life–death struggle.

Typically, he fought with aggressive determination. When his oncologist told him to drink five glasses of water a day, he drank fifteen, one after another without pause. That is an athlete going the extra mile, doing one more training ride up a mountain, one more 10 kilometre row, one more hour on the tennis court, twenty more drop-kicks on the rugby field, in pain, exhausted, but determined just to get an advantage over the opposition. In Armstrong's case, cancer was his new opposition. And he beat it.

In 1999, less than three years after his diagnosis, he won his first Tour de France. Most people thought it a miracle he was even competing. Then he won six more, in succession. 'Without cancer I would never have won a single Tour de France,' he has said. 'Cancer taught me a plan for more purposeful living and that in turn taught me how to train and to win more purposefully ... Pain and loss are great enhancers.'

It is impossible to know if the pains of my illnesses and the loss of my greater powers as an oarsman spurred me on to the 2000 Olympics. I don't know, but I do know that against any visible signs of physical weakening there was a growing belief in myself. If I had overcome the depression, the panic and fears I felt in South Africa, then winning a gold medal was not beyond the bounds of possibility. Maybe I was just being stubborn, but I didn't just think I had a chance. I had a strong conviction I'd win.

When Lance Armstrong lined up for the 1999 Tour de France he, too, thought he could win. He trained, as he said, like a geek. Planning meticulously, eating healthily and riding, every day, up and down mountains. Not just mountains. Alps. He trained through sleet, rain and wind. He would ride for six to seven hours at a time. I reckon, in another life, he could have been a rower.

He believed cancer had realigned his body. It felt thinner, leaner, sparer and all the better for the cruel mountain climbs, but his other advantages remained. He still had an aerobic capacity of 83.8 ml/kg/min. His heart was thirty per cent larger than the average male. Most crucially for the business of riding 3,500 kilometres in a month around France, scaling the most precipitous climbs, plummeting down the most vertiginous drops, among a field of almost 200 competitors with whom collisions, bumps and clashes could occur at any time, Armstrong has spectacularly low lactate levels, resulting in a freakish ability to ward off muscle fatigue.

I was never quite such a convenient freak. I had a good uptake of oxygen with every lungful of air, but not as good as Matt Pinsent, although I do remember when I was tested for the volume of air I was able to shift in and out of my lungs with every breath that it was greater than that of anyone else the doctors had seen at that time. I'm still not a physical freak, though, and perhaps I have to concede that Armstrong would be a better rower than I would ever be a cyclist, except it might blow his mind to race backwards.

Armstrong pulled on the yellow jersey, the iconic top worn by the leader of the Tour de France, after the very first stage of the 1999 race. He was wearing it again when he rode down the Champs Elysees a month later, the unexpected champion. Many people in France were astounded that such a recent survivor of cancer could conquer an event so gruelling. It looked like a miracle. And then he produced six more victories, reeled them off one after the other, as the world looked on in shock. He put it down to the belief that cancer cured him of laziness. He wanted to keep proving, and celebrating, and confirming the fact that he was alive. I can't lay claim to any of those feelings. When I won my fifth gold medal I wanted to celebrate the fact that I could lie on the sofa and watch TV for a while. But I was older than he was. Unlike Armstrong, I was never going to mount a comeback after Sydney. I was thirty-eight. That was it. End of career. That was the point where belief in my performance as an oarsman would have become delusion. Now I'm just deluded about golf.

Armstrong was twenty-seven when he won in 1999. There was a lot of pedal power left in the guy. He even came to compete in the Sydney Olympics, though I didn't realise it at the time. I didn't meet him, but that's not so surprising as I don't think he joined us in the Olympic Village and I am not even sure whether he attended the opening ceremony. However, he wanted to be there to eradicate bad feelings about his previous two Olympics.

When Matt and I were having our most beautiful row in Barcelona, Armstrong was blowing up with an immature performance that left him nowhere. Four years later in Atlanta, when Matt and I were having a terrible time, he was struggling – unbeknown to him – with a dozen lung tumours and finished out of the medals again. In Sydney he wanted to put that right. He didn't do badly. He finished thirteenth in the 148 mile road race, but he won a bronze in the Individual Road Time Trial, so that's one thing we have in common. We've both acquired an Olympic bronze medal that nobody ever remembers. We forget Armstrong's because he went on to become a multi-millionaire superstar far more famous for winning his seven Tours de France. And people forget the bronze medal that I won in the coxed pair in Seoul because I went on to win five gold medals. I still have the bronze though. It's in a cupboard somewhere in the house.

I'm not blind to the ambivalence that people feel about Armstrong, I'm just saying that here is a man who virtually came back from the dead, who suffered to an extreme that I've never known and then used his ferocious willpower to climb back to a position of utter dominance over his sport. He turned suffering on its head, he used it as inspiration – and then he worked like a dog. There is so much to admire in that.

OSCAR PISTORIUS

I like Oscar. I find him very down to earth and refreshingly normal, which is unusual in this day and age in most sports. He's been in the limelight for so long I expected him to be different when I met him for the first time at the first Paralympic World Cup in Manchester, but he was clearly a very nice, unpretentious guy and by then he was already world champion and record holder in the amputee 100 metres, 200 metres and 400 metres.

I remember what he told those children. 'I'm not disabled, I just don't have any legs.' I wouldn't be surprised if the children came away thinking that to run on two blades was one of the biggest thrills in the world. This is someone who did not so much triumph over adversity as refuse to believe in his fate as any kind of adversity at all.

He gives much credit to his family and I'm sure he's right. His mother and father took the decision to have both legs amputated below the knee when he was eleven months old after he was born missing the fibula bone in both legs. They scoured the medical world for a solution, dismissed the on-going trauma of reconstructive surgery and then set about treating him as a 'normal' boy, just like his older brother Carl.

'I got teased a lot at school,' he said, when we talked about it, 'but I had an elder brother with a big hand and he used to come and swing a few shots for me. Eventually I took up boxing and learned to look after myself. I remember my dad coming to pick me up from school one day when I was being bullied. He saw what was going on, but decided to stay in the car, because he knew he wasn't always going to be there to protect me. There's a stupid saying, "What doesn't kill you makes you stronger." It's a cliche, but it's a cliche because it's true. In the end it taught me tolerance and patience, and the fact that when I got big enough I just hammered the blokes who'd been tormenting me was pretty good, too.'

Oscar's strength of mind and purpose have come in handy,

I didn't grow up with a father who pushed me. If anything, Dad prepared me best by letting me get on with my sport.

The school crew.
Left to right: Nicky Baatz, Clive Pope, Robert Hayley, me, Peter McConnell.

...ing out on the river in school time? What a skive! But for four solid years we beat ...ost everyone we rowed against.

In Mike Spracklen's boat with Eric Sims, Adam Clift and Julian Scrivene in 1980. However, the boycott of the Moscow Games would thwart any Olympic hopes that year.

Sometimes a team just clicks, like ours did at the Los Angeles Olympics in 1984.

I achieved my goal of one gold medal in Los Angeles, ahead of schedule. Why didn't I stop then? I thought I could do better and win another one.

Andy Holmes and I won the World Championships in Copenhagen in 1987. If you can spread your self-belief into the minds of your rivals, some races are won on the start line.

...asing my second Olympic ...tory in Seoul in 1988 with Andy.

My family had started a fund-raising campaign to get me to Seoul and I was able to repay them with a gold medal.

Barcelona, 1992. Back in the boat after being diagnosed with colitis only a few weeks previously.

Jurgen's final words to us had been 'Have a good race. I think you'll win.' Funnily enough, we did.

My daughter and Matt's goddaughter, Natalie, was there to congratulate us.

Atlanta ❧ 1996

Despite the huge glare of a self-inflicted media frenzy, Matt and I went on to win gold in Atlanta in 1996.

You rarely saw me celebrating at the end of a race. Partly because was too exhausted, partly cause the major emotion was relief. Job done.

My fourth and final medal... or so I thought at the time.

But my obsession got me back to the gym, even after I was diagnosed with diabetes and struggling in 1997.

I battled through my conditic and back into a place in t boat. Training with the Sydn crew at Henl

All I know is that by the time I reached Sydney in 2000, I was truly fired up and inspired to give everything for one last assault on an Olympic gold medal.

...att, Tim and James – fellow conjurers of gold in 2000 and friends for life.

...ere is an aura when a team ...s right that is almost magical. ...had that.

My family were all there in Sydney. They had been put through the wringer by one man over the years – me.

A piece of my gold medals belongs to my coaches throughout my career.
Left to right: Mike Spracklen, Francis Smith and Jurgen Grobler.

Through it all my family have
been incredibly supportive
and an inspiration.

Beyond the age of thirty-eight, belief
in my performance as an oarsman
would have become a delusion.
Now I'm just deluded about golf.

especially in 2008 when the IAAF banned him from competing in able-bodied competitions (despite having invited him to compete in their own races in 2005 and 2007), citing the 'unfair advantage' allegedly supplied by his carbon fibre blades. He fought the decision and it was overturned by the Court of Arbitration for Sport (CAS) five months later.

Lesser men, and you have to remember he was only twenty-two when all this was going on, might have surrendered but he believed the claims against him were wrong and superficial. Clearly, CAS thought so, too. I'm no scientist. I have no idea whether the J-shaped blades, manufactured for him by a company that produces helicopter blades, provide any measurable kind of advantage, but I can see that Oscar also suffers disadvantages on the track. Traction suffers in the rain, wind blows him off course and he needs more energy than able-bodied athletes to get off the starting blocks, so it sounds like swings and roundabouts to me.

The thing I like best about Oscar is that he actively wants a level playing field. He isn't looking to win gold medals through some kind of favouritism. 'If the IAAF ever found evidence that I was gaining an advantage then I'd stop running.' As he said to me, 'It's not necessarily about winning, it's about being the best you can be.'

All that I applaud, but I have to be honest. When it comes to the principle of Paralympians competing in the Olympics, I think it's wrong. I understand where the desire comes from – to challenge yourself against the best – I think it's fine in exhibition races, but if we say to Paralympians, 'Someone among you is so good we're allowing them to jump ship to the Olympics,' we are denigrating and diluting the Paralympics themselves. I think Oscar should be considered a great Paralympian as it would raise the profile of the event and inspire athletes with disabilities all over the world to try to emulate his achievements. I'd like to see his competing in the Paralympics as the highest of aspirations, not a second-best option. That's just my opinion. I don't expect Oscar to agree and it doesn't mean I wouldn't love to see him race the world's greatest able-bodied sprinters at different events round the world. One thing is definite, though – he would beat me over 100 metres.

The funny thing is, he hated athletics at school. He was a rugby player by nature. When athletics came on the agenda he used to forge notes to his teacher, along the lines of, 'Dear Ma'am, Oscar is terribly sick. Thank you for understanding his predicament.' He said he used to go through the thesaurus to find the longest words to substantiate the forgery, as though the letter had come from his mother, but he was instantly found out every time. He was both forced to do athletics and walloped when he arrived home. Somehow a champion was born.

In fact, he took up athletics seriously only when a rugby injury forced him to abandon the team sport for a while and use running as part of his recuperation. He found he was surprisingly good. That's what I always said about rowing. I found it by accident and because I kept winning, I kept going. Oscar was the same.

'Blade Runner', as he is known, was only eighteen when he took bronze in the Paralympic 100 metres for amputee runners in Athens. He fell in the preliminaries for the 200 metres, but recovered and won gold. Four years later in Beijing, despite failing to qualify for the Olympics (he was fourth fastest in the able-bodied 400 metres in the South African trials), he became a triple gold medallist.

Still, I'm pretty sure he'll never allow himself to turn into a hero in his own mind. His favourite athletes are the ones who remain rooted to the ground. Joe Calzaghe is one of his idols, because he still goes to the same barber he went to before boxing made him famous. He has a great deal of time for Colin Jackson, the former British 110 metres hurdle world champion, and Valentino Rossi, the Italian MotoGP star. I can see what they all have in common. He told me, 'What makes them great sports people to me is not what they have accomplished, but the type of people they still are. With Colin I can sit down and chat for ever. You'd never guess he was once one of the world's great athletes, because he's such a humble guy. I'd like to think when I retire that I had a gift and I didn't waste it. I'd always want people to feel they can come up and chat to me, not put me on a pedestal.'

I think Oscar will achieve his wish. He is a poster boy, he is box office, but the one thing I do not describe him as is 'disabled'. He is the living example of someone whose apparent disability has been turned into something entirely positive.

MATT HAMPSON

As Armstrong would say, 'It's about getting back up on the bike,' but sometimes that isn't an option. Sometimes getting back to where you once were is impossible. What if you face the most basic choice of all – do you live or do you die?

Matt Hampson was a prop forward in his former life. He was a twenty-year-old from Rutland on the Leicester Tigers team with four Under-21 England caps to his credit and a reputation for fearlessness. The muddier, harder, more brutal the game turned out to be, the happier he was in the battle. In his first match for England against Wales he was smacked in the mouth and sin-binned. He loved every second of the initiation. He loved his sport. He loved his life.

In March 2005, in a routine training session prior to a match against Scotland, he settled himself for the scrimmage and heard his favourite word in the world: 'Engage.' The scrum locked, collapsed and he felt the weight of his team-mates fall on top of him. That was the last time his body would register feeling. He blacked out. His neck was dislocated under the press of bodies. He spent the next seventeen months in Stoke Mandeville Hospital, having acquired a new description. He was now a 'quadriplegic', paralysed from the neck down.

It is not, however, a description that sticks. Matt Hampson is still a prop forward. He is a prop forward in everything but deed. He loves rugby. He writes a column about it for the local newspaper, he works for a rugby magazine, he coaches the forwards at the local boarding school in Oakham, he helped organise a sponsored walk/barge ride from Rugby to Twickenham to raise money for charity. In the event, he took the barge option himself, despite recognising the obvious pitfall. 'The only trouble is I know the wheelchair – with me in it – will end up in the canal at some point. I've always been an accident waiting to happen.'

Sportsmen are often called heroes. I've never felt like a hero. To be honest, I see myself as two different people. The athlete and the person. The athlete is the one that people admire. They respect what he's done and I know I have to embody him for their sake. He has to exist for the purpose of the myth, but it's not me. It's somebody else, someone quite similar to me, but not the same. The real me is hardly different from the person I was before five gold medals came along. I am not a hero to myself, but in Matt's case I can't think of many words that would suit him better. To lie in a hospital bed, for week after week, month after month, at the age of twenty, unable to feed yourself, move yourself, even breathe by yourself and in the gathering knowledge that perhaps these things will be beyond you forever; to lie there and not surrender to bitterness is the greatest heroism I can imagine.

I gather it didn't come immediately. For an all-too-understandable while he lay there and cursed fate, not to mention the members of his family who surrounded him. He vented his rage and frustration on them, but his mother and his sister wouldn't take it. He had a hole in his throat to pump air into his lungs, and tubes and wires running all over his body, but they refused to make themselves victims of his anger any more than they refused to see him as helpless. 'If you go to bits, what use are you to him,' said his mother, Anne.

He began to look around. He saw people in the hospital, a specialist spinal unit, with similarly debilitating problems. Some had cancerous tumours of the spine, others were paralysed from traffic accidents or falls. All were severely disabled. There was a difference. They did not have the World Cup-winning England rugby captain, Martin Johnson, visiting their bedside. Nor a stream of stars, friends and team-mates from the rugby community. Nor a family telling him to get his act together while bringing him home-made food and DVDs. Many of the ill and injured were completely alone.

Matt decided he had a reason not just to live, but to live well. He looked around some more. He became aware of a businessman, Paul Tiana, in a nearby bed, partially paralysed by a fall from a horse in a point-to-point race. They became friends. Matt noted that Paul was so determined to keep his business afloat he would crawl out of bed in the morning, no matter how 'dizzy and crap' he felt, and go to work on his laptop. Unconsciously, Matt absorbed the scene and converted it to example.

He decided to become a prop forward who might not be able to scrummage any more, but could still delight in feeling the sun on his face or the sound of a beer fizzing as the ring pull is torn. He decided he could still go dancing at Stringfellows – in a wheelchair, but so what? – and still enjoy watching his old mates, the Leicester Tigers. He didn't just come back to life, he embraced it.

'When I was in hospital in my wheelchair, I'd look around at someone else and think, "God, look at that poor bloke in a wheelchair." I'd stopped thinking of myself like that. I never looked at myself from that moment on as being disabled. I'm probably a bit stupid. It's difficult sometimes. I do occasionally find myself thinking . . . what if? Then I pull myself together. If you go down that line you get bitter and twisted, and I'm not that type of person. It wouldn't be a very good reflection on myself, because I've had so much support from my family and the rugby community. I look at it like this: It was a freak accident and I'm kind of over it. I feel I must keep strong. My life isn't over. It's just changed.'

Matt came home to his village in Rutland and lived in a barn conversion attached to his parents' home. Funds were raised, much of it through the tight-knit rugby community, to supply twenty-four-hour nursing care. He needs a care team of ten people with two always on duty. It takes him three hours to get up and be ready for action every single morning. He still breathes via a ventilator through a hole in his throat. One of his dearest wishes is to be rid of it, yet people who visit always meet a bloke with a smile on his face. His father is building him a new home in the village to give him greater independence. He can't wait to move in and look out of the picture windows on to the view over the rolling Rutland countryside. That is the official version. The unofficial version is that he can't wait for the parties.

He has never seriously considered 'Plan B', as the patients in Stoke Mandeville, with typically dark humour, used to call suicide. There have been other men, other young rugby players, who have taken the view that life is not worth living as a quadriplegic. Matt went to talk to one of them. He tried to express the sense of fun and purpose he has found in his reconditioned existence, but it is an individual's choice. To some, to many, perhaps to most, being attached to a machine that breathes on your behalf is a burden that simply cannot be borne. Matt is more attached to hope. 'I might not walk again. I might not get any feeling back in my arms, but they're making progress with the research, so there's always hope.'

A number of his former Under-21 team-mates have done well for themselves. James Haskell, Tom Rees, Toby Flood have all earned full England caps and, instead of being grudging or resentful, Matt is delighted for them. He goes to matches at Twickenham to watch them and enjoys a few beers after the game. There cannot be many better definitions of generosity.

I know how I feel when I'm confined to barracks. It is the most awful feeling in the world and I generate huge amounts of misery every time it happens. Even though I don't like to talk about it, my conditions are life-threatening and restrictive. I have to walk around with an insulin drip attached to my stomach and a patch that reads my blood sugar levels. The wires get tangled up in bed at night. Sometimes I'm tied up in knots. This does not compare with Matt, attached as he is to a breathing machine at all times, but maybe I have an inkling of what he goes through with such astonishing cheerfulness.

I know my lifespan will be affected by the diabetes. How could it not be? But what do you do? You either accept it and live on, setting yourself new challenges, or you waste away. I can't, maybe won't, do that.

Like me, I suspect, Matt put a high value on being active. He was always big and strong as a child. His mum said he was banned from pre-school play group for being too boisterous. At twenty he was already a professional sportsman and an international, and then his world fell apart. But that is me talking. It isn't him. I'm imagining it all from my point of view. From his, the world didn't collapse, it just rearranged itself.

He still works out. He has a specially adapted cross trainer. His carers lift him from his wheelchair to a seat on the trainer, he is winched up into a standing position and strapped in place by his arms. He does a physio session to music. Why would he bother? I can tell you why. It is what any sportsman would do. It is how we see ourselves. As he says, 'Although physically I'm not an athlete any more, mentally I always will be.'

He's a brave man. Braver for the fact that he doesn't think so. 'I know it might sound surprising, but some aspects of my life are better since the accident. I've grown up. I think about people a lot more now. I appreciate the simple things in life, like a steak on the barbeque, a good conversation, a beer with my mates, a laugh and a joke. There are other people much worse off than me. I am just enjoying being alive really.'

FRANZ KLAMMER

I love skiing. I think it's magical. It's rescued me at some of the worst times of my life. I went off skiing with Ann and the children after that wretched time in South Africa. I didn't tell Jurgen. Basically, I went AWOL. The only person I called was Tim Foster, to ask him what he thought about me going. He was surprised. I'd never talked about anything personal with him before. He reckons to this day that the only reason I chose him over Matt and Jurgen was because I was sure he'd say, 'Go!' He may be right about that. He was always the unconventional one.

You can lose yourself skiing. I love the mountains and the peacefulness of it all. I like the freedom. When I was younger I'd watch the Winter Olympics and *Ski Sunday* on TV and reckon that if I'd been born in the mountains I'd have been one of those downhill racers. I sound like Muhammad Ali. 'I'm great at ski racing. I just haven't done it yet.' The reality is that the better I become, the more I realise I'm not that good at it, but it doesn't stop me trying.

One of my most memorable moments was meeting Franz Klammer at the Salt Lake City Games in 2002. He was a heroic figure in the history of ski racing, yet he came up and recognised *me*. 'I know you,' he said. 'You're Mr Olympics.' I've had many flattering moments in my life, and I try and take them in my stride, but it was difficult not to feel a thrill of pride when a guy like Klammer said that.

What do they say about pride before a fall? In theory skiing should be a smooth-running business, taking lifts to get you up and using gravity to get you down, but that isn't necessarily my experience. You get wild weather, pock-marked terrain, ground like corrugated steel, ice ruts and potholes, raving nutters, helpless novices and, in my case, trying to teach the mother-in-law how to snowplough. But the slopes in Salt Lake City were filled with unblemished twinkling white powder. They looked lovely to approach. They were the devil to escape.

On one of my outings I got a bit ahead of myself and ended up crashing headfirst into that powder. It was like falling into a three-foot deep duvet. My goggles and ski hat went flying; more to the point, so did one ski. I surfaced with a mouthful of snow and looked around for the missing items. The bobble hat was visible, standing up on a sea of white like a man buried up to his ears. The goggles were alongside, but a ski had vanished. I couldn't walk back without it, I'd be wading through snow up to my waist, so I just had to wander about like Long John Silver on one ski, searching for its long-lost fellow. It seemed to take hours, but I did eventually find it and came back down the piste a chastened man.

It's a strange business. I was sure of myself when it came to rowing. Self-belief was the vital factor in my achievements, but when it comes to any other sport confidence can be a dangerous beast. You can all too easily end up with your legs in the air and your head in a self-made snow hole, literally and metaphorically.

So I may be Klammer's Mr Olympics, but he certainly has all my admiration when it comes to the piste and, although the adversity he overcame was of a different order to those sportsman who have suffered terrible illness and disabilities, I still see much to admire in his approach to life off the piste, too.

The man they called the 'Klammer Express' was a giant in 1976 at the Innsbruck Winter Olympics. Only twenty-two, he won the downhill race in his home country, flinging himself down the treacherous course of the Patscherkofel, descending 2,854 vertical feet at 70 mph, flying like a rag doll over the murderous bumps, dangerously off balance, teetering on the verge of disaster with every slithering inch and winning, to the roar of 60,000 Austrians lining the course, by 0.33 of a second.

It was an amazing, death-defying run, a legendary descent and one that cemented his reputation as the greatest downhiller ever. He won the World Cup title in four successive years, 1975–78. He was in his prime. There seemed no end to his domination and then, suddenly, it stopped. He went through a profound, prolonged slump – some believe a training accident suffered by his younger brother in 1977 affected him greatly. Klaus Klammer was a teenager and already an Austrian junior ski champion when a spinal cord injury paralysed him from the waist down. His elder brother immediately set up a foundation to help young athletes in all sports who suffered disabling injuries. 'Klaus had no insurance, but doctors cared for him because his name was Klammer,' he said. 'Others are not so lucky. I want to help.'

It was a noble aspiration. The foundation flourished, but Klammer's career disappeared. His form dipped so dramatically he didn't even make the Austrian team to defend his Olympic title at Lake Placid in 1980. A psychologist might say that his brother's accident had awakened his sub-conscious mind to the fact that skiing – especially the way he skied – was a fickle and potentially damaging business. His style had been based on inelegant fearlessness. He revelled in speed. The introduction of a scintilla of caution destroyed his relationship with the sport. On the other hand, he had a new set of skis. Maybe they just didn't suit him. There's one more thing that strikes me, though. Think about it. He won an Olympic gold medal, in extraordinarily exciting circumstances, in his home country. Not much tops that. Perhaps even against his will, one part of his ultra-competitive nature was satisfied by that. It does happen. It is human nature. I was approached for a chat once by the New Zealand professional golfer, Michael Campbell, who won the 2005 US Open. He explained, 'My long-term goal was to win a major. Well, I won one and my drive has just gone. I've done what I wanted to do, but I'm still quite young. How do I get going again? How do I drive myself forward?'

I could understand all that. In some ways, the passion, the determination, the drive to achieve had lessened because he was satisfied. My advice, for what it was worth, was that it's always possible to reset your goals. I was lucky. After every gold medal I won, I was able to shoot for the next one. Old campaign over, new one begins. I just reset myself. 'Well, that's done. What am I going to do next?' But it's hard. When you are successful there are many more distractions. You get recognised more, you are invited to more things. It is so easy to lose focus and motivation. I do wonder whether the 'satisfied syndrome' was partly responsible for Klammer's dip in form.

I might ask him about this one day. We've met up a few times since that initial get-together in Salt Lake City, always on the golf course. Needless to say, we don't have in-depth, emotional conversations on the tee, especially when we're on opposite sides in the Alfred Dunhill Links Championships at St Andrews (the year I made the cut). However, whatever the nature of Klammer's problem, he did not give up. That attitude was already wired into him.

His origins in the sport were more humble and off-piste than the conventional ski-boys from Salzburg and the Tyrol. His parents were farmers in a rural community called Mooswald and, as the world's media gleefully reported from Innsbruck to dramatise his transformation from bumpkin to champion, he grew up mowing hay and milking cows. It is certainly true that the first thing he bought with his new-found wealth after the Olympic victory was a milking machine, an item not on my list when I won in Sydney.

The fight back to form was as treacherous as any of his downhill races, but much, much more protracted. Still he refused to retire. A corner was turned when he won a World Cup race at Val D'Isere in 1981 and two years later he was hailed again at the World Cup champion after a gap of five long years. I can only imagine what that meant to him, but a clue comes from a TV interview he did in Austria many years later. He was asked about his 'greatest moment' and instead of choosing his Olympic gold medal, he settled instead on a downhill victory in Kitzbuhel. The date is probably the key. It was 1984 – seven years after he had last won there. He finally retired, perhaps properly satisfied, in 1985.

But what am I saying – 'properly satisfied'? Few athletes ever know that feeling. Klammer, in later years, became a regular contestant in legends events and was a pretty consistent winner. Three times he won a sponsor's Jeep for finishing first in the competition and three times he gave it back. 'I race for the glory of being fast, not for a prize,' he said. 'Well, unless the prize is a Mercedes.'

4

OBSESSION

It's 1980 and I'm in my single scull, racing from Cookham to Marlow against Adam Clift. We're full pelt and there's an island coming up. I'll go one side, the Buckinghamshire side; he'll go the other side, the Berkshire side. Mike Spracklen, our coach, is following in the launch. This is one of his cunning set pieces, designed to pit us against each other and find out who is the fastest. I'm eighteen years old and have a shot at the Olympics. The competition is incredibly intense. This is my chance to impress. I must win. I must get there first.

I'm hauling the oars, exerting all the power I possess to make sure I emerge beyond our island in front, but I know that Adam will be doing the same. I can't see him and so I imagine him flying through the water, being pulled along by the eddies that run close to the bank, cleverly avoiding the low-lying branches that reach down into the shallows.

'Thhwackkk!' I hear the collision of boat and branch from the Berkshire side. Then I hear a colourful parade of four-letter words. Grimly, I smile. Adam has just suffered a water traffic collision with an inanimate bush. It's all over now. I can relax, but not for long. If I am to achieve my goals it is days like this – repeated over and over and over again – that will ensure I'm in with a shot of winning. There won't always be a branch to help me. If I'm to go on winning, I'll have to go on working.

*

When I was that boy wondering how long I could keep the winning feeling, I never imagined I'd retire just before I was thirty-nine. The age of forty would have seemed impossibly ancient to me then. I was only thinking one Olympics at a time. In fact, unbeknown to me, I was facing another twenty years of intense competition.

For two decades, if I ever went out to dinner I'd think about whether or how much I was going to drink. I'd worry about what time I'd go to bed. I still do. I'm probably obsessed from that point of view. My life revolves around my sport. Perhaps I'm too intense in some ways and too affected by my results. I ought to be able to switch off and think of something else now, but I haven't learned that trick yet.

I suppose I'm obsessed with winning and to win you have to train hard. You have to dedicate the time. I didn't like having to do the training. Sometimes I dreaded a hard session, but it is what you have to do to win. I like the feeling of crossing the line first and I want that feeling to last for as long as it possibly can. There is even a strangely satisfying pleasure that stems from a really hard training session, but it is not an end in itself.

I'm a typical human being. I don't want to cause myself any more pain than I have to. We are a race programmed to survive, but we're also a lazy race. We want to do the bare minimum to achieve our version of success. It's just my bad luck that an Olympic gold medal can only be produced by hours – make that years – of staggeringly hard graft. Not many people want to push the boundaries of comfort. I didn't either, but I had to. I was inspired by the need to win. I was inspired by the strength of my obsession.

This was always fine for me – it was my dream I was chasing – but it was different for Ann. We married just before the Seoul Olympics in 1988. She was an Olympic oarswoman herself (fifth in Los Angeles in 1984 and silver and bronze at the Commonwealth Games in 1986) and I was convinced she knew what she was getting into. She says she didn't and I must admit that in terms of the longevity of my career, the illnesses I've suffered and my slight reluctance to pick up the Hoover she hasn't had the easiest of times, especially as she worked as a doctor and we have had three children. I acknowledge everything she has done, but not necessarily out loud. She understands . . . I think.

Ann Redgrave: Steve and I have been married for over twenty years and, after all that time, he is still the most bizarre person I know.

I am taking on the role of narrator here, because it's futile to ask any sportsman to describe how they are obsessed. To them it is the most natural thing in the world to focus on one sporting goal so determinedly that every other aspect of their life is minimised. That isn't obsessive behaviour. It's necessary behaviour. They don't notice what they're missing, because they're not missing it.

I have certainly noticed that I am married to a stubborn individual who won five Olympic gold medals and never did any housework. He still doesn't. It didn't bother me then, when Steve was training. I did the shopping, cooking, cleaning, everything, as well as setting up my own osteopathy practice, because, if I didn't, it wouldn't get done. I took on the role of supporter for better or for worse, and, to be honest, we've had plenty of both.

I know what Steve's response would be. He'd say, 'You knew what you were getting into,' and to an extent that was true. I was an Olympic rower myself. I competed at the LA Olympics where Steve won his first gold. Two years later, at the Commonwealth Games in Edinburgh, I asked him out. We were both in relationships with other rowers that were fizzling out. He was an attractive bloke, a bit of a rebel, we'd been friends for a while and so I just asked him. He said yes, we went out and a year later he asked me to marry him. He said he knew a long time beforehand, but kept quiet because he just wanted to be sure. The proposal was vaguely romantic. He went down on one knee in a restaurant in Marlow, but the funny thing was he wouldn't tell anyone we were engaged. 'It was nobody's business,' he'd say. That is very typical of Steve.

I don't really know what I was expecting after we were married. None of it was normal. It was the run-up to the Seoul Olympics. Steve was going for his second gold medal, I was working as a doctor and in training for the Olympics myself. In the end I didn't get selected, so only went out as a spectator. Steve duly won his gold.

So we entered our married life, one athlete, one doctor, one house in Marlow Bottom, a bridging loan and crippling debt. We simply didn't have any money. Lottery money hadn't come on stream, sponsorship was minimal and Steve, being a professional athlete, couldn't go out and get a job. Then I became pregnant with Natalie and I do wonder whether the stress of the situation brought on Steve's colitis. Don't get me wrong, he was delighted to discover he was going to be a father, but he was acutely aware he had an additional responsibility. He thought I was adult enough to look after myself, but a baby was a different proposition.

His illness began in the summer of 1991, the same year Natalie was born. I thought it was acute gastroenteritis. He blamed it on some dodgy chicken. He was in hospital, on a drip. It was all very dramatic, but we both thought it was an episode that would soon be over. It wasn't. It persisted. Meanwhile, he was losing nourishment, vital electrolytes he needed to cope with training, and a lot of weight.

'Oh, you look lean,' one of the rowers told him at a training camp. No, he didn't. He looked as if he was suffering from malnutrition. Tell someone, I kept saying to him, but he wouldn't. He wouldn't let me say anything either, even though by then I was doctor to the women's rowing team. Strictly speaking, being a man, he wasn't my responsibility, so I respected his wishes and kept quiet.

In the end, though, he had to tell Jurgen, because he under-performed at the trials in Nottingham and he finally realised he couldn't go on suffering. Once it affected his rowing it was serious. He was sent for a biopsy, colitis was diagnosed and he was lucky, because the consultant agreed that as it was so close to the Barcelona Olympics they would throw every available drug at the problem. Usually, doses are mild to begin with and ramp upwards. Steve started at the top.

It seemed to work and I remember the sense of relief we all felt when a professor of physiology sat us all down and told us that Steve's strength would flood back once he was on medication. He was right, it did, enough to win his third gold in Barcelona, his first with Matt. It was only afterwards that he reacted against the medication and the symptoms came back with a vengeance. I suppose his body knew better than to play up during the Olympics themselves.

I might sound matter of fact when I discuss Steve's various illnesses and ailments. That's partly a function of being a doctor, I suppose, but it's also due to the sheer number of scares and alarms we have had down the years. I always remember the time I was supposed to be going on holiday with the children to Spain. It was the night before we were due to leave and we had gone to sleep when I was suddenly woken by him writhing around in pain, knees drawn up to his chest. I said, 'Oh, it's just the colitis, you'll be fine,' but even as I said the words I knew I was kidding myself. It was more serious.

I drove him to hospital and, sure enough, it was appendicitis, so my holiday consisted of flying the children to Spain to stay with Steve's mum and dad, and then flying straight back to sit at a hospital bedside. When they opened him up the appendix was so inflamed that they said it would undoubtedly have burst if they hadn't gone in as soon as they did. They complimented him on his high pain threshold, but we knew about that already. Rowers regard pain as inevitable, but even by an oarsman's standards, Steve has endured more agony than most.

The two years leading up to Atlanta in 1996 were, I think, the hardest we ever had. We were going through a strained time in our marriage and had been to see a counsellor. I don't think Steve was enjoying his rowing either. He and Matt always seemed to be critical of what they were doing. They were favourites for the Olympic medal and demanding perfection of themselves, plus they had gone out and said they would win it – Steve does have a tendency to open his mouth at inappropriate times – and that put extra pressure on them.

They did manage to win, but that was the famous occasion when Steve told the world to shoot him if he ever went near a boat again. I thought it might be the adrenaline speaking and I was proved right. Within twenty-four hours he'd changed his mind. He knew I would have loved him to stop rowing. Just to have a weekend as a normal family was my dream, but I never went so far as to give him an ultimatum. That would have been completely pointless. When you're confronted by someone whose whole life is competitive, you only create more friction by being confrontational yourself.

I suppose that was why he was all the more stunned when I supported him and encouraged him to carry on after he had been diagnosed with diabetes. I remember that phone call from South Africa when he said he wanted to give up and I suppose he was surprised that I didn't immediately say, 'OK, come home. Let's have a life,' but I genuinely didn't feel like that.

Giving in when the going was tough – that just wasn't him. That is not Steve. I didn't want him to give in to the disease. I couldn't bear the thought of him living the rest of his life with regret. He'd come that far. I may have been his exasperated wife, but I was also his supporter, so proud of the way he had fought through so many painful difficulties. It was a particularly low time for him and I just gave him my backing.

Anyway, we reached the ultimate goal – Sydney. By now there were three Redgrave children, including Zak, along for the experience and I was still working as team doctor. Perhaps people would find it strange that when we reached the Olympic Village I'd go to my room somewhere on the campus and Steve would pair off with his usual partner, Matt, and head for a nice little twin room overlooking the Olympic flame. Those were the team rules, though, and no one was arguing, especially not me, as I'd far rather Matt dealt with Steve's fidgeting and sleeplessness.

I drove the crew to the lake at some ungodly hour on the morning of their final. It was dark outside and very, very silent inside the bus. No one said a word. The air was fraught with nerves.

In Atlanta I'd been in the drug test marquee when he won the gold. This time they wouldn't let me hide and I sat in the stand with the children, holding Natalie, who was sobbing desperately because she thought Daddy had lost. From where we were sitting it was possible to think that the Italians had chased them down on the line and she took a lot of convincing that he'd won.

It was such a wonderful moment. I don't really know what I was thinking, but later I realised it was a sense of 'job done', perhaps for both of us. Steve had come through all his health problems, and I was just enormously happy for him. From a medical point of view, I thought then, as I still do, that to overcome the effects of all his illnesses was not just a triumph; it was an inspiration.

And he didn't change. Steve is just Steve. Thankfully he wasn't transformed by fame. His biggest ambition was to be a single sculler and it still disappoints him that he didn't make it. That tells you all you need to know.

None of this is a moan. I consider myself very fortunate to live where we live, have the life we have and possess three such well-adjusted children. You don't always see things clearly from the inside, but someone, a journalist, said to me once, 'You have a very functional family.' I thought about it and realised they were right. I have much to be grateful for.

Steve didn't compete for the applause. That was the furthest thing from his mind. He competed to see how good he could be and, as an ex-athlete myself, I suppose, deep down, I always understood. He is incredibly driven – sacrifice and focus, even tunnel-vision, are essential to achieve what he has done and, for all the ups and downs, I'm glad I've been here alongside him.

If I knew then what I know now, I'd have still asked him out that day in Edinburgh. As he said, 'You know what you were getting into.' Actually, I didn't, but we're both still here.

Tony McCoy

Rowing has its pitfalls – oxygen deprivation, kamikaze ducks, anglers throwing maggots at you from the bank – but it is hardly a life-threatening occupation. Horse racing over jumps, on the other hand, looks like a masochistic form of madness to me. For a start, no race horse on earth would bear my weight, but it's the rest of the picture I find so incredible.

To fly along at 35 mph on the back of half a ton of horse; to leap through the air alongside upwards of forty other competitors just as hellbent as you on the finish line; to endanger life, spine, brain and limb every time you go out there; to risk being either crushed or kicked to death or at the very least breakages; and to do it almost a thousand times a season, sustained by a spoonful of tea and half a chocolate biscuit, travelling crazily from Kelso to Wincanton seven days a week – someone explain to me the sense in that. I thought rowers were mad, but at least we get to eat 6,000 calories a day. A jump jockey can only stare longingly at a peanut.

I've owned a horse, well, a leg, and I've sat on a pony, but that's about as much as I know about equine sports. I had a share of a race horse known as Five Gold, which came seventh in its first race, won the second, and was runner up in the third. Then it caught a virus and unfortunately had to be put down, so not such a great experience. And the pony I 'rode' at an adventure camp, with my great friend Robert, when I was about fourteen, was a plodding beast that knew exactly where it was going, which meant I didn't have to do anything except bounce around like an idiot on its back. So I have no idea of what it must feel like to be any kind of jockey. They are a breed apart. If anyone thinks I, as an oarsman, was obsessed, let them consider the life of A. P. McCoy.

First things first. Aged eighteen, in Ireland, Tony McCoy broke his leg falling off a horse. It was a hideously loud snap, like gunfire, heard by everyone in a hundred yards' range. Tony looked down at his leg and could see the end of two splintered bones pressing against his jodhpurs. He was screaming in agony, blankets were brought, an ambulance called and he spent a desperate thirty minutes riding over the bumps and potholes of the road to the hospital in County Carlow, pumped full of the gas normally supplied to women during childbirth.

As soon as he was better, he went back to work riding horses. His boss wasn't desperately impressed. 'You want to be a jump jockey. You're some fool,' he said witheringly. 'I heard you crying like a baby with a broken leg. You're not hard enough. You're not tough enough to be a jump jockey.'

To me that would have been a sign. Do something else. To McCoy it was an invitation. Go right ahead. He rode his first winner, Legal Steps, at Thurles, Ireland, in March 1992. He won the Conditional Jockeys Championship three years later and then just about everything else the adrenaline-fuelled sport had to offer. To keep it brief: he was National Hunt's Champion Jockey (with the greatest number of winners in a season) 1995–96 and every year afterwards without exception. Now, in 2009, he has become Champion Jockey for the fourteenth successive time, with a body that is chronically under-fed and broken more times than a footballer's contract.

In April 2002 he rode more winners in a season than anyone else in the history of British horse racing (289), surpassing the record of the great flat-racing jockey Sir Gordon Richards (269) fifty-five years earlier. That same year he broke Richard Dunwoody's national hunt record of 1,699 lifetime winners and by 2009 the tally was over 3,000 – almost twice as many as any other jockey. I called myself an endurance sportsman, but McCoy takes the concept to a new realm. I suppose what he does for a living would be the equivalent of me taking a single scull over a waterfall into a crocodile-infested river seven times a day.

He is an extraordinary sportsman, one who always gets up, wipes the blood off his face, leaves missing teeth in the ground, wilfully ignores broken bones, dismisses the hovering ambulance, and defies medical advice and disbelief to pursue his over-riding goal in life – the next winner. He claims it is fear that drives him: 'Fear of someone else in my place, fear of someone catching me, fear of someone getting my job, fear of someone riding my horses, fear of someone saying, "He's not as hungry as he used to be."' I don't think there's very much danger of him looking relaxed.

If ever there was a sportsman who looks more miserable than me, it is Tony McCoy. In fact, the people who know him say he is fabulous bloke, with a deadpan sense of humour and great generosity, who is deeply appreciated by his fellow jockeys, many of whom he has put up at his various houses over the years. However, the years of wasting away to a weight well below natural for a man two inches short of six foot, breaking most of the bones in his body at least once, and sustaining between sixty and eighty falls a year, ten per cent of which are really bad ones, take their toll. He calls the endless weight-watching the 'most depressing thing in the world'. I can't imagine how terrible it would be. I ate to compete. He starves. It might be a joke – or it might even be true – that one jockey kept a noose outside his sauna for when the wasting just became too much.

McCoy's strength is a mystery to me. I know how I felt when I didn't eat enough after the onset of my diabetes and yet he is often described as, pound for pound, the strongest athlete in Britain. He doesn't necessarily agree. 'I don't know if I'm the strongest. Joe Calzaghe would maybe be tougher. I probably wouldn't beat him in the boxing ring, but I'd give Ricky Hatton a go at ten stone.'

You can only conclude that what drives him is a magnificent

obsession – to win or bust, often literally. He is now in his mid-thirties and people have suggested he might soften, but he scoffs, 'I would never soften. On the race course I'm unbreakable. This is a terrible thing to say, because people have died in this sport, but you need to be nearly prepared to die to win. And there's no excitement if you don't, to be honest.'

The medical staff at race courses have grown used to his attitude. They have come to understand that, with a little room for exaggeration, if he's not dead he'll be riding. He broke his back in a shattering fall in January 2008 and his doctors told him it was curtains for the Cheltenham Festival in March, but he threw himself into a fitness campaign that included ice chamber treatment, involving spending up to two and a half minutes in temperatures as low as minus 130 degrees. I understand the mind-over-matter approach to pain, but standing naked in the equivalent of Arctic temperatures would not be my idea of a pleasant time. I am happy to say I've never done it and I don't plan to.

As for injuries, they are an occupational hazard he mentally and physically surmounts all the time. He has no feeling down the left side of his face. 'From the top of my nose down to my upper lip is totally numb. I'm well aware that I'm not going to be in great shape when I'm older. Maybe it will be different then, but at the moment the pain is worth it. The good thing about being injured is that it's the only time in my life when I'm completely out of it and nothing hurts. As the morphine kicks in, you're high and couldn't care less.'

I share McCoy's attitude to injury to some extent, especially the part about mentally blanking what might happen later when you are older. The day we all sat down – Jurgen, Ann, my specialist, a sports scientist and I – to discuss my diabetes is still vivid in my memory. Jurgen asked a question that hadn't even crossed my mind. He said, 'Is Steve going to do himself any long-term harm if he continues to row?' I was shocked and actually quite moved. This was Jurgen Grobler, once attached to supposedly the most ruthless sporting machine – the East German system – that man has ever invented, caring about the future health and well-being of one of his athletes, even to the detriment of the team. It shocked me to discover how much I lived in the present, but it didn't change anything.

We still don't know what those final years of competition did to me. Maybe there will be such a thing as Redgrave Syndrome one day, brought on by the overload of stress I caused my body. Maybe I'll reach fifty in 2012 and that will be it. At least I'll get to see the London Olympics. The problem is, as far as we know, no diabetic has ever trained as long and hard as I did, with the same combination of volume and intensity. There's no model and nobody knows what will happen. I suppose I have in the back of my mind, however ridiculous this sounds, the words of a palm reader/medium I saw in my teens. She was some relative of my girlfriend at the time and I remember her telling me I'd have a heart condition by the time I was fifty. Mind you, she didn't tell me I was going to win five Olympic gold medals, which you might have thought would be relevant, so maybe she wasn't so good at her job.

Athletes have a mentality that doesn't dwell on problems. You have to move on. Quickly. I certainly did that as a competitor. I was never a good patient. I remember fantasising in training about being ill. 'Wouldn't it be lovely to have a cold and be tucked up on the couch instead of doing this bloody work,' I'd be thinking. Then I'd catch a cold and go training anyway. You imagine illness will give you a few days of beautiful escapism and then you don't take it when it's offered.

I still do it now. I went skiing a little while ago, took a tumble, cut my lip and hurt my arm. First of all, like an idiot, I put snow on my lip, which instantly increased the blood flow and left me standing in a huge red puddle. Meanwhile, my left arm was becoming more and more painful, and I thought I must have snapped a bone. What would normal people do at this point? Tell someone? See a doctor? I said nothing. I wasn't going to miss three more days of skiing, even if I did have to do it with a fractured arm.

Maybe McCoy and I are on the same wavelength. Plenty of stories demonstrate the scale of his obsession, from the uncontrollable mare he rode as a child (he fell off nine times out of ten) to his meeting with Sir Alex Ferguson at the 2002 Cheltenham Festival when McCoy's dream horse, Valiramix, lurched on to his nose and crashed to the ground after the third last jump in the Champion Hurdle. McCoy's physical injuries were the least of it. The horse did not survive and even the strongest men have their breaking point. He sat in the weighing room, head in hands, and cried. It was a desperate time. He went about his business afterwards, a gaunt and haunted man. Everyone on the race course, everyone in the industry, could see the extent to which Valiramix's death had affected him. No winners came as consolation. Perhaps out of desperation someone asked Sir Alex, a great racing aficionado, to have a word in the paddock. They had met many times before, but the Manchester United boss, a proven man-manager of sensitive thoroughbreds, took one look at the blank-faced misery in front of him and decided not to.

He told Tony later, 'I thought it might be a good idea to have a chat with you, but I took one look at you and thought it would be like trying to counsel Roy Keane after a defeat.'

When someone tells you that you remind them of Roy Keane at his most uncommunicative you know you've got entry to the obsessives' club. If I understand it at all, it is about being so hard on yourself you feel the joy of winning only fleetingly, but the torment of defeat drags on unbearably. Jockeys seem to specialise in self-punishment. Richard Dunwoody, twice winner of the Grand National and partner of the great Desert Orchid, called his autobiography *Obsessed*, which is a pretty good clue as to where he stood.

He wrote, 'It used to be said I would ride over my grandmother to get to the winning post first. The reality is that I wouldn't have seen her. My focus was that narrow. I saw only what I wished to see. Such single-mindedness came with a price. There was much that I missed along the way. World War Three could have broken out, but as long as it didn't mean the postponement of Fontwell, it wouldn't have affected me.' I don't think I was as ruthless as that. It was probably one of my weaker areas.

Obviously I was competitive, but I didn't want to seek

advantages I didn't think were fair, because, I suppose, I was confident in my own ability. I say that, but I still used to pull a few tricks for fun. At one point, the four of us – James, Tim, Matt and I – were invited up to Durham to take part in a few races as the prelude to a fund-raising dinner. We were split up and settled into two separate eights and then it was a question of winning – no matter what. There was to be what we call a 'floating start', which means you are not tethered to any kind of landing stage and just start to row when the flag drops. As we sat in the boat, waiting for the start, I told every member of the crew, 'Don't bother about the flag dropping. When you hear the word "Attention!" we're going to go.' You could hear the gasps from the crowd as we set off, but I was unrepentant. If we hadn't done it, the other boat would.

However, I justify these actions as 'a bit of fun', not ruthlessness. I also remember a time when I was rowing in a pair with Matt in 1990 and we were invited to train with the Canadian team, just before the World Championships in Tasmania. We were seasoned campaigners by then and they were so naive in comparison that I found a little 'tease' irresistible. We were doing practice starts. They were in a double scull. They would have a big advantage off the start, so Matt and I began bouncing up and down. The waves radiated outwards. By the time the flag dropped, our boat was in dead calm and they were bobbing about, completely unstable, thanks to our efforts. We won, I think.

A sports psychologist diagnosed Dunwoody as a compulsive perfectionist, driven to self-punishment if he didn't live up to his own expectations. As his expectations were of nothing less than perfection he caused himself terrible harm. He records dreadful incidents of unbridled rage, when he banged himself into the walls and doors of his own house after what he believed was a costly mistake on the race course. On one occasion a horse had unseated him at a ditch at Huntingdon, a routine matter in the life of a jump jockey, but he had taken it personally and furiously. The next day he appeared with a badly blacked eye and facial bruising. He had administered the punishment himself. That may explain why, when Dunwoody sent McCoy a text saying 'not to worry' at that morbid Cheltenham so-called Festival 2002, McCoy fired one right back, which read: 'That's a bit rich coming from you.'

Dunwoody retired in 1999, the legacy of the neck injury, despite a global search for *one* solitary specialist who would tell him it was safe to ride on (I know that feeling), and became the standard bearer for those athletes who never find the addictive adrenaline-rush of their chosen sport in civilian life. He could only be a sports junkie in remission, never cured. In 2008 he reached the South Pole with a fellow explorer after a forty-eight-day trek along a route previously attempted by Ernest Shackleton. Now who does that remind me of?

JAMES CRACKNELL

James Cracknell, two-time Olympic gold medallist in the coxless four, retired from rowing in February 2006. He had already enjoyed a sabbatical rowing across the Atlantic with the TV presenter Ben Fogle, an event which almost killed him, took forty-nine days, nineteen hours and eight minutes, and seriously annoyed his wife.

In April 2006 he ran the London Marathon in three hours, nearly an hour faster than his fellow Olympic gold medallist, Matt Pinsent (and about two and a half hours faster than me). In February 2008 he covered over 1,400 miles from Britain to North Africa in ten days, rowing, cycling and swimming the distance to raise money for charity. In January 2009 he took part in the Amundsen Omega 3 race to the South Pole, skiing up to fourteen hours a day in temperatures as low as minus 40 degrees, pulling 70-kilo sleds across 430 miles of ice, suffering weight loss, bad blisters and a chest infection.

I'm saying nothing.

NICOLE COOKE

Here's my take on cycling. It's not easy. I remember roaring downhill on a mountainous stretch of the Cape and taking hairpin bends under no control whatsoever, as the wind wobbled the front wheel dangerously and 16 stone of cyclist leaned nervously over the handlebars. I was paying attention to the fact that there was no barrier between me and land a few hundred feet below. I am full of admiration for Nicole Cooke.

Physically she is as tough as they come. Mentally she is rock hard. Emotionally she has been taken to breaking point, contemplated retirement and still found the strength to carry on. She's nobody's fool. She's fought all kinds of political battles in a sport where Britain had no track record whatsoever. She's blazed a new trail, won her Olympic gold medal and then set up her own road racing team. She is some athlete.

She has known injury and pain like the rest of us. A knee problem almost destroyed her racing career. She has suffered the typical crashes that come with racing in a peloton at high speeds, among 150 fellow racers, with the width of a bicycle tyre between you and a French gully a few hundred feet below. She's held her cycle helmet in her hands – split into pieces – and pondered the fact that it could have been her skull.

Then you ask her about 'sacrifice' and she responds as though you are clinically insane. 'Sacrifices! Everything I get from cycling is a positive gain, not a sacrifice. Even when I retire I shall always ride.' When she goes away on holiday the first thing she does is go for a ride on her bike. Maybe that qualifies as obsessive behaviour – at least I don't go rowing on my holidays – but if you ask Nicole, she marks herself right down for obsession. Say, six out of ten. In her mind, she is just doing what she enjoys. She admits she is highly competitive, but obsessed? Like the rest of us, she reckons she is just a normal-ish, highly motivated human being playing at something she's good at.

The word 'obsession' has unhealthy overtones, but that's not how it feels to the competing athlete. I think of it like this. People like doing things they're good at. Then it's easy to be motivated. If I'd lost every race I'd ever rowed, then I'd have been obsessive to pursue it so devotedly, but when you're winning it's just logical to carry on. That, I suspect, is how it is with Nicole. She's not just good, she's brilliant. She's world champion. She's Olympic champion. Why wouldn't you carry on?

In 2007, the year before the Beijing Olympics, Nicole had a second operation on her injured left knee and was close to enforced retirement. 'I reached the point where I thought, "Right, I might actually stop this. It's really sad. I'm not really enjoying the cycling. It's giving me a lot of emotional pain. I'm going out and all I'm thinking are negative thoughts about the negative situation I'm in. My Olympic dream is getting further and further away."

'I had the operation in September and by mid-November I started getting the pains again. I was thinking, "Oh my God, I've had an operation to correct this and the problem's still there." Something that had given me so much freedom – the buzz, the whole pleasure of being outdoors and riding under your own power – had turned into something I was just hating. I was riding so slowly and in so much pain. Also, one of my big dreams – to try and be Olympic champion – was looking as though it wouldn't happen.'

Nicole had joined the club of Olympian doubters, membership open to all with on-going injury and illness. I certainly was a member of that club over the years, but it's funny how often the most persistent, determined, tenacious athletes end up cancelling their membership. It isn't just fate that decides the outcome, it is the furious search for an alternative to failure. That isn't obsessive behaviour. It is good, practical common sense.

In Nicole's case, it was a word from her bike mechanic that salvaged her career. He took her to see a doctor he had worked with before and, thanks to the new medical advice, she began to make slow but marked improvements. The culmination was the 102.6 kilometre road race in Beijing, which she won on the finish line, in a tumultuous thunder storm, pelting past Emma Johansson of Sweden and Tatiana Guderza on the last uphill climb to claim her first Olympic gold medal. It was the first of nineteen golds for Team GB, the greatest haul in a hundred years. It seems apt that Nicole started the rush after a lifetime of landspeed records on her bike.

When she first arrived on the scene, some assumed she might be the victim of 'Pushy Father Syndrome', because her father, Tony Cooke, had been a competitive cyclist himself and was a visible presence in her life. When he was arrested (then released without charge) at the Athens Olympics for painting her name on the course in advance of the road race – a traditional encouragement in the cycling fraternity – that cemented the idea of paternal dominance, but it wasn't true.

Tony was indeed enthusiastic on his daughter's behalf, but, frankly, he had little choice. 'I remember mornings at home when a gale was blowing and the rain was lashing down, lying in bed at 6.30 a.m., inwardly praying that I wouldn't have to get up. But, sure enough, the door would be flung back and Nicole would burst in. "Come on, Dad!" She was eleven at the time.'

Nicole was the author of her own career. 'Dad and my brother Craig, who also rode, never seemed to have the same urgency as me. It was always me that wanted to get out of the house. I think I suffered from Pushy Daughter Syndrome, not the other way round.'

She was so good so quickly in British and international road races that in theory she qualified for the Sydney Olympics. She was seventeen. The world governing body had an age-limit of eighteen and the British authorities refused to fight it. She made a stink. They didn't like that. She didn't go, but she is not one to nurture bitterness. The injustice merely fuelled her desire to win more. You would like to think that her phenomenal record of success in the next few years – pointedly including an Olympic gold medal – has rewritten official attitudes. It began with gold in the Manchester Commonwealth Games and has continued to include virtually every single prestigious road race open to women in the world. She has won the female Tour de France, the Giro Donne (the Italian Tour over ten gruelling, mountainous days), the Thuringen Rundfahrt (the German equivalent), every event that takes heart, strength and competitive steel to still be in fighting at the end. She is a genuinely tough athlete, a mixture of mind and muscle.

I thought it was significant when one of our victorious coxless four, who won the gold medal in Beijing, thanked her personally at the Sports Journalists Awards during a speech. He turned to face where she was sitting in the audience and told her first hand that the whole rowing team had watched her win that first gold for Britain and credited her with the rush of GB triumphs that followed. She seemed stunned, but she certainly wasn't contented.

After the Olympics she narrowed her eyes and decided to go for a new record. No rider – male or female – had ever won a World Championship and Olympic road race in the same year. Now they have. At the age of twenty-five, she won the world title in Varese, a 138 kilometre road race, holding off the challenge of the 'flying Dutchwoman' Marianne Vos. 'Straight after the Olympics I realised there was a chance to write cycling history. It was an inspiration to me when I got back into training.' That makes sense to me. Get off the bike, reset the goals, climb on again and go.

JONNY WILKINSON

Few of us have a life that turns on one single, solitary, stand-alone moment. Jonny Wilkinson does. In the public perception at least, his fame, reputation and glory all stem from one kick in the 2003 Rugby World Cup final which earned England the title of champions; one moment, one chance, one precise execution changed his life for ever. 'Thirty-five seconds to go . . . This is the one . . . It's coming back for Jonny Wilkinson . . . He drops for World Cup glory . . . It's up, it's over . . . He's done it . . . Jonny Wilkinson is England's hero yet again . . .' How many times in the intervening years have we heard that snatch of commentary from Radio Five's Ian Robertson. With the score against Australia tied at 17–17 and thirty-five seconds remaining, he received a pass from Matt Dawson, the scrum half, and set himself for a drop goal. The world watched as though the whole process was in slow motion. Tense, gripped and worried, I was watching it with Roger Black in a hotel in Portugal, where we were supposed to be speaking at a conference, but that could wait.

Jonny dropped the ball to his feet. It landed slightly off-centre, bouncing towards him as he struck it with his right foot. The power was reduced, but the accuracy was deadly. He looked up. He could see the posts. He knew the ball's trajectory would take it between them. The deadlock was broken, as the white half of the crowd roared and the gold half stood silent. England would win the Rugby World Cup for the first time in history.

Did it take courage? Yes and no. For those watching – almost breathless with the tension and intensity of it all – it was a hugely gutsy performance, but for Jonny, for the athlete who had trained so long, so hard, so obsessively, it was an act committed on automatic pilot. That is what I believe it was like for him. When I came off the water in Sydney, so many people asked me about the race. 'It must have been incredibly tough,' they said. Yes, it was the usual, draining, hellish, painful six-minute experience, but actually, no, it didn't kill me. It is what we geared up for. We were racing. We expected it.

Jonny, I am sure, felt the same. Throw a novice into that situation and they would have panicked, but for someone who had trained and primed himself to face such a moment without flinching it wasn't courage that buoyed him in that brutal moment, it was the years and years of commitment beforehand.

Without that breadth of preparation it could never have happened. He has said so himself. 'I was left to do exactly what I had spent an unhealthy amount of time doing already in my life. All the hours of isolation, of dreaming, of crying, of screaming and of cheering, the practice sessions in car parks, on football pitches, in swimming pools, in hotel rooms and in my sleep added up to perhaps this one repetition. In a strange way that drop kick symbolised the bigger process of winning the cup. I had learned over time, with practice, with the influence of others, how to make something I wanted to happen, happen. This time of all times, it worked.'

We met – well, we were in the same place at the same time, Jonny and I – at the 2003 BBC Sports Personality of Year awards, when I received the all-time Golden Sports Personality of the

Year trophy for the sportsperson of the last fifty years. Clive Woodward told me that some of the England players were sitting in the audience sending texts to vote for me, even though, strictly speaking, we'd been told to turn our mobiles off.

At the same time, Jonny was winning the individual award. I think that was an embarrassment from his point of view. He seemed very uncomfortable about being singled out for a special honour and I identify completely with that. I had no business winning the same award in 2000 when rowing fours is a sport from which it is impossible to select one individual. Fair enough, if I'd achieved my dream of being a gold medallist in the single scull, but without Matthew, James and Tim what could I have achieved? One man in a coxless four would be as much use as a rowing boat without oars.

I've always felt I had something in common with Wilkinson. He was obsessed, intense, although I am sure he has mellowed a little now. In the days of the World Cup he practised to the point of irrationality. He reckons he has kicked a million balls, up to 300 place kicks the week before a game, 250 punts with the left foot, 250 punts with the right foot. Daily (six to seven times a week) he struck twenty drop goals with either foot and fifteen to twenty restarts. He is infamous for remaining out on the practice field for two, three, even five hours if he wasn't happy with his kicking. Sometimes, if he thought a successful kick was a little flukey, he would go through a whole set of kicking challenges again. He would never cheat himself just to go home and collapse in front of the TV. He defined perfectionism and the dreadful exaction of commitment that being a perfectionist imposes. He sacrificed relaxation and enjoying himself to the higher purpose of kicking a ball.

It sounds crazy, but I understand. Throughout my career I behaved in ways that could easily be dismissed as mad. Under that crude label you could list: not drinking beer on a Saturday night as a teenager, competing despite colitis, competing despite diabetes, competing despite being thirty-eight, even training through the night to limit the effects of time difference before going out to Australia . . . I could go on. Wilkinson lived a life that looked insane to anyone outside it – why would you spend five hours kicking rugby balls when you were already pretty brilliant at it – because he could not bear to feel under-prepared.

At that World Cup in Australia he was the mainstay of the team, because the grinding style of rugby they played required him to amass points with his kicking. Flamboyant tries were a rarity, Jonny's kicks were a necessity. His preparation allowed him to turn on the game brain, the automatic pilot, and succeed. Panic had been expunged by repetition.

From afar I have watched Jonny Wilkinson's subsequent career; the catalogue of injuries and the determined quest to go on playing. I don't think anyone could fail to admire him, not just for the kick that crowned England rugby's finest achievement, but for the million stubborn, dogged, obsessive, committed and determined moments that had gone before.

5

COMPETITIVENESS

I AM NOT SLEEPING. I am lying here awake in a hotel room near Crawley, tossing and turning, my head plotting and planning to win tomorrow's competition. By the time dawn comes I'll be exhausted, and yet this is the day that matters most: the final. How we made it this far is a minor miracle, given my physical condition, and now I am going to have to survive on adrenaline alone.

There are four of us in this together, but as the leader, the team captain, I feel the responsibility hugely. I may be the oldest competitor, I may be overweight, but I still believe in my capacity to win. I don't want to let the other three down. They're my team-mates, they need me, they rely on me to some extent. Above all, I can't bear the thought of doing less than my best. I am not the same athlete I once was, but, trust me, I shall be massively, desperately disappointed if by the end of this day my team are not crowned winners of the 2008 televised edition of *Superstars*. Someone must take home that small plastic trophy and that someone must be me.

A competitor competes. That is what we do. I may have won my last Olympic gold eight years ago, but competitiveness doesn't fade away with the last strains of the national anthem. It survives, getting older, getting fatter, even getting beaten. The goals may change, but the principle remains: in competition, I will do everything I can to win. That explains why I haven't slept properly all week.

Superstars, which has been around for years, is a televised competition that pits athletes against each other in all sorts of different sporting competitions. Swimming, running, climbing, gym work, cycling . . . Kevin Keegan caused a famous moment by falling off his bike and suffering a horrible graze. Joe Frazier made even more of a splash in the 1973 series in America. He dived into the pool and nearly drowned. He couldn't swim. The producers were aghast. Why didn't he tell them? 'How was I to know I couldn't unless I tried it,' he said. Typical athlete.

I had been in the competition twice before. I came third both times. Not bad, given the opposition, but this time I wanted to win and I knew it would take more than brute force to do it. I decided to be cunning instead, so I learned the rules. I learned the rules so well, I knew them better than the production team. That was a good start, but it was going to take more than that.

On the first day we walked into Crawley Leisure Centre and the first thing I saw was the climbing wall. 'Oh bloody hell,' I thought, looking upwards about thirty feet. The four captains (Dame Kelly Holmes, Roger Black, Mike Catt and myself) had to race to the top to decide which order we would pick our teams. 'Oh bloody hell,' I thought again. I'm 19 stone these days and there's a lot of weight for gravity to pull on. On the other hand, there's competitive bloody mindedness.

Kelly reached the top, the rest of us fell off at roughly the same point, but I reached that point the fastest. I had second pick – result. Then came the advantage of plotting. I knew that Alain Baxter, the former Olympic downhill skier, had won *Superstars* a couple of years ago. He was going to be my first pick, if Kelly didn't choose him first. She didn't, preferring her old friend in athletics, Iwan Thomas. Good, I'd remind Alain of that when I needed to goad him. 'Remember, Kelly didn't pick you when she had the chance.' There's nothing immoral about that. It's all part of the game.

We ended up with a fabulous team: Alain, Shelley Rudman, winter Olympic silver medallist in the skeleton bob, Lee Sharpe, the former Manchester United footballer, and the fat one, me. All the teams were good, but now I liked my chances.

During that competition I don't think I won anything as an individual, but as a team we held our own. My biggest kick was winning the tug of war against Mike Catt's team, officially the chunkiest of the series. Captained by the world champion rugby player, it featured Jane Crouch, the female world welterweight boxing champion, Mark Foster, the Olympic swimmer, and

Martin Offiah, the rugby league star whose physique was good enough for him to have posed naked for *Cosmopolitan*. And we still beat them in the tug of war.

It's all about technique. You can have all the strength in the world, but a rower understands the dynamics of getting low and using leg drive as leverage. It was just as well that we were victorious in the tug of war, because there weren't many other out-and-out wins, but it didn't matter – I was still world class at cunning strategy.

Take the 'dips' round. One of the gym exercises would pit Shelley against, among others, Martin Offiah. She was, understandably, worried. 'I don't want to embarrass myself,' she confided to me before the start. She didn't have to worry. I'd already worked out my plan. 'Don't do it then,' I said. 'Oh, I've got to. It'll look so bad if I pull out.' 'Yeah, but not if I pull you out. You're going to lose anyway, so why waste your effort. I'm going to save your energy for something you can win.' She was happy with that.

So, just before the start of the dips contest, I threw in the towel. 'I'm saving my secret weapon for later in the series,' I announced. The other captains looked surprised. They may not have known it was an option, but, as I said, I knew the rules. Put it this way, I knew there was nothing in the rules against it and, furthermore, I'd made friends with the referee, Graham Poll.

So it has come down to the final and, thanks to those sleepless nights, we are in it. Head to head with Kelly's team, a formidable line-up, including Thomas, the footballer Roberto di Matteo and cricketer Graham Thorpe. I have injured my hip flexor muscles, but that is pretty well balanced out, because Thorpe has pulled his hamstring. There are three more events to go – winner takes all.

First is the archery and my team wins pretty convincingly. Then canoeing and we lose pretty convincingly. It all comes down to the outcome of the triple-test in the gym. It is perfectly possible for us to finish level on points. I think the producers would love that outcome. 'That would be nice and dramatic,' I bet they're thinking. But athletes don't do nice. I am going to find a way to win.

First test: squat thrusts. I choose Shelley to fight it out with Roberto. She knows I have faith in her and she's phenomenal. They race to complete sixty squats and she only finishes six seconds down. We carry that penalty into the next test, but it will be possible to overturn such a tiny deficit.

Second test: cycling. The first one to complete a kilometre wins. I pick Lee Sharpe to take on Iwan Thomas, the only trouble being that Iwan was a BMX biker in a previous athletic life, and we go into the third and final test now trailing by thirty seconds.

I suppose, dimly at the back of my mind, I know that this is not an Olympic final and that my whole world does not rest on the outcome of a 'dips' contest between Dame Kelly Holmes and Alain Baxter, but try looking into our eyes – it is only the present that matters. We are warring for a piece of plastic on semi-primetime TV and we are behaving as though we would sell our souls to succeed. It's ridiculous. It's crazy. It's the nature of competitiveness. It doesn't come with a gauge. It is either on or off. Now, in this moment, it is on full.

First one to sixty dips wins, but Kelly gets a thirty-second start. She has completed forty-two dips before Alain even begins. We roar him on. It's a mountain to climb and he is only used to going down them, but I had the sense (or the mischief) to have a little word with him before he started. 'Remember Kelly didn't pick you . . .' I mentioned casually. Now he's fired up and the gap is closing, but Kelly still has a formidable lead. When Alain reaches thirty, she's already in the fifties. Less than ten to go, but she is slowing. The tiredness, the emotion, the pumping adrenaline is draining her, and she falters on her fifty-eighth dip. She has only two to go. She puts in one more massive effort . . . fifty-nine. Only one more to go, but the bell sounds suddenly. Alain has finished. Incredibly he has performed sixty dips in twenty-eight seconds. If it isn't a world record, it ought to be. We've won. Our team celebrates, hugs all round and Kelly . . . Dame Kelly Holmes, the double Olympic gold medallist, is gutted. Absolutely wretched. Her gold medals will mean everything to her again soon, but at this precise moment that little bit of plastic is the only thing that matters. And it's mine.

Tanni Grey-Thompson

Tanni is as bad as I am. Maybe worse. I've known her a long time. Her first Paralympics was Seoul, my second Olympics. Her fifth and last Paralympics was Athens, the one after I retired. Our paths often crossed and in all that time I have never doubted for a moment that she is one of the most competitive athletes on the planet. The outcome is therefore predictable: eleven Paralympic golds, over thirty world records and six victories in the London Marathon.

Tanni retired as Britain's greatest wheelchair racer in May 2007 and was happy to do so. Her body was slowing down – I know that feeling – and she moved out of the sport with no regrets. However, as I've said, you can be in remission from competitiveness, but never cured. The urge for combat is in the blood and she just became competitive about other things – work, public speaking, training for recreational triathlons, arguing with her husband.

I asked her about it. 'Ian and I are competitive about everything. Absolutely everything – except chess, which I can't stand because it's so tedious. I would rather lose it quickly than play it. I don't have the brain to think two to three moves ahead. But apart from that, everything else is a localised war game. I have to have the final say. He's been involved in coaching me for years, so it must sometimes appear that we're having a permanent argument, but actually we're on very equal terms. If I'd married someone who agreed with me all the time it would never have worked. If I'm wrong, he'll tell me. He doesn't let me be a drama queen.' Four days after she gave birth to their daughter, Carys, Ian said impatiently, 'Are you coming to training camp, or not?' Tanni said she'd have been fuming if he hadn't done so.

Like me, Tanni took care never to extend that competitive spirit into overt hostility with rivals. Why react? Let them worry about you. 'I want to beat everyone at everything. I'm quite confrontational with Ian, but with fellow competitors I always went the other way. It was part of the process of focussing. It would be a terrible mistake to get involved in some scrap. If people were pushing me into parked cars during a road race I just made sure it wouldn't happen again next time. I treated it as a learning process.'

That doesn't mean she didn't enjoy mixing things up a bit, though, and there were loads of ways to do that. She told me that if she knew one of her rivals preferred to focus quietly before a race, she'd sit beside her and chat. If she knew people preferred to be chatty, she'd be quiet. On some of the longer road races, when they formed a peloton like the cyclists, she'd conduct a loud and bizarre conversation in German with one of the girls. All good fun at nearly 20 mph.

'I can't help it. I was always competitive. I can't remember when I wasn't. My mum was very driven and I suppose I take after her. I have a sister, eighteen months older than me, and it never occured to me not to compete with her because I was born with spina bifida. I competed with her whether she wanted to or not, over everything – how fast we got dressed, how long it took to eat dinner. I don't think it registered with her what I was doing. She certainly wasn't competing with me.'

When Tanni went to school she competed at everything there too – spelling tests, general knowledge, anything. Then, when she was about eleven or twelve, she started to enter school sports competitions – wheelchair racing, swimming, field events, archery. It didn't matter what it was as long as it was always her against everybody else. She tried team games, too, but it would confuse her when other people on her team weren't so bothered. How could they not be bothered?

'If you want to be a recreational athlete that's fine, that's brilliant, but if you're sixteen years old and you're claiming you want to be an athlete for your country at the 2012 Olympics, yet you're only training twice a week and you're not watching your diet, then I think, "Hmmmm. Not good enough. You don't want it enough."'

Tanni trained twelve times a week as an athlete, often with Ian on his bike beside her, pushing her. It wasn't losing that terrified her. It was the thought of being on the start line and not being in the best possible shape. The thought that there was somebody out there better, stronger, tactically more aware, so terrified her that she trained 150 miles a week until she was close to collapse.

'Because, as an athlete, competitiveness works. It's phenomenal. It can carry you through an awful lot of trouble. Your body and mind are the raw materials, but it is the thrill of competition that drives you. It is the catalyst. When it clicks, it carries you through. You can overcome anything. It's about never giving up.'

I recognise everything Tanni says. It is a process that any winner would understand and any loser wouldn't. There was a race in Athens, two races in fact, that sum up the Grey-Thompson killer instinct. The first was the Paralympic final of the 800 metres wheelchair race. This being her swansong, her final Paralympic Games at the age of thirty-five, she was the favourite and the focus of heavy attention. As well as the nation's expectation, she had her own personal supporters in Greece: husband, parents and daughter. The stage was set, the competitors lined up and then it all went to hell.

'I made a stupid, stupid tactical mistake. All those years of experience counted for nothing. I boxed myself in and as we went through the bell for the final lap I knew there was no way back. I tried. There was nothing I could do. I finished seventh. It was horrific.

'I found my family afterwards. They were all crying. It was probably better that way. It was so bad, that I was given the option by the GB Paralympic team of going home. Can you imagine that? To be given the option to flee the scene of some criminal racing. I said, "No, I'm staying." A few days later was the Paralympic 100 meters. Even now I remember everything about that race. Everything.'

Tanni was sick twelve times on the warm-up track. She was so nervous, more nervous for a race than she'd ever been in her life. When they called the athletes on to the track in the Olympic Stadium, she was almost beyond moving at all. The other girls went for a warm-up lap, she just sat rooted to the line. She couldn't move her hands. She was shaking. She just sat there quaking with nerves.

'The race was due to start at 6.03 p.m. I looked at the clock. It said 6.00 p.m. I remember the click of the stadium clock as each minute passed. 6.01 . . . 6.02 . . . It was as though time had been suspended and my arms with it. Then through this fog I heard it. "Ready, set, go."

'It's a bad start. I'm faltering, still badly hampered by my nerves. The Italian, Francesca Porcellato, has made an amazing start. She's out in front of me, but I'm not panicking. A tunnel seems to come down round my lane. I am staring straight ahead. Moving now. Moving faster. By 50 metres I'm catching her. By 60 metres I'm past her. I don't see anyone in front of me again.'

Tanni remembers every second of that race. It makes her feel sick even now to think of it. She crossed the line with this demonic look on her face. Not happiness. Something much darker than that. 'I felt, if this is not too biblical a word for it, a sense of redemption. I believe to this day that I was carried to that gold medal not by years of training, years of experience, years of winning. I was carried to that gold medal by my will to win. It was all I had left and it was enough.'

EMIL ZATOPEK

I never met Emil Zatopek, so why do I feel we would have enjoyed common ground? Probably because, to achieve what he did he trained, and trained, and trained like demon, and so became the greatest long-distance runner of the twentieth century. Zatopek died in 2000 at the age of seventy-eight, coincidentally the year I retired, but the stories of his prodigious endurance have been handed on as legend.

I have to like a man who said, 'It is at the borders of pain and suffering that the men are separated from the boys.' I thought my training was punishing, but I don't remember pounding for miles through Eastern bloc snow in heavy boots at night with only a hand-held torch as a guide. Nor turning up at an Olympics, winning two gold medals and deciding to enter my first marathon as well to pass the time, then winning it by a clear half mile. The feat of the little army colonel from then Czechoslovakia at the 1952 Helsinki Olympics was so extraordinary it surely cannot be repeated.

Sometimes sport throws up a story that is almost too much to grasp. How can we, in our age of specialism, understand an athlete who trained in his army boots, without a coach, who won that improbable triple in Helsinki (5,000 metres, 10,000 metres and the marathon) and who retired having broken eighteen world records, from 5,000 metres to 30 kilometres.

He became a national hero in Czechoslovakia and an athletic icon round the world, celebrated for his results, revered for his determination and respected for his domination. Funnily enough, no one says much about his competitiveness, mainly because the competition was invisible, so, more often than not, he competed against the clock. He raced against time and his human rivals were usually left behind like trailing bridesmaids by his rhythmic, relentless, torturous stride. But he was just as much a competitive animal as the rest of us. He had to be. No man has a track record like Zatopek's without a burning will to win.

He was little more than a child, sixteen years old, working at the Bata shoe factory in Zlin when, as he told it, 'One day the factory sports coach, who was very strict, pointed at four boys, including me, and ordered us to run in a race. I protested that I was weak and not fit to run, but the coach sent me for a physical exam and the doctor said I was perfectly well. So I had to run

140

and when I got started I felt I wanted to win. But I only came in second. That was the way it started.' Those are the emotions of a competitor. Coming second is not enough. Wanting to win is a way of life. It is significant that although he had never run with any serious intention beforehand, this one taste of racing was enough to turn him, the son of a Moravian carpenter, into a would-be Olympian.

His whole life was a study in competitiveness, initially against himself. He wasn't the most natural, most fluent of runners, so he introduced himself to a furious regime of training, modelled on the Flying Finn of the twenties, Paavo Nurmi. Zatopek was one of the first athletes in the world to seriously adopt interval training – fast sprints and recovery jogs – to build stamina and speed muscle recovery. I can't accuse him of masochism, given the painful lengths I went to myself, but maybe even I would have baulked at riding a bike from Prague to Berlin just to take part in an international sports meeting.

The result of his efforts was a running style so torturous spectators actually feared for his survival. The legendary American journalist, Red Smith, was horribly disconcerted. He said, 'Zatopek ran like a man with a noose around his neck . . . the most frightful horror spectacle since Frankenstein . . . on the verge of strangulation; his hatched face was crimson; his tongue lolled out . . .' Zatopek didn't care. 'I was not talented enough to run and smile at the same time,' was his response – so he was a forerunner in the field of soundbites as well, then.

But whatever Zatopek's top half was doing, his legs were churning out stride after stride of metronomic running that broke the heart and resistance of even the most iron-willed opposition. He won the London Olympic 10,000 metre title in 1948 by running a succession of seventy-one second laps that crushed the field. He broke the world record by 11.8 seconds.

Then came his fight against the laws of probability at Helsinki. By now his reputation had spread around the world. The Finnish crowds were gathering to hail this human running machine. He obliged first with victory in the 10,000 metres, beating his own world record by an astonishing forty-two seconds. Four days later he was crowned the 5,000 metre champion and attention was turned to the marathon, an event he had never run in his life. This bothered him only slightly. He was secure in his powers of endurance, but a novice in pacing strategy. He decided, not illogically, to run in the footsteps of a master.

He noted that Jim Peters of Great Britain had run the fastest marathon in history only six weeks beforehand and, having carefully noted the Briton's racing number from the local newspaper, he introduced himself on the starting line. It's a wonderful thought. 'How do you do. I'm Emil Zatopek from Moravia, double gold medallist. I'm just going to track you, old boy, if you don't mind, because I might have a little bit of trouble with my pacing.'

It is hardly surprising that Peters bolted off at an alarming rate and by 15 kilometres was already running out of engine. Zatopek and Gustav Jansson of Sweden had caught up with him and at least one of them was growing a little concerned. 'The pace? Is it good enough?' enquired Zatopek. Peters did what anyone in the same desperate situation might do. He dissembled. He pretended he was fine and that, if anything, the pace was too slow. Zatopek needed little further invitation. 'Are you sure the pace is too slow?' he double-checked he had heard Peters correctly and then forged ahead, taking Jansson with him.

Zatopek, still learning from his new environment, noticed that the Swede took a slice of lemon at a feeding station. He was unsure whether to follow suit, having never taken any sustenance during racing or training. He decided to watch Jansson's progress. 'I thought, "If he runs well, at the next feeding station I will take *two* lemons."' Jansson faded. Zatopek never did pick up any lemons.

Instead he made triumphal progress to the finish line, so far in front that he chatted amicably to policemen, supporters and cyclists en route to the Olympic Stadium. When he entered the arena he was hailed by a huge crowd chanting his name and as he went through the finish line, after 2 hours, 23 minutes and 3 seconds, he was hoisted on to the powerful shoulders of the Jamaican 4 x 400 metre relay team who carried him around the track on a lap of honour. He was already signing autographs when the silver medallist, Reinaldo Gorno of Argentina, arrived in the stadium. Zatopek broke off his socialising for a moment to greet the runner-up with a slice of orange.

It can only have been a slight consolation to all his trailing rivals that his muscles seized up the following day. He was only marginally superhuman after all. 'I was unable to walk for a whole week after that, so much did the race take out of me, but it was the most pleasant exhaustion I have ever known.'

He entered the Olympic marathon four years later in Melbourne at the age of thirty-four, but six weeks before the Games he developed a hernia – from trying to train with his wife, an Olympic javelin champion, on his shoulders. Jurgen never suggested we try that one. Following an operation to relieve the problem he began training immediately, in contravention of the orders of his doctors, who suggested a two-month break. In the event, he came sixth, which was still a phenomenal feat.

Zatopek competed against everything – his own lack of raw talent, the elite distance runners of the world, the clock, Olympic records and even the Communist Party. Although nominally a prominent member of the party, through his position as a lieutenant colonel in the Czech army, in 1968 he signed a manifesto which supported the establishment of freedom in his country. For his rebellion he was expelled from both the party and the army, and sent to work for a geological survey team in a uranium mine for six years. He never recanted and by the end of his life was restored as a national hero.

There are two stories that best reveal Zatopek's personality. The first takes us back to 1952. Zatopek and his wife Dana had both won gold medals on the same day. Jovially chatting to reporters afterwards, the competitive husband decided to credit himself with inspiring his wife by his performance. His wife got to hear about this. 'Really?' she said tartly to the world's press. 'OK, go inspire some other girl and see if *she* throws a javelin 50 metres!'

The second story shows another side to Zatopek's character –

a side that shows true champions also know when to keep their competitive nature in check. It involves Ron Clarke, the famous long distance Australian runner, who, despite his many record-breaking feats never did win an Olympic gold medal. He went to Prague to compete in a meeting in 1966 and Zatopek, long-retired, drove him back to the airport. Just before they parted the Czech pressed something into the Australian's hand, wrapped in paper. Fearful it might be something to smuggle out of the country, Clarke kept it hidden in his pocket and only opened the small parcel once the plane had taken off. Inside was one of Zatopek's gold medals from the Helsinki Games.

*

The trouble with competitive drive is that it can carry you over a cliff. The will to win minus integrity can take you into dangerous areas. Balco, the Eastern Block, EPO, fixed matches, rigged elections . . . the list of means by which humans cheat never ends. Where there is ingenuity minus honesty, anything goes.

I couldn't do it. I just couldn't take drugs to artificially enhance my performance. That's what it boils down to – artificiality – and that would bother me. I wanted to win those gold medals without fraudulent help. Every time I got into a boat to compete, I was challenging myself, not some profit-hungry hot-shot chemist in a lab. I didn't want to be a junkie, a lab rat experiment. I just wanted to be a champion.

I would hate to be sitting here now thinking that I had won an Olympic gold medal by pulling the wool over people's eyes. I didn't want to be part of a sport where technology ruled over athletes, either. In Formula One, the sophistication of the cars makes an incredible difference, but in rowing I'd like to think it is the athletes who make the difference. That's where F1 gets it wrong, I believe. Although maybe not as wrong as I think, as F1 drivers are multi-millionaires and I'm not.

I hold true to my original thought, though, that drug-taking is a pointless exercise if you want to win on merit. I was there in the stadium in Seoul when Ben Johnson infamously won the 100 metres. Ann and I were sitting there watching and our first reaction was to be amazed by what we had just witnessed. However, a few days later – I was in the dining hall – not a rare occurrence – the news came out that Johnson had tested positive for Stanozolol. I was saddened, but not surprised.

Of course, he protested his innocence at first. Most sportsmen and women do when they are on drugs. Marion Jones protested her innocence as vehemently as was humanly possible and ended up in prison for lying to federal agents in the Balco steroid investigation. It turned out that the American heroine of the Sydney Olympics had taken the designer drug tetrahydrogestrinone prior to Sydney. That is how far ahead the cheats had pulled from the authorities. She had been tested over sixty times and had never once tested positive.

I hate drug-taking and I applaud the British Olympic Association's lifetime ban from the Olympics on those who test positive, but I still think I understand the temptation. It must be staggeringly annoying to push yourself to your limits and still see someone else beating you. You either push yourself further and hurt like hell, and still risk failure as the outcome, or surrender to outside aid. There's money in winning in modern sport and where there is money there will always be corruption.

However, what truly horrified me when I was competing and what horrifies me still is the thought of governments colluding with the cheats. In 1984 I remember being really shocked that one country had pulled two weight-lifters from the Olympics because a random test had revealed drug use. They didn't announce it. They didn't punish the athletes. They preferred a cover-up to losing national face.

I don't claim that British athletics hasn't had to face the issue as well. Linford Christie tested positive for pseudoephedrine following the same notorious 100 metres in Seoul. He was later cleared by the IOC on the grounds that the substance might have come from a permitted source, ginseng. Then, when Linford tested positive in 1999 (in semi-retirement) for the performance-enhancing drug, nandrolone, it was reported that the UK athletics authorities accepted that there was reasonable doubt whether the drug had been taken deliberately, although the international governing body imposed a two-year ban. Linford has to live with the fact there has been doubt about his sporting credentials, which is why to me drugs are such a no-no. If you hear of a positive drug test, your first reaction is that the athlete is guilty; when someone performs outstandingly, your mind involuntarily wonders, 'What are they on?' No one ever came up and asked me outright during my career, but they did ask colleagues of mine in the early days, 'What does Steve Redgrave take?' It's truly saddening and such a shame. Athletics has a highly publicised battle with drug cheats and being the biggest

Olympic sport it taints the other sports, even the ones with less problems. I would argue that rowing is mainly clean worldwide these days and definitely clean in this country, and it's a terrible shame we all suffer the same kind of cynical suspicion.

There was a time around 1988 when someone said to me, 'Why don't you make more of a stand against drugs,' and I thought, 'Yeah, why don't I?' but it was soon explained to me why not. If there was an industry, a mafia of some sort, organising and promoting the use of drugs, then becoming the voice of an anti-drug campaign would make you a target. It would be so easy to spike a drink. It would be very, very easy for the drug criminals to get volunteers in the sporting world. The door is wide open to volunteers. If I tested positive, everyone in the world would think I was guilty.

In rowing we were so wary of this that when race organisers threw us bottles of water after a race we wouldn't touch them if the seal had been broken, even if we were gasping with thirst. As an Olympic athlete you are constantly aware of the risk.

That case of the weight-lifters in 1984 has stayed in my mind, though. When national governing bodies appear to work with cheats rather than throwing them out of sport altogether you create an environment in which doping is seen as a minor misdemeanour, not something that wrecks the whole concept of sport. That's truly why I hate doping. I would say it destroys the point of sport as we know it. The Ancient Greeks had their cheats. When they were caught, their marble busts on display at Olympia were deliberately smashed. It was the literal destruction of their image.

However, there are some problems with my argument. One is

Jurgen Grobler, our coach. Jurgen was coaching in East Germany when there was a doping regime in place. There is no doubt about that, because every coach in East Germany in the seventies and eighties had to be exposed to the system or they would have been ostracised. However, Jurgen says that the GDR was aware in the eighties that steroids had no benefit to rowing as it is an endurance sport. East Germany was a country that defined itself by its sporting prowess. It only existed from 7 October 1949 to 3 October 1990 and yet it lies ninth in the all-time Olympic medal table, with 409 medals, 153 of them gold. We are often too fast to place all that success at the hands of the doping system, but we should also remember that East Germany had a coaching development programme that was second to none. There is no doubt other nations participated in doping but the East Germans' meticulous record keeping means that they have been in the spotlight.

My view of Jurgen was perhaps typically pragmatic. He arrived at the Leander Club in 1991 with the reputation of being one of the world's greatest coaches. I had an open mind, I reserved judgement and before long I had accepted him as a coach and a decent man. We asked questions. I asked him about the GDR's doping regime. He explained very clearly that it was not him, that it was very politically motivated, designed to prove that Communism was better for the people. This is an issue he has been asked about many times and his answer is always the same. He says, 'I have to live with what went on in East Germany. I was born in the wrong place. It was not possible to walk away.' My view is very clear on this too, the system, not the man, was to blame.

You have to be very naive to say that, if it was me, I would have rebelled. That was their world, controlled by the Stasi, imposed by the Communist regime. It is very easy to say that had I been a brilliant rowing coach in East Germany I would have renounced that system, but who can say what we would do under that kind of pressure?

All I know is that Jurgen is a brilliant rowing coach. He has never, ever mentioned drugs to me in his role as British men's head coach. He coached us to be better, winning athletes and for that I will always be grateful. If Jurgen had harmed his East German athletes I think he would have been treated with hostility whenever he went back there. There were certainly plenty of coaches and doctors who faced court cases brought by injured or illness-suffering former pupils, but when Matt and I accompanied him to Germany, to race one of his former crews in a training exercise, we were struck by the affection that everyone showed. They were shaking his hand, calling him 'Mr Leander'. They seemed genuinely happy to see him. That told me a great deal about him.

The other exception to my argument, and something that worries me still, is my insulin. I take up to sixty units a day to stay alive, but since I started competing as an athlete it has been added to the banned substance list. I had to receive official permission for my insulin at the Sydney Olympics and prove there was a medical necessity for me to take it. Ann really stunned me the other day by telling me insulin can be described as a 'growth hormone'. I didn't know that. It shocked me. I find it hard to believe that insulin would have any positive effect on an athlete. If their blood sugar plummeted, they could face a coma or even death as a side-effect. Still, it gave me this little niggling sense of doubt. Maybe I shouldn't have been allowed to compete in Sydney? Mind you, it definitely didn't enhance my performance. In fact, I've never performed as badly as I did in those first four years of having diabetes, but, even so, it makes me feel uncomfortable.

Finally, on this subject, I have a serious confession to make. Just before the Junior World Championships in 1980 we were training at Thorpe Park, but it was one of those downtimes between sessions. To pass a couple of hours a few of us, including my rowing mate Adam and his girlfriend Mel, were playing Monopoly, but I cheated. Mel was passing me Monopoly money in secret. Adam was absolutely horrified. He still is. He and Mel came round for dinner the other night and he was still going on about it, nearly thirty years later. Look, it was a one-off.

JACK NICKLAUS

I have seen sportsmen and women behave with fantastic generosity and integrity, though. You might think the red mist would come down in battle and obscure every last decent human impulse, but there have been memorable occasions when that killer instinct turns to mercy. Do I have that in me? Of course – don't you remember when I competed in the London Marathon with Ann and we held hands and stepped over the finish line together? Actually I did make sure I was just a fraction in front for every split time and the only reason I didn't do that at the finish is because I was too bloody exhausted. Fortunately fate intervened and, according to the official results, I finished one hundredth of a second faster than Ann. She always claims it was a fix by the organisers.

Possibly the finest example of sportsmanship I know took place a long time ago now, in 1969, during the closing stages of the Ryder Cup at Royal Birkdale, when the destiny of the famous trophy depended on the outcome of the Jack Nicklaus versus Tony Jacklin singles match on the last day.

Jacklin had won the British Open a couple of months previously. Nicklaus was anchoring the singles leg for the Americans. The match had been dramatically close for the first two days. On the final day Great Britain charged into the lead, winning five of the eight singles matches. In the afternoon the US roared back, winning four of the first six games. The outcome was poised, almost theatrically, for two great players to go head to head in the deciding showdown. As they drove down the eighteenth fairway, all-square, Nicklaus asked the Open champion if he was feeling nervous. 'Bloody petrified,' Jacklin returned. They laughed.

They both hit good second shots on to the green. Jacklin settled about thirty feet from the hole. Nicklaus was conspicuously nearer. To a hushed gallery, Jacklin putted first and left the ball a couple of feet short. There were sighs and groans. Nicklaus, putting for the trophy, sent his ball five feet past the hole. Calmly the American holed the comeback putt and picked the ball out of the hole. While he was bending down he also picked up Jacklin's marker, conceding the putt.

The crowd must have been bewildered. What was happening here? One of the most important putts in the history of the Ryder Cup and Nicklaus wouldn't let his opponent fail. As he handed

Jacklin the marker, he explained his behaviour. 'I don't think you would have missed that putt, but under these circumstances I would never give you the opportunity.' The match was halved, the tournament ended in a tie for the first time in its forty-two-year history and the two players walked contentedly off the green, arm in arm. However, the Americans retained the trophy as the previous winners, so Nicklaus hadn't exactly let the side down.

Funnily enough, his team-mates were not all best pleased that they had been denied an out-and-out victory. Neither was captain Sam Snead. But Nicklaus's philosophy was this: he believed good sportsmanship should be as much a part of the Ryder Cup as good competition and 'the concession' is now immortalised in golfing history.

These days, the Ryder Cup is one of the most thrilling, exposing, ruthless episodes of sport on the worldwide calendar. At the Belfry in 1989 Seve Ballesteros and Paul Azinger had a dispute over a damaged ball. They resumed the hostilities at Kiawah Island two years later. In 1999 'the Battle of Brookline' raised the temperature to new levels with the competition between American Justin Leonard and Jose Maria Olazabal of Spain erupting in controversy on the seventeenth green. Leonard was facing a forty-five-foot putt for a birdie, while Olazabal was better placed twenty-two feet from the hole. If the Americans won the hole, they won the Cup.

The American stood over the putt, perhaps visualising the one of thirty-five feet he had holed earlier in the round. The putter went back, the ball was rapped towards the hole, it sailed across the green and to a rapturous response from the boisterous crowd, sank into the hole. The spectators went mad and a few ran on to the green. Leonard went mad, his team-mates went mad, the players' wives went mad and it was with some difficulty that emotions were restrained so that Olazabal could square up to his own match-saving putt. However, the Spaniard was unable to regain his concentration. He missed the putt and Europe lost the trophy.

Strictly speaking no rules had been broken, but etiquette had been ground into the manicured turf. The so-called 'gentleman's game' had appeared decidedly yobbish by its own upright standards, all because competitive fire had burned out of control. 'Nobody died,' as Boris Becker once said about losing at Wimbledon, but perhaps the Corinthian spirit took another turn for the worse.

Frankly, I do think that the advent of professionalism has eradicated the noble approach to sport. To me, the reason I want to win is to prove to myself I can do it. I don't want to win if I've had to bend the rules or cheat. I partnered the model Jodie Kidd in a charity all-star golf match some time ago and afterwards she told me that she thought I had been too generous with my concessions. Matt and I, when we play golf, often concede putts of two feet, just to go round more quickly. That way you make it a genuine pleasure rather than murderously competitive.

The best way to win is fairly, with the opponent at their best. That is why it was so special and so poignant to me when the Italians who rowed us so close in the 2000 final said afterwards that it was their best row ever. It is so much more satisfying to win over another team at their peak.

I remember one Slovenian rower who always had an excuse. It was never that our boat rowed better, it was always that the conditions suited us or their boat had a technical problem. It was never that we were just superior, although in the end that is what I had to conclude, as in my whole career I only lost to him once. Sport is this: you compete on the day and you're either good enough or you're not. End of story.

ERIC THE EEL

What are they even doing in the Olympics? The Eels and the Eagles. Given my competitive attitudes you'd expect me to be a campaigner against no-hopers at the Olympic Games, but funnily enough I quite enjoy it. Put it this way: I see the point.

I remember an international rowing regatta where a Kuwaiti team was entered. Rivers not being a prime feature of desert landscapes, they were not lining up as favourites, but they made an impression on me at the team weigh-in. The lightweights obviously have to prove they are below the weight limit, which means climbing on a set of scales, and it was their cox I recall so clearly. 'But I can't be over-weight,' he was saying in distress. 'I didn't have breakfast.'

I was an elite athlete – my slightly spare tyre means I can't exactly claim to be one now – but I defend the right of people to kick-start the popularity of sports in developing countries by entering, er, less well-prepared competitors in the Olympics. Although there are limits. I believe Eddie 'the Eagle' Edwards over-shot those limits at the 1988 Winter Olympics in Calgary when he came a plummeting last in both the 70 metres and 90 metres ski jump. I can see that people associated with the sport, not least the other competitors left in the shadows, felt he was making a mockery of the event. On the other hand, around the world ski jumping received more attention than it ever had before.

Two things happened as a result. Eddie the Eagle, with his bottle-thick glasses completing the picture of hapless failure, became temporarily famous – or infamous. He was like Stan Laurel on skis, a disaster waiting to romp down the ski jump, and the world loved it. The International Olympic Committee, by comparison, hated it. The 'Eddie the Eagle Rule' was subsequently activated, which required Olympic hopefuls to compete in international events, finishing in the top thirty per cent or top fifty in order to be considered for selection.

However, as we saw in Sydney, there have been concessions. There are times when, to encourage sporting participation in developing countries, rules have to be relaxed. They were for the Republic of Equatorial Guinea at the Sydney Olympics. One of the smaller countries in continental Africa, with a population of half a million, it did not boast many Olympic swimmers, but the two they sent to Sydney made Ian Thorpe, the Australian swimming sensation, only the secondary story in the pool. Eric the Eel and his compatriot, Paula the Crawler (who recorded the slowest ever time in the women's 50 metres freestyle), were the stars. I can't remember whether I knew about them at the time or whether, having been safely locked in my pre-race bubble, I only discovered the details afterwards, but they provided two classic moments in sport.

If we are being brutally honest, Eric Moussambani could scarcely swim. He won his heat in the 100 metres freestyle, but only because the other two swimmers were disqualified. That would be a good pub quiz question: for what failure are Karim Bare of Niger and Farkhod Oripov of Tajikistan rightly famous? Answer: they were both thrown out of the Sydney Olympic pool for false starts, leaving Eric swimming the heat all by himself.

So it was a farcical scene from the start. All three 'swimmers' had been invited to Sydney under the friendship funding programme organised by the world governing body. As it happened, neither Bare nor Oripov had a particularly friendly time. Perhaps over-awed by the occasion, they both wobbled on their blocks and dived into the water too soon. They were cast out of the race on the one-start rule and despite the furious booing of an 18,000-strong crowd the officials refused to reinstate them. Only Eric, in his blue swimming trunks and goggles, had entered the water legitimately. It just took rather a long time for him to come out again.

We later discovered that he had only learned to swim six months before and 'swim' was a very generous description of the progress he made in the water. It turned out that he had never seen a 50-metre, Olympic-sized pool previously as his training headquarters had been a hotel pool in Malabo, Equatorial Guinea's capital city.

Spurred on by sudden lone star status, he started swimming as hard as he could, but a huge emotional and physical toll had been extracted. After one length he soon looked seriously exhausted. Now he had to turn and swim one more. He heroically pushed off for the homestretch, but he soon looked as though he was drowning. The crowd had initially been derisive, but they were being won over by the aquatic acrobatics on display. They identified with the underdog (and underwater) spirit. As he flailed, thrashed and fought his way down the pool, apparently wrestling the water as opposed to scything through it, his audience rose to their feet, cheered him and willed him on to the finish line. He made it to a standing ovation and probably chronic chlorine poisoning. My favourite quote from him was: 'The last fifteen metres were very difficult.'

Eric had recorded a time of 1 minute 47.48 seconds, over a minute slower than the world record soon to be set by the Dutchman Pieter van den Hoogenband. But who do we remember? I would wager my golf clubs that Eric the Eel is a bigger name than the gold medal-winning van den Hoogenband. In a way, that's wonderful. Widening the scope of sport is never a bad thing. Politicians put up the barriers, sport kicks them back down again, and anything the Olympics can do to unlock aspiration is fine by me.

It was ridiculous, but how can you knock a guy who tried his best and reached his goal? That is all I ever did. It was sad for Eric that his bid to compete in Athens (after bringing his personal best down to 57 seconds) was thwarted due to a visa problem. He didn't take part in Beijing. Perhaps he'll show up in London. As you may recall, I'm building a swimming pool in my garden (well, I've dug the hole), so maybe I'd better get a move on in case he needs a high-performance training centre for 2012.

6

TEAMWORK

IT'S NOT LIKE KING ARTHUR and his sword. I wasn't strolling by the Thames one day in Marlow when an oar broke the surface of the water like Excalibur and that was it – I was anointed the world's greatest rower. It's not as though it is my destiny to come here to Australia to win this fifth Olympic gold medal. It is simply my goal.

It's 10.25 a.m. on 23 September 2000 and I'm at the Olympic rowing lake in Sydney. In five minutes I will begin the quest in the Olympic final of the coxless fours. But there is nothing mythical about it. The pain will be only too real, just like the sweat, fear, tears, drudgery, strain, illnesses, accidents, faith, hope, friendships and teamwork that brought us here in the first place.

Teamwork – how utterly reliant we are on one another. If one man in six minutes, 2,000 kilometres, 240 back-breaking, muscle-screaming strokes, fails, quite literally, to pull his weight, the dream for all of us dies. My fifth gold medal, Matt's third, James's and Tim's first will disappear like mist in the Australian sun.

But I don't think we will fail. Four years we have been together – through friction, experiments, trauma, in sickness and in health, and if that sounds like a marriage vow then it's not surprising. I've seen far, far more of Matt than I have of my wife. I've put up with his snoring, marvelled at his eating, sneaked off to the golf course with him. We've played stupid pranks on Tim and James, and cried with laughter. We've all suffered times of despair and cried with frustration. Maybe not Matt, he's a pretty smooth pond, but the rest of us have been through a torrid time. We know each other deeply by now. We don't need words to describe the bond, but I think we all know it is there for life.

And then there is Jurgen Grobler, our coach. We have complete and total faith in him. The coxless five. We are, as Jurgen says, all for one and one for all. And we are – unless you count the times I've chipped my elbow, or Tim's slashed his hand, or James has had an emotional melt-down or Matt's done his back in – but that's all history now. It is what happens next that decides our mutual destiny.

Last night, when we had our final team meeting before the race, it was different. Usually, we go through tactics, practicalities, we rehearse the race to come, we take a matter-of-fact, hard-nosed look at the professional job we are about to do. Last night, though, I don't know what happened, but it became much more poignant and emotional. I found myself speaking about the difficulties I had had overcoming my diabetes, how much I wanted to convert the rotten ergo tests, the exhaustion and frustration, the struggles to find the right insulin balance, the times I had to acknowledge human limitations, all of those, into one last assault on a gold medal. I wanted it to be for a purpose. That purpose was to win.

Then James spoke. This was his third Olympiad and he'd never even made it to the start line. He could have been a 'spare man' in Barcelona, but refused to go because he knew he couldn't bear the frustration of being a spectator. In Atlanta it was even worse. He was there, but not there. He had a virus and to prevent the rest of the team being infected he was locked away in a room on his own. He felt like a leper. This was his chance to make all that had gone wrong before come right.

Tim expressed a similar need. He and Matt had been juniors together, but then their paths had diverged. While Matt and I had struck up a partnership that consistently won titles and medals, Tim had taken a more tortuous route. He had rowed in the coxless four that began the final in Atlanta as co-favourites, but could only finish with a bronze. Since then he had incurred a self-inflicted hand injury and a horrendous back problem that made his seat in our boat highly precarious, but he was here now and hugely sensitive to the fact that this was one last opportunity.

You know, it's funny. I can't remember what Matthew said, even though it was just last night. Maybe he hasn't suffered enough. I'll have to change that on the golf course. But Jurgen made an indelible impression on me. He wants us to vindicate ourselves. To show the world how good we can be. Like every good coach he wants it for us, but, in our turn, we want Jurgen to maintain his extraordinary record of winning at least one gold medal at every Olympics he has attended since 1972.

He wants it for himself, too, I suspect. His East German past has made him a target for media-digging. As our profile has grown higher, so has the intensity of the questioning about his background. It must have been a huge pressure on him, but the whole team has supported him. We're clean athletes. He is the best coach in the world. That was and is the end of the story as far as I am concerned.

Jurgen came to this country back in 1991, hardly speaking the language, bringing his wife and son to a place they had never seen. As he was driven down into Henley on that first visit he was staggered by the size of the houses down Remenham Hill. 'How many families live in that one,' he asked the driver. He was even more staggered by the answer. 'One little old lady.'

When I first met Jurgen – I think it was at the Henley Regatta, which he described then as being a totally different world to the one he was used to, a world where there were ladies with big hats – I asked him what he wanted to do. He answered quite simply, 'To help you win your third gold medal.' This was Barcelona. I said, 'Not just a third gold medal. I'm going to win a fourth one as well.' 'No, no,' he said quickly, 'just concentrate on the next one.' That impressed me. He was completely right. In sport you can never take your eye off your immediate goal to daydream about the next one, because if you do there won't be a next one.

It was a big change and it must have been quite lonely for him at first, but he didn't ask for anything as enormous as those houses down Remenham Hill. He only asked for a rabbit for his son who needed something to help him feel at home, and some assistance re-laying the flooring at his flood-damaged little house in Henley. I was one of the workmen that helped with that floor. Jurgen never moaned or complained. He was completely professional, but reading between the lines it can't have been easy facing the consequences of having been part of a totalitarian culture. In some eyes, he was tainted, but never in ours.

So now I'm sitting here, watching the seconds tick down, thinking how lucky I have been to work with two of the best coaches in the world: Jurgen and Mike Spracklen. Somewhere in my head is the small but persistent thought that since I have worked with them and because Matt and I were – arguably or not – the two best rowers in the world, perhaps we should have done better than we did? There's no time for that now, though. This is no place for regrets, only the summoning of willpower and a sense of comradeship with the three men who sit in the boat with me – the team.

The 'Redgrave Four' they call us, but that's wrong. I am not the most indispensable member of the team. That would be Matt. He is the strongest athlete amongst us.

Maybe you could replace all of us or none of us. We'll never know now. What I do know is that we can win an Olympic gold medal in a few minutes' time. We have the character and the track record. We have the mental strength and the physique. We have Jurgen. We have balance. We have James's perpetual negative matched by Tim's perennial positive. We have me – a little bit grumpy – offset by Matt – a little bit cheerful. We are united. More than anything in the world at this precise moment we want to clamber into a Kevlar shell, row like demons and reach the finish line first, If we do, we'll be part of Olympic history. If we don't, I'll still have three friends for life. Three miserable, disappointed, haunted friends. So let's not fail.

The light turns green and we're off with a great start. After only eight strokes we are ahead, rowing hard, but with control. 'Keep it solid' I say through the first 500 metres. We are 0.88 seconds ahead of Australia but the Italians are coming back at them with the fastest second 500 metres in the field. At 1000 metres our lead is reduced to 0.46 seconds. As usual we try to assert ourselves in the third 500, 'Gold medal catches' I say to inspire the guys. It works. With 500 metres to go we are back up to 0.99 seconds ahead. I call out to step it up. Last 250 metres, 'First lift – go.' 'Up again – go.' 'Last time – go.' The Italians are coming back strongly. I see the finish line under my armpit. Only a few strokes more. We cross the line. We are first. We are Olympic champions. We are gold.

The Sydney Five

James – the first thing you need to know about him is this: one year at training camp he was looking for ways to boost his meagre funds to pay his share of the Sky satellite dish we always bought to stave off boredom. We were walking through a field when James spied an electric fence. 'OK,' he said, inspired, 'I bet you

I can bite that electric fence with my teeth longer than anyone else.' There weren't many takers. I certainly wasn't one of them, but he did it. He held on for quite a long time and then refused to take the money because he said it didn't hurt enough.

In some cultures, James would be considered a madman. Even among rowers, he is extreme, but the truth is that he was the hungriest of us all; the angry man who won't let the rest of us be lazy; our one man-motivator. He wore his emotions on his sleeve. For him life is always about the here and now. He doesn't seem to believe in perspective and as he has admitted himself, he was always, always moaning. 'We're not trying hard enough . . . We're not going fast enough.' He had to get it off his chest. Sometimes his intensity wore you down a little bit, but he's also a lot of fun. He changes moods so quickly, unlike Tim, who's just happy all the time. James will be in a black mood one minute and fifteen minutes later the sun is shining.

We used to know all about his love life. When his relationship was going well, he'd be higher than high. When it went wrong, it was the end of his world. That's how highly strung he can be. Sometimes I felt like his protective older brother. After he broke up with his girlfriend I spent a bit of time with him and took him out on a couple of occasions. I remember once saying, as a joke, that if he was struggling he could 'come and move in with us'. That made everyone smile, even him.

There is a ten year age gap between us and he admitted to me recently that it is only now that – with a wife and two children of his own – he has begun to understand what makes me tick. Back in the pre-Sydney days he had no idea. To him life so revolved around rowing that his day consisted of: shave, post letter, row. Me, I had a bit more going on. A wife, three kids, diabetes, sponsorship appearances, mortgage and the pressure I was putting on myself of going for five gold medals. James has described himself back then as 'Just the bloke that rowed with Steve Redgrave. I'd either get no credit for our win or be blamed for making him lose.' I think he was joking. I am sure he was because he was so much more than that description.

So what made our particular foursome, our team, so special that we came home with gold medals round our necks? Each of us has a different take on what the magical ingredients were – and perhaps that's where the secret lies. At any one time we took different strength, support, inspiration from each other. Whatever was needed, we could find in the others.

According to James, my best quality was my stubbornness. There is no question that is a hugely beneficial sporting attribute. Especially in the face of a severe setback. James doesn't mince his words when he describes how my diabetes affected me, and him.

'No matter how many people told him he had diabetes, he didn't really think he did. It took him a long time to get through that, but the stubbornness that prevented acceptance was the same stubbornness that let him cope. It affected his training badly, but he never let it dominate him. He always came back. Always just in time. His mental strength was unbelievable.

'I remember how he survived that struggle with himself in South Africa. I'll never forget the mental strength he showed to overcome that. It wasn't like me being rubbish at all the training.

It was the greatest rower in the world being rubbish. In the cycling he was so slow compared to the rest of us it was like me taking my son out, aged five. I just don't know how he got through that, especially as never, not once, did he fail to complete an exercise.

'I suppose you could say that I was insensitive, but my view was that I didn't really care what illness he had or didn't have. The question was whether he could row or not, and he proved time and time again he could do it when it counted. I'll be honest with you, he was awful in the spring before Sydney. He shouldn't have been in the boat. He shouldn't have been in the team on merit. I think if he had been anyone else Jurgen would have dropped him. I would have dropped him. I'd have tried Ed Coode, who had rowed with us when Tim was injured, in the boat. We'd gone as well as ever, if not better, with Ed. I thought it worth the risk.

'But maybe that's why Jurgen is one of the greatest coaches in the world. He knew better than me. Steve made himself, through attitude and stubbornness, get better. At the Olympics he probably rowed his best race in the final. I could feel how powerfully he was rowing, because he was sitting right in front of me. I would definitely say that Steve is a pretty special competitor.'

I am not surprised James says he would have dropped me. After missing out in Atlanta he was determined to succeed in Sydney. He didn't know what it took to win an Olympic gold medal, whether he had the necessary ingredients. So he always wanted to get the best out of everything we did, in training, in the gym, at camp.

It might sound strange, but James wanted to be the weakest in the boat. Not because of any inferiority he felt, but from a fundamental point of view: Matt and myself were bigger and stronger and therefore we should have been doing better than him. So he was always the one pushing us to get the best out of ourselves, winding us up. He has told me he didn't care if we didn't like him. He knew he was playing a vital role in the team and that was a good thing, even if he did get overtired. Sometimes Jurgen would have a quiet word with him and say, 'Sacrifice yourself this week. Work extra hard and push the others with you.'

James agrees that the four of us brought different attributes to the boat. He regards Matt as being very confident, but not in the same way as me, perhaps because of his Eton schooling, perhaps just because he is naturally like that. But James recognises that this confidence is not arrogance. It is more of a case of Matt knowing what he can do and then doing it when it matters. He is gifted with huge power. Lots of people with a gift like that wouldn't have used it properly, but Matt was able to in the races that mattered. 'That huge engine would power up and you would have to call him a phenomenal competitor. Even to cope with Steve, the big beast, for as long as he did – that's an achievement.' James has nailed it with that description of Matt.

Tim he sees as being the technician in the team, a different style of rower. Where Matt and I tore through the water, Tim finessed. This variance in our techniques is reflected in an interesting take James has on how Tim viewed his place in the team. 'If we're honest, he would rather have won an Olympic gold medal without Steve and Matt, to prove it could be done another way. That was always his slight frustration, I think. He'd competed in Atlanta in the coxless four and it didn't end very well. They were beaten not just by the Australian 'Awesome Foursome', but by the French, who put them into bronze position. Tim wanted to try and win a gold his own way. Joining Steve and Matt in a boat was always going to be a more physical experience.'

Getting the job done to the highest standard was what mattered to James. No compromises. So it is no shock that he was furious when Tim went out partying and put his hand through a window. James regarded that as irresponsible and immature behaviour – especially as we weren't getting the best out of the team at that stage – even without Tim's setback. So he ignored him. His view then was 'I'd rather try and win without him.' I don't think he would feel or behave the same way now. But back then, for James the goal was clear and all the team had to be pulling in the same direction at all times.

But even with this reaction, James also understood the power of a team that clicked, that performed as a unit in a way that it is hard to explain. That was what happened to the four of us who lined up in Sydney. James 'blames' Tim's reinstatement into the boat on himself. 'Ed had come in and done really well, but I just had this feeling that the boat was faster with Tim. Then we won the pairs trials together. QED. Tim made the boat go faster.

'Perhaps the trouble was that the four of us became undroppable. However different we were in terms of experience (Steve had four Olympic golds, Matt had two, Tim and I had none), temperament (I let all my emotions out, Steve rarely let one escape), and size (Matthew was a bear, Tim was a reed by comparison), something about us had bonded. I suppose in the end the bond was created by having a common goal. We focussed on nothing but winning a gold medal. Someone's fifth or someone's first, it didn't matter, it was the same goal, the same challenge, and it brought us together in a way that will never change.'

Respect and admiration are critical for a team to perform at its peak. There was no one-upmanship. Matt and I listened to Tim and James, just as much as they listened to us. As James puts it, 'It was a straight twenty-five per cent split.' He is right. Matt and I may have been the 'bigger names' with the 'bigger reputations' but that didn't matter one tiny bit. We were a unit. We used to laugh when photographs of us were being taken, ensuring that James and Tim were positioned in the middle with Matt and me on the outside so that they couldn't be cropped out.

James's determination and focus on being the best it is possible to be are perhaps most clearly illustrated by his answer to the question of how he felt as we crossed the finish line in Sydney. 'I felt thoroughly pissed off. I was really angry that we let the Italians get so close. We were so much better than them. I wanted to show the world how great we were. We didn't do that, but Steve would say I was being unnecessarily negative. "We won, didn't we?" he'd say, ever the pragmatist.' He's right on that score. I am very glad indeed that James didn't go down in history as the man who made Steve Redgrave lose.

Tim – always the jolly guy with a smile on his face, good to have around. On the surface, some might say he was a million miles away from me, and yet of the four of us I feel he is most similar to me in nature. He's a loner. I don't mean he hasn't got any friends. He has loads of friends and is very sociable. I just mean that he would never come to me for advice. I don't know why that is, but while James needs a hand on his shoulder, Tim is quite happy to walk alone.

Of course, he has had his personal wars with, for instance, his on-going chronic back problem and other, what you might call more self-inflicted, wounds. While James was seething over how Tim injured himself, I wasn't. With Tim, my role could be more a father-figure than an elder brother, and this was one of those occasions. James was making a drama of a crisis, but I wasn't angry. How can you wrap people up in cotton wool? We're athletes, but you have to have a normal-ish life, whatever that may be.

While James ranted I remembered the time in the heart of winter, training for the World Championships in Indianapolis, when one of the rowing eight, Ben Hunt-Davis, organised a full contact game of rugby. We used to play touch rugby every Sunday for our last season of the year. Our abilities were mixed. This was organised when Jurgen had gone back to Germany for Christmas. Because we'd played a fair bit we naturally thought we were fantastic. The only trouble was, since all rowers are built like second row forwards, that's exactly what we had – a bunch of second row forwards. No one knew how to play any other position. So I got landed with centre. I lasted about ten minutes before I ruptured the ligaments in my acromioclavicular joint. I remember walking off the pitch, clutching my arm, thinking, 'You bloody idiot, what have you done?'

There was also the time, unbeknown to the press and only a few months before Sydney, when Matt and I had been working out at the gym and I'd fallen off a medicine ball and chipped the bone in my elbow. All in all Tim's physical injuries never seemed so bad.

As for Matt, well my best friend became the best rower in the world. He overtook me to that title in Atlanta. He had everything. All the benefits of a powerful physique, the maximum oxygen take-up capability, attitude, focus and, above all, the ability to pull his finger out at the crucial time.

We became friends when we started to row together, but I could count on the fingers of two hands the number of times we have had really close conversations about our love life or children. That wasn't our lifeblood. There's never been a daily diet of agony aunt stuff going on between us.

Sometimes Matt got a bit lazy. I suppose complacency is bound to be a problem when you are as gifted as he is, but I always knew that when it mattered – like in Sydney – I was going to get one hundred per cent from Matt. There was another gear to unleash and that gave all of us confidence. One of the frustrations with Matt was knowing that the other gear was there in training, but it might not necessarily appear. It used to wind James up, but I learned to live with it. You cannot raise your level to its peak session, after session, after session. Matt saved himself for the big moments.

In all these years, incidentally, I have never seen him really angry. Not once in my life. He is a true gentle giant. That doesn't mean I haven't been angry with him, especially for being able to go to sleep anywhere, anytime.

If I've been angry with Matt, well, he has admitted to secretly wanting to punch me on a regular basis. But he never did, I am glad to report. Good job too, because he is godfather to my oldest daughter, Natalie, and behaviour like that wouldn't have set a very good example.

Matt reckons I have definitely softened with age, and he is probably correct about that. But as he would be the first to acknowledge, I was never the 'hard bastard' of legend. That role was pinned on me by accident. But I think the reputation probably played a factor in the success I had. It certainly helped Matt and me when we first got together as a team. The reason I got known as an awkward bugger was that I tended to go round the side of the system, such as it was, and that made me a target. People resented the fact that I was a full-time professional rower while so many others were obliged to be part-time with other jobs. I could sense there was a distinct antipathy towards me – it sometimes felt a bit like everyone else on the entire British rowing team was out to beat me. That proved to be a real motivation.

And then suddenly, in 1991, Matt joined me as a pair. From that point on it was no longer Redgrave versus Pinsent and the rest of the British rowing team, it was Redgrave and Pinsent versus the rest of the British rowing team. That is a powerful bond.

The 'them versus us' feeling didn't evolve out of spite though.

It was just the way things were set up. It was very adversarial. It was the old Boat Race dynamic, as old as the hills. An individual wants to beat everyone else to get a place on the team, but once on a team you pull together. That's exactly what Matt and I did – and we became equals in the boat and friends out of it.

I like to tell Matt that he got the job of rowing with me by default. And even then, only just. Matt was one of two blokes who had been chosen to try out for the pair – the first guy didn't show up for the trial, and Matt was late because he overslept. I bought him an alarm clock for his 21st birthday; he thought I'd bought it in honour of that first day on the water as a team. It was hardly an auspicious start for what was to come – three gold medals.

Mind you, after Atlanta in 1996, Matt was convinced that that was it. After the tough, gruelling time we'd had he thought that I really would stop there and then. I thought so too, at the time. But from such low points new teams can be born, if the people involved want it badly enough.

Matt then turned up at Leander for the start of the season and the first person he saw was Jurgen, who told him I was going to carry on. 'No, I don't think so, Jurgen,' Matt said with authority, 'I think he's done.' 'You'd better go and talk to him,' Jurgen replied. Matt went off immediately to call my mobile from the little office on the top floor at Leander. 'Jurgen thinks you're carrying on,' he said. When I responded, 'I'm thinking about it,' he translated my answer as, 'It's done.' That was clear from what he said next. 'We're not doing the pair any more.' He felt that we'd had enough and was laying down a condition. We'd been unbeaten for four years. What more could we possibly do? We were just waiting to lose. I could see that way of thinking. But the idea of jumping into a four – taking on Australia's 'Awesome Foursome' – all of a sudden that provided a different impetus. 'OK,' I said. That's how Tim and James arrived in our boat.

Matt's view on what motivated the two new members illustrates very well how different dynamics can still act as bonds within a team. From Matt's perspective, 'James always, always motivated himself out of fear. He scared himself to do his best.' He sees James's approach as being very different from how the two of us coped. 'Steve and myself, we controlled the fear. We used to tell ourselves, "We deserve to be here, we deserve to win." Steve and I were hardened practitioners at keeping fear under wraps. It was weird seeing how different James was. He let all his feelings out into the open.'

Tim, of course, was different again. He appeared to be incredibly chilled and relaxed. But in Matt's view that was just an act, because Tim changed after he put his hand through that window. He realised his Olympics were hanging by a thread. Ed came into the boat in 1999 and we carried on winning. So Tim's driving focus was to earn back his place.

But then Matt believes that medal could have been won without any one individual of the four. 'It's a sobering reality ten years on. We made our future that day. It is Steve's, Tim's, James's and my achievement, but I wonder if we were, all of us, individually expendable.' I am not at all sure that we were. I think each member of a winning team brings something unique and vital to the overall endeavour. Change one of the components, and the team changes. Whether a new team would be able to gel in the same way and cross the line first, it is impossible to say. But for me, it was those four team-mates in Sydney, with our individual trials and tribulations, our separate characters, and our different styles and approaches, that were needed to win. There is an aura when a team feels right that is almost magical. We had that.

But apparently Jurgen wasn't as impressed. Matt remembers a celebration rowing dinner in late 2000, when everyone got completely trollied. At some stage, about 2 a.m., Jurgen came and put his arm around Matt's neck, holding him in a virtual headlock, and whispered raspingly in his ear, 'Ah, Matt, we could have won by more.' As Matt said to me afterwards, 'Yeah, OK, maybe this is the reason Jurgen is head coach. He never stops wanting to be better.' It is for that very reason I talk about the Sydney coxless five.

Matt may wonder if any of us were expendable on that day in September 2000 – perhaps because there was such a high standard of British rowing then, with the eight also winning gold – but he also acknowledges the incredible power that a close knit team can produce. When he reflects on the roots of that victory, he can see that they go way, way back, long before the medals were decided.

'That gold,' Matt concludes, 'was won on the Thames two years, three years, four years beforehand during one – or all – of our 20 kilometre rows. It was something to do with the commitment we all brought to the same task. We inherited one another, but we became a band of brothers. We all felt the same.

People might say that sport is trivial, an overgrown hobby, a pastime, but we all thought our existence depended on the outcome. It was the focus of our lives for four years. The ups and downs were extreme. We went through them together. The bond is now a given and I am sure that bond stays forever.

'Going out to row for the gold medal, it feels as though your life hangs in the balance. That's ridiculous, of course, it doesn't, but in those moments before a race, and probably in life leading up to it, it is as important as anything you have ever known. I think that's why sport makes such compelling viewing. It's a drama, only the characters are not acting. Their whole life turns on this moment.'

Matt is correct in what he says about the individuals coming together for that one, incredibly important moment on the lake. We had earned our place in that starting line-up. The hard work had been gone through, but we did also have some fun along the way, which is critical to building that bond he talks about. Matt tells the story of a rather inglorious moment for both him and me in the run-up to the 2000 Games.

'We had a game of golf just before Sydney. We called it the Coxless Four Ball. Obviously Steve and I played together as the established pair, with Tim and James as our opposition. Tim is OK, but James we called Harry Half-swing, because he attacked every ball like a cricket shot. We gave him thirty-odd strokes to balance the arrangement.

'Unbelievably, Steve and I lost on the eighteenth hole. The penalty was not money, but a bet we had that the losers would act as butler/man servants to the winners when we embarked on our next regatta. I had to go to James's house and pick him up, carry his bags to the car, drive to the airport, unload his bags, check them in and then do the same at the other end, all the time calling him "Sir". Steve had to do the same for Tim. We had a double-or-quits fallback position, where the losers had to do all the above, with the addition of wearing black tie. Unfortunately, that contest never came about.'

The jokes and the banter were part of the sporting equation. They helped quell the boredom and drown the nerves and contributed to our sense of togetherness. For Matt and myself, it was the simple jokes that we enjoyed the most. Tim and James were both given sponsored matching Vauxhalls in the run-up to Sydney, with which they were inordinately excited. So of course Matt and I resolved to sabotage them somehow. During training we found the opportunity to reach into their bags and switch around their keys and the remote controls and the next day we would swap them back. This went on for weeks. Fortunately they parked in different areas of the car park. At training they couldn't understand why one day the key fob would open the car and the next it wouldn't. James kept ringing the manufacturer saying there was an issue with the locking system. It only came to light when eventually they parked next to each other and one of them went to unlock their car and the other one's doors opened! Pathetic really, but the two of us were crying with laughter in a corner.

I didn't escape scot-free either. In a hotel on one occasion I remember opening the door to my bathroom and finding a huge statue that should have been in the corridor, staring back at me courtesy of my team-mates. I jumped a mile when I saw it.

These shared memories and experiences have bound the four of us together for the rest of our natural lives. That is something very special, although Matt tells me I should regard this as bad news because, according to him, his golf gets better all the time . . .

The fifth member of the Sydney Five is Jurgen. Jurgen's simple motivation is to help other, more talented, athletes succeed. What better vision could a coach have?

Jurgen was born in Magdeburg. His father was an architect, but he knew from a young age that he was more interested in sport. He has told me that he played everything he could – football, handball, table tennis, water polo. He was also a rower, but, as he puts it, 'a low-key one'. He was too small.

Jurgen's world changed at a party in Berlin that he attended with his wife in 1989. Up until then he had been a successful rowing coach in the GDR sporting empire. He had no reason to expect anything to change, but while at the party someone put on the TV and they listened, unbelieving, to the announcement that the gates to West Germany had been opened. The news was greeted with incredulity. 'That can't be right,' they thought and carried on with the evening. The Berlin Wall was a fact of their life. It had stood for a quarter century. It must have been almost impossible to imagine it not being there. By around midnight, the rumours had kept coming and eventually Jurgen said to his wife, 'Come on, let's go and have a look.' And when they got there they saw that the unbelievable had become reality – with a stamp in your passport you could just walk through to the West.

That's when Jurgen realised he could move on. High performance sport had always been very important to the GDR, but it was clear to him that everything was about to change. Suddenly here was his chance to prove it was not just a system that made him a good coach.

When Jurgen finally arrived in the UK to take up his position, he and his wife and son stayed in rooms in the Leander club and he quickly became very integrated into my life and my career. But he has always maintained a degree of distance. He feels he has to be independent as a coach or the whole arrangement would not work. For Jurgen, quite rightly, it was important that all the rowers in the team knew they could trust him. And we all did without question.

As coach, Jurgen looks at the boat from the outside, and as a result his views on what made the Sydney team work offer a new perspective to those of the rest of us.

Jurgen Grobler: Four men and a boat. And three big problems. And a lot of small problems, too. The gold medal in Sydney was not guaranteed. So much had happened in the space of four years and I was confident, I had faith in them and I thought they would win, but would they? You don't know until it's over.

My first problem was Steve. He was the figurehead of the team, there was no question of that, but the greatest athlete in the world was suffering, sometimes very badly, with his health. It may have been a sign that in 1997, when, after a wonderful start to the season I officially selected him for the

Olympic coxless four crew, he was in hospital with appendicitis.

In a way it was funny. He was in High Wycombe Hospital and when he left, because he is such a well-known person, they asked him to come back in the autumn and open their new Diabetes Centre. Then he was their first patient.

The effects of the diabetes were so difficult. It was a really, really tough time and yet he was so strong. There were periods when it was really hard, really awful. I remember that time in South Africa. The bike ride. He started everything well and then he had a total breakdown. This is a four-times Olympic champion. You can't help but be sorry to see him struggle so badly and yet he finished everything he did. He always finished. He never gave up. He had my biggest respect for that.

I think what kept him going was his competitiveness. He wanted to be the best at whatever he did. Rugby, football, sprinting, throwing shoes into a rubbish bin. It didn't matter. He always had to be the best.

The second problem was Tim. Well, there were really two problems with Tim, his hand injury and then his chronic back trouble. James reacted strongly to the hand injury. He was a very principled guy. I remember it was a big deal for him. He felt they had a gentleman's agreement not to put themselves in dangerous situations. I said to him, 'I totally agree it shouldn't happen, but in life, it's different. We should learn from it.' James was young. He thought everything should be perfect and he wanted to close the door on Tim, but I said we should discuss it. I had been through enough to understand that life is not always black and white. It seems so when you are growing up, but life teaches you not to be so sure.

And my third problem was James himself, when he was splitting up with his girlfriend. It was a very critical time. He wanted to walk away from the boat. He told me, 'I don't want to row any more.' He was very sensitive in that area. We had a lot of discussions. Although it was nothing to do with rowing, we had to take it very seriously. Steve played a very important part. He had discussions with James as well. We all wanted to be supportive, but I also had to mention quietly that he had a responsibility to the other three guys. I think that helped his decision to carry on. They were a great team, a good combination, all different, all contributing to one goal, but, believe me, it was never easy.

In the coxless four we had hugely talented athletes. Matt for his physical capacity, Steve for his experience and being a mastermind at reading races, Tim for the feel of the boat and his ability to give feedback afterwards, and James who nearly killed himself with effort every day. We always knew James would give everything. It became routine for me to stand behind his ergo machine and catch him as he fell off. His lips would go blue and his last ten to fifteen strokes would always take place in darkness. Basically, he would black out.

They were such a good combination. Everybody put something in. Matt, of course, never put more in than he had to. No question he was the most gifted physically. He was a natural, mentally very strong and always capable of giving you that little bit extra to make him a winner.

Tim was a sunny boy and very nice person. His technical input was very valuable. Physically, I wouldn't say he was weak, but in the ranking of the four of them, he came fourth. Somebody has to be ranked in that position, but, when he wasn't punching through windows, he calmed things down a little bit.

This makes it sound as though the coxless four were a solid unit from 1997 to 2000, but that isn't how it happened. The guys have said we were a coxless five, if you include me, but we were also a coxless six. Ed Coode was introduced to the boat when Tim had his serious back injury in 1999 and they performed brilliantly in the World Championships. In the end, Ed lost his place again to Tim and I thought it was the right decision, but it was very hard. He had the option to go into the eight, which also won a gold medal in Sydney, but he turned that down. He chose to race in the pair with Greg Searle instead. They came fourth, just out of the medals. When he rowed with Matt in the coxless four that won the gold in Athens, I just felt wonderful relief for him.

However, as Sydney approached there were voices campaigning in the media to bring back Ed, even as a replacement for Steve. He had won four gold medals and still Steve's place in the boat was questioned, but I had big faith in him. He didn't. He came to me, more than once in the run-up, when he was struggling with his illnesses. He couldn't predict them – the colitis, the diabetes – he couldn't predict when they would make him feel so bad he could hardly train.

He'd say, 'Jurgen, I don't like to lower the chances of the other guys' or 'I don't like to hold the guys back.' I had to tell him to go away. He had to trust me. At the end of the day my job as chief coach is to find the best possible boat to get the best possible result. You can't be sentimental. You put three other guys at risk if you do that. I always believed Steve could do it. I was totally convinced he would make it. When the time came, look how he rowed. He won his race. He was so strong, so focussed, so up for it. It was his day. Mentally and physically, he was on top.

Typically, he did his job really well, but it was still a hard race. Favourites are always presented with a more difficult task. Something hampers you a little bit. There is so much to lose. I've always said that if we had to row that race again we'd win a lot more easily.

I still have the BMW the boys bought me after Sydney. It has over 100,000 miles on the clock. A coach has to be detached, analytical, sometimes ruthless, but for some reason I can't explain, I still don't want to part with that car.

BARON DE COUBERTIN

It's odd to think I owe most of my adult life to a French Baron. The Olympics were the idea of Pierre de Frédy, otherwise known as Baron de Coubertin, or at least he was the man who stubbornly clung to the idea when all around him were telling him it was impossible. Why would I identify with a man like that?

I've been stubbornly clinging to ideas all my life: that I could win an Olympic gold medal, that I could overcome the effects of illness, that there is no harm in that seventh jammy dodger. There, however, the comparison ceases. Baron de Coubertin had a slightly more exalted background than mine. I was a secondary modern schoolboy with no access to money except what I could make lugging boxes in the local fruit shop, whereas this French descendant of a chamberlain to King Louis XI of France had a mother who apparently was descended from aides to William the Conqueror. I can't really compete with that. I've met the Queen a few times, including the day of my knighthood, but I don't think we could say I was related.

De Coubertin was a true visionary. He knew that the Olympics movement would prosper when all the politicians around him at the time were dismissive or derisive, regarding the concept as an utter triviality. He pursued his dream with total conviction, abandoning careers in both the military and law, much to his aristocratic parents' consternation, and it comes as no surprise to me whatsoever to know that he was also a bit of a rower. I think stubbornness must be a fundamental part of the oarsman's character.

The Baron succeeded against enormous odds. You could say he was the greatest sporting team-builder of all time. He formulated a movement that has grown beyond even his wildest imagination, but for him the matter was simple, perhaps simplistic. He wanted the Olympics to overcome political and religious differences between nations. He also wanted 'youth' to be inspired to great deeds and higher learning, thanks to the discipline of sport.

'I shall burnish a flabby and cramped youth, its body and its character, by sport,' he said and his invention certainly burnished this flabby, cramped youth and many others on the British rowing team. Without the Olympics every four years, the sporting world would just drown under football. You can't see handball getting a mention, or the triathlon, or even cycling were it not for the ruthless quest by hundreds of athletes for a bit of gold-leaf-covered metal.

Ann would remark that his ambition did not extend to the female of the species, but he was a man of his times. Women in Britain did not even have the vote, let alone the sanction to run the 100 yards. Lady tennis players were encased in corsets, and females in general were reputed to exist on bottles of smelling salts, so prone were they, poor souls, to fainting. (As the father of two daughters, I do not recognise this view of womankind.) What he would have made of the Press sisters, the Soviet field sports specialists who mysteriously disappeared from sport, allegedly when gender testing came into being, you cannot begin to imagine.

He may have been a man ahead of his time in many respects, but he was also part of a culture that decided women should not be allowed to perspire in public. In one of his more famous pronouncements, he advised that the role of women was to merely 'crown the winners in garlands'. I suspect if I said something like that to my Olympic sportswoman wife, she would crown me in the kitchen with a frying pan.

His most famous pronouncement of all, however, is the one we hear at every Olympic Games and the one with which I profoundly agree (as long as I have won): 'The important thing in life is not the triumph but the struggle, the essential thing is not to have conquered but to have fought well.' I like to think I was invariably gracious in defeat, because I just wanted to do my best. If someone else's best was better (which I didn't believe it would be), then I could only congratulate them. If I was poor on any given day, then I deserved to lose.

The Baron was certainly possessed of premonition: 'Sport has grown up within a society in which lust for money is threatening to rot to its marrow. The imposition of an individual oath on all participants will be the best way of bringing sport within the realm of honour again. The renewed Olympism will be the force best able to undertake this charge of purification . . .' He couldn't possibly have known that alongside his vision of providing a lesson to youth, there would grow a rising tide of profit-generating, performance-enhancing, professionalism – all of which we have today, for good or ill – but he said this in 1925.

Of course, purification never did quite happen. We all know the depths into which the Olympics have been dragged: from internal corruption to systematic doping to terrorist atrocity; from boycotts to blatant political manipulation, from Ben Johnson to Marion Jones, the cheating, the accusing, the doubting that we can trust the evidence of our own eyes. And yet. I owe the way I live my life to the Olympics. I sit here in a house named 'Casitas', after the lake in Los Angeles where my sporting adventure really began. I owe many of my greatest memories to the Olympics and the establishment of my greatest friendships. Sometimes those friendships are brief, but they remain in my mind nonetheless. I'll never forget meeting a guy from New Zealand before the Sydney final. 'I really want you to win,' he told me. I thanked him. 'The only trouble is . . .' he added, 'you're rowing against my son.'

I don't know whether the twenty-first century Olympics are quite what de Coubertin had in mind, but he ought to know that at least one old athlete is grateful he stubbornly stuck to his convictions when his critics were only scornful and dismissive.

SIR ROGER BANNISTER

It is easy to imagine Sir Roger Bannister achieved his place in sporting history on his own. I've seen the picture of the moment when his gasping figure, wearing the number forty-one on his chest, breasts a finishing tape watched by seated members of the press in raincoats feverishly writing in notebooks. He is the action figure, they are the passive onlookers. He looks like a man alone with his feat – and exhaustion. I sympathise with the feeling, but it wasn't like that at all. The loneliness of the middle distance runner had nothing to do with it, the way he tells the story. It was teamwork, among all the other attributes of courage, conviction and ambition, that led him to break one of the most resonant landmarks in the history of sport. The sub-four minute mile.

Some ill-informed doomsayers with no concept of sports science or human willpower believed it could ever be done. A certain mythical significance had grown up around the number, but by the early fifties athletes like Bannister and the Australian John Landy believed the number four could be beaten and began an all-out assault on the record. It may have helped that Bannister, as an Oxford-educated, trained doctor who would go on to become a distinguished neurologist, was no believer in myths.

His first attempt on the mile record was a response to coming fourth in the 1,500 metres at the 1952 Olympic Games in Helsinki. His time was a new British record, but he had experienced a palpable sense of disappointment and so decided to set himself a new goal: to be the first man to run a mile in under four minutes.

He intensified his training while still working full-time as a doctor and made the first attempt on the record in May 1953. He failed by 3.6 seconds, but remained convinced the feat was possible. Two months later he tried again, running the third fastest mile in history but still two seconds outside his goal. As the year wore on, news came through from half the world away that John Landy was running similar times in his repeated attempts on the record.

A new date was set for Bannister's attempt – 6 May 1954. Training intensified still further and, crucially, he was not alone. Every lunchtime he would leave hospital to train on a track in Paddington with friends who shared a passion for running. They became known as the Paddington lunchtime club. Bannister's friend, Chris Brasher, joined him for the hardest sessions and on Friday evenings they went along to Chelsea Barracks where Brasher's Viennese-born coach Franz Stampfl, who pioneered a scientific form of interval training, held a training session. At weekends they were joined by another friend and Olympian, Chris Chataway. 'In this very friendly atmosphere the very severe training we did became most enjoyable,' said Bannister.

I understand exactly what he meant. Our training could be peculiarly satisfying even when it was hellish. There was a certain perverse pride to be taken in completing brutal exercises and it felt all the better for knowing that your team-mates were suffering alongside. Of course, it also meant we would be competitive with one another, but when a race came round all rivalry was forgotten and we were locked in that musketeers' mentality again.

When Bannister and friends became 'bogged down', when the body refused to break barriers no matter how hard it was worked, they would insert an adventure – rather like my bobsleighing – to freshen up the physical regime. In Bannister's case, he went climbing in Glencoe, until it struck him most forcibly that he was in danger when Brasher fell climbing a rock face. Ankles, at the very least, were at risk. They came home and, mysteriously, the timings of their quarter-miles improved.

The race day approached. Both Brasher and Chataway gamely volunteered to be pace-makers, although Chataway doubted his ability to run three-quarters of a mile in three minutes as he would have to do. Nevertheless he vowed to try. Training was lightened and trials were run. Friends were volunteering their services in all departments. The McWhirter twins, Norris and Ross, who went on to publish *The Guinness Book of Records*, were keen supporters who acted as time-keepers, media-informants and chauffeurs. 'Sometimes I was not sure whether it was Norris or Ross who held the watch or drove the car, but I knew that either could be relied upon,' said Bannister.

As the appointed date got nearer and nearer, Bannister could scarcely contain his impatience. He imagined he was developing a cold or he worried about the weather. The day before the race he slipped on a highly polished hospital floor and developed a temporary limp. If he imagined the start line in his mind, he would find his body trembling with nerves.

God, yes, I remember that. The number of times I used to imagine I was coming down with a sore throat, a mysterious ache or some niggling injury. I'd be in all these glamorous places round the world and all I would do was prowl the hotel and gaze balefully at four walls as I waited impatiently for the hours to tick down to race time.

Our team would test ourselves obsessively to check we weren't dehydrated. We were constantly on the watch for something that might be wrong and the joy of not having to care about it when the race was done was almost as wonderful a feeling as winning. Even if I earned a calamitous hangover, it was fantastic to know I could hurt and it didn't matter. Perhaps Bannister, being a doctor, never took it quite to that extreme, though.

The race day dawned. It makes me smile to think of Bannister's preparations. While we might have been in a training camp for weeks, honing and tapering and using every available method of sports scientific expertise to reach our peak, he was in his hospital that morning, sharpening his spikes on a grindstone in the laboratory. 'You don't really think that's going to make any difference, do you?' said somebody going past at the time. He caught a train to Oxford and quite by chance met Stampfl. It was a fortuitous meeting. Bannister had been in a high state of nervous apprehension, worrying especially about the strong winds. He had almost decided that unless the near-gale force winds dropped, he would postpone the attempt. Stampfl understood, but offered valuable advice. What if this were to be Bannister's only chance at the record? Why not take that chance when it presented itself instead of looking to a more suitable future. The future often does not behave as expected. 'With the proper motivation,' said Stampfl, 'your mind can overcome any sort of adversity.' Bannister heeded the advice. How would he ever forgive himself if he rejected this one opportunity which might never arise again? By the time the train arrived at the station, he had willed himself into a positive frame of mind.

A friend, Charles Wenden, met him at the station and took him home to lunch with his family, which was a perfect distraction. Chris Chataway arrived, in good humour as ever, and firmly described the weather as perfectly fine, when the evidence through the window was a gale. Warming up on the Iffley Road track in late afternoon, Brasher and Chataway remained hopeful that the wind was now blowing a little less strongly and a little more fitfully.

Throughout the day, a subtle team of running mates,

well-wishers, close friends and supporters had buoyed him to the start line. As he stood there, taut and nervous on the brink of history, a complete silence fell over the track. Even the wind, which had been whipping the flag, seemed to drop in sympathy with the mood. The starter gun fired – but it was a false start. Bannister felt a momentary anger that precious seconds of a lull in the weather were slipping away. The gun fired again – a clean start this time – and Brasher took up the running as planned.

Slightly misled by his nervous energy, Bannister tried to push the pace along. 'Faster!' he shouted to Brasher, who had the common sense to ignore him. The first lap time was 57.5 seconds, on course for the record. Had they run any faster at Bannister's request, the attempt would have failed due to premature exhaustion. His friend and colleague had saved him, but Bannister continued to worry about the pace until he thought he heard a voice from the crowd shout 'Relax!' and he obeyed the injunction unconsciously. He later learned it was Stampfl, recognising the signs of his over-eagerness.

The half-mile point was reached in a time of 1 minute 58 seconds – still on course – and Chataway took up the running, willing himself to perform the three-quarters of a mile in a time of three minutes. They managed 3 minutes 0.7 seconds. Bannister knew he had to run the last lap in 59 seconds. Chataway led round the next bend and then Bannister smoothly drew past him with 300 yards to run.

The crowd was no longer silent. From every corner of the track came a roar of encouragement, all eyes and hopes on one man. Bannister's description of the closing moments still makes my spine tingle: 'I had a moment of mixed joy and anguish, when my mind took over. It raced well ahead of my body and drew my body compellingly forward. I felt that the moment of a lifetime had come. There was no pain, only a great unity of movement and aim. The world seemed to stand still or did not exist. The only reality was the next 200 yards of track under my feet. The tape meant finality – extinction perhaps.'

The nearer he got to the tape, the more he became aware of his physical distress. He doubted his legs would carry him over the line, he feared the tape was receding. The last few seconds seemed an eternity. He collapsed over the line, virtually unconscious, caught by his arms on either side by unseen friends. 'I felt like an exploded flashlight with no will to live,' he said. He had no idea of the time he had run. He was caught somewhere in limbo between dead and alive.

The voice of the stadium announcer – Bannister's friend Norris McWhirter – intoned the result, perhaps the most teasingly drawn-out in the history of athletics. 'Ladies and gentlemen, here is the result of event nine, the one-mile: first, number forty-one, RG Bannister, Amateur Athletic Association and formerly of Exeter and Merton Colleges, Oxford, with a time which is a new meeting and track record, and which – subject to ratification – will be a new English Native, British National, All-Comers, British Empire and World Record. The time was three . . .'

Anything else Norris might have said was drowned in jubilant cheering as it became clear that everyone present had witnessed the dawn of a new age – the sub-four minute mile. Bannister grabbed Brasher and Chataway, his vital and generous team-mates, and together they scampered round the track to celebrate the momentous occasion with the crowd. 'We had done it – the three of us!' said Bannister. He knew, better than anyone, that he had not been alone.

The story of Sir Roger Bannister and the four-minute mile only comes back to us now in black-and-white footage. It is ancient history as far as sport is concerned, so many international runners have now gone under the time, but for me it is one of the most uplifting stories in British sport, not merely for the achievement of Bannister, but also for the quiet, heroic and generous nature of the people who supported him.

7

LUCK

IT'S 2001 AND I'M at a local hotel, speaking at a diabetes conference organised by my consultant, Ian Gallen, and I'm here to provide the 'patient' experience, while Ann is alongside me to talk about the disease both from the perspective of rowing team doctor and spouse.

I have been diabetic for four years now, but I can remember as clearly as yesterday how it all began. The first warning was years ago, even before the Barcelona Olympics in 1992. I was in the throes of my painful colitis and, for some reason, the treatment for that condition triggered an episode of diabetes symptoms – the raging thirst, the roaring blood sugar levels. The doctors matter-of-factly taught me to inject myself with insulin.

Needles didn't bother me. I did as I was told and after a couple of weeks the symptoms just faded away.

They did warn me then that it might come back in later life, but I never imagined it would be during my lifetime as an athlete. I thought of my grandfather, who had diabetes, so, if I imagined my future diabetic self, I imagined myself as an old grandfather figure in my sixties or even seventies, long after retirement age, long, long after the days when I was required to be fit enough to pull a boat along. How we deceive ourselves.

Five years later, in the autumn of 1997, it was my first day back in training after the pleasure of a three-week stay in the Caribbean where I had startled holiday makers, and probably Ann, by taking to swinging on a trapeze on the beach. I think it was worse than that. I think – no, I know for a fact – that on my last day I gave a performance with a troupe of local trapeze artists. Thank heavens no footage survives of the event.

Sydney was in our sights and our thoughts. There were only three years to go and our workload was going to be enormous. I was going to have to push my body through every barrier it had ever known to compete at the Olympics at the age of thirty-eight.

It had been a busy time. We'd come back from holiday and I had done my usual rushing around. I'd given a speech at a dinner, and then we had all congregated at a restaurant one day for Mike Spracklen's surprise sixtieth birthday. It was, as I say, busy, but not stressful. The first day of training was fine, too. Just a couple of easy sessions on the water, so nothing unusual there.

I drove home, walked through the door and suddenly I felt

this desperate thirst. I drank pint after pint of blackcurrant juice and water, yet I still felt thirsty. 'Uh-oh, this is a little familiar,' I thought, remembering the previous occasion I had suffered these symptoms. I rooted around for urine dipsticks that I'd used on training camps to monitor hydration. We had used these so much that through sheer boredom we had come to know all the measurement indicators. One of these was for sugar in the urine. It came back positive.

I phoned Ann. She was calm, as she always is, and told me I'd better make an immediate appointment with the GP. They could see me the next morning, so I cancelled training – I didn't tell Jurgen why – and took myself off to the surgery. They took a more accurate reading of my blood sugar level. It was thirty-four. 'Is that bad?' I said. It was. The highest it should be is seven. 'I think you'd better see the diabetic consultant at High Wycombe Hospital,' my doctor advised and phoned immediately. By good fortune, the consultant was available and I was given an appointment at the end of the day.

I trundled home and had four or five hours to think about it. I was typically matter of fact with myself. 'That's it,' I decided. 'Career over. I can't go on with diabetes. You've won four Olympic gold medals. That's not a bad stab at it. Now you've just got to get on with whatever happens next.'

I drove to the hospital and expected to face the grim but necessary prospect of retirement. Instead, I met Ian Gallen. At first he took me through the practical side – the diagnosis, the treatment, the insulin jabs, the diet. To be honest, there was so much information I couldn't take it all in. On top of the trauma of suddenly discovering you're diabetic, you've just got too many facts to process at once. We were together about ninety minutes and only at the very end did Ian say the words that saved my career. He said, 'Yes, you have diabetes, but I see no reason why it should stop you achieving your dream in three years' time in Sydney.'

I was stunned. I hadn't been expecting that or anything remotely close to that. I was sure my career was over, but then I thought, 'Well, this bloke's the expert. If he thinks I can do it, why shouldn't I? There is no way I'm not going to give it my best shot.'

It was only later, much later, that he told me he didn't really have any idea whether I could do it or not. There was no medical precedent. He had searched for it. There was none. As soon as he had heard I was coming to see him that day, he'd switched on his computer, accessed the internet and looked up 'diabetes – elite sportsmen'. There was nothing, except the case history of Gary Mabbutt of Tottenham Hotspur, but his sport and his experience were vastly different from mine.

Ian even told me that the first time I competed after I'd become his patient he had to watch the race on TV like a kid watching *Dr Who*, virtually hiding behind the sofa in terror, yet he had seemed so confident to me. I trusted him completely.

There were no guinea pigs in the field of elite endurance sport who had tried to do what I was doing. No one had gone before. If we did not get the balance between insulin, blood sugar and exercise in the right proportion, I could be in trouble. Too much insulin and physical exertion could cause blood sugar levels to plummet. I could pass out in a glycaemic coma or, worse, die. On the other hand, not enough insulin and I could suffer from heart problems, loss of eyesight or even have to endure amputation.

Much of this was trial and error. In the early days I didn't take enough insulin and my energy would just vanish like a light switch being turned off, but I didn't want to overdose on insulin either. There is a specialist magazine that covers diabetic issues. It's called *Balance*. When I first saw it I thought, 'That's not a very catchy name,' but it didn't take me long to realise how appropriate it really was. To explain in the simplest terms possible, food and drink pushed my blood sugar up, and insulin and exercise pulled it down. Finding the perfect balance between them on any given day was an imprecise and, on many occasions, frustrating experience.

I'm not sure that everyone in the sporting world completely understands what diabetes entails. I was annoyed with a journalist once, who knew me well, but still asked me at the London Marathon in 2001 if I was going to need to inject myself with insulin on the way round the course. If I had, I wouldn't have made the first five miles; I would have gone into a coma or died!

Eventually, by Sydney, the savage ups and downs of energy had been resolved. Even so, I was extra cautious on the day of the final. Imagine if that light switch suddenly turned to 'off' after a thousand Olympic kilometres. I was confident it wouldn't happen, but I wanted an insurance policy. I strolled into the canteen and surreptitiously took two sugar sachets, which I then taped to the bottom of the boat, just in case. The crew noticed but didn't comment. In the event, I didn't need them.

Those little packets of sugar didn't cross my mind again until the River and Rowing Museum at Henley put our victorious boat on display and there they were, still taped to the bottom of the boat. The museum wanted to keep them as exhibits. Unfortunately, the cleaners had other ideas. To be fair, two ancient and water-ravaged packets of Australian sugar are hardly up there with the Rosetta Stone. The cleaners clearly had every good reason to rip them off and throw them away or perhaps someone kept them as a souvenir. Either way, they've gone now.

So that's what I've been sitting here remembering as the conference proceeds and we address this audience of people of considerable expertise. I'd better pay attention, because we are now throwing ourselves open to questions from the floor. A member of the audience gets to his feet and says, 'Steve, you're a very lucky guy.' Huh! 'Cheeky sod,' I'm thinking. I've worked incredibly hard for everything I have achieved. I begin to articulate a polite version of these thoughts. 'No,' he interrupts, 'you misunderstand. I'm not talking about rowing. I'm talking about your specialist. If you had come to me, or to most of the people in this room, I would have told you to forget about the rowing for ever. My advice would have been that your body simply would not be able to cope with the workload.'

There are assenting voices round the room. Specialist after specialist tells me that in their opinion the maintenance of an elite endurance sport career with diabetes is unlikely to the point of impossible. They would have said what I expected Ian to say – game over.

I am stunned and then I realise the importance of what they are saying. It just so happens that the specialist in my area to whom I was recommended is just about the only consultant in the world who was prepared to break new ground and thought I could carry on. It was blind luck in the post-code lottery. The only specialist in the world who thought I could still do it was up the road in High Wycombe Hospital.

I like to think I have repaid his faith a little by proving him right. Ian has now become an acknowledged expert in the field of elite sport diabetics. His work has had worldwide significance. He has pushed the boundaries of knowledge, just as I have pushed the boundaries of physical endurance. I don't claim credit for that. Once we decided to go for that gold medal in Sydney it's just what I had to do, but we don't always realise how much in our lives hangs by the thinnest of threads. There was Ian, so confident, so obviously the expert I could trust, and all the time – he tells me now – he didn't really know. 'It was just gut-instinct,' he said.

*

Sometimes you work for your luck, but at other times it seems to be a little miracle with no effort on your part whatsoever. We were burgled at home. No one was in, but, fortunately, the monitored alarm swiftly summoned my parents and the police. The thieves took off with quite a haul: laptops, Ann's jewellery, my grandfather's retirement watch engraved with his name, 'Harold Stevenson' that he earned after working on the buses in Birmingham for forty years and three of my awards, including the special gold BBC Sports Personality one I received in 2003.

However – and how is this for good fortune – having ransacked the office and gone through all the drawers except one, they didn't find my five Olympic gold medals, because they were in that one drawer they didn't open. I don't believe in fate, so what else could it be except pure, wonderful luck.

I know the medals shouldn't have been in the drawer in the first place. Don't worry, I'll buy a safe, but it seemed easier to have them to hand when I used to take them out with me so often. You could see how much joy it gave to people just to be able to handle one. They would look at them with a touch of awe on their faces, kids would light up and follow a medal round the room. I have loved being able to do that, but there came a point when I daren't do it any more. The medals became visibly worn and slightly damaged. The fifth has a slight dent and its ribbon is slightly singed where it came into contact with a candle. The previous four are little better and I've had to become more protective, although I've never put anything on display in a trophy cabinet at home. I do have one, though. I made it myself in my famous woodwork class at school. Mum and Dad had it for while, then gave it back to me when they moved, so it's in the garage now and I use it as a wine rack.

My medals haven't always been with me. After Atlanta, the River and Rowing Museum borrowed the four of them for display and it was two and a half years before I got them back. In fact, the lengths I had to go to were quite drastic – I had to win a fifth in Sydney!

I was asked if they could be brought over to Australia for photographic purposes if I won that last medal. Of course, I flatly refused to give my permission, but, secretly as a surprise, everyone decided to send them anyway and so they were flown over to Sydney under the personal protection of a British Airways pilot in his cockpit. The first thing I knew about it was when they were produced at the post-race celebration with friends and family in a nearby hotel. I admit I was pleased to see them. We go back a long way.

TONY NASH AND ROBIN DIXON

I can drop a few names if I need to – the Queen, the Prime Minister, Sir Matthew Pinsent – but there is an Olympic gold medallist who is way ahead of me in the connection stakes and way ahead of everyone, I imagine.

Lord Glentoran, then Robin Dixon of the Grenadier Guards, was having breakfast one morning in the late fifties in a hotel in San Moritz, enjoying a break, a sort of military package holiday, organised by the Services' Winter Sports Association. All of a sudden – 'pure chance' he always insisted – he bumped into a second cousin once removed. 'Ever been down the bob run?' said John Bingham, the removed cousin. Dixon confessed he had not. 'Like to have a go?' Dixon confessed he would and he did, later saying, 'I got in the back, didn't look at the course and when we stopped I realised I had quite enjoyed it.'

It is a footnote to the story that John Bingham eventually became Lord Lucan and, accused of murder, famously disappeared. There cannot be many athletes who can claim that their careers were kick-started by one of the most notorious figures in English criminal history. There Lord Lucan leaves the story, but what followed became one of the most unlikely and heart- warming tales in British sport.

Those were the days of real ice and amateurism, and Dixon, having caught the enthusiasm for the crazy sport in which four grown men crammed into a large sardine can and rattled down a swirling chute of ice at ninety mph, became something of a hot property.

A ferocious sprinter, who could cover 100 yards in 10.3 seconds, he was ideal as the brakeman, the character at the back who has to push the bob on its perilous journey before leaping into the back seat at speed. Within weeks of his initiation, Dixon was competing as brakeman in the British number two team four-man bob at the World Championships. 'We finished last – significantly. In fact, the closest team to us was the British number one team, who finished second last.' This acted as no deterrent whatsoever, though, as Dixon, an accomplished all-round sportsman, was hugely enjoying this new challenge. The sport, fairly rudimentary in Britain at the time, was equally delighted.

He finished second in the European four-man Junior Championships in San Moritiz, where his driver was a farmer called Henry Taylor, who also happened to be an F2 racing driver. They raced in the 1958 Bobsleigh World Championships together, but in 1959 Taylor was given his opportunity to race in Formula 1.

By now another individual had been added to the four-man team: Tony Nash, an officer with the Royal Tank Regiment, who was now promoted to driver in a new two-man arrangement, although Dixon admitted, 'I was a little unnerved at first, because Tony was entirely self-taught and he was as blind as a bat.'

Their first major competition together was the 1961 World Championship in Lake Placid. They led the opposition after the second run, but would eventually have to settle for sixth place. However it was not a wholly disappointing experience. Despite finishing out of the top three, they felt enough progress had been made to think seriously about the up-coming 1964 Olympics in Innsbruck.

The problem was money, as it so often is. These being the days of relative austerity in the sports world, there was no government funding. Dixon and Nash raised the money required to buy old Italian cast-off sleighs thanks to the efforts of their wives, who organised fund-raising dances and balls. Why didn't I think of that? Surely Ann could have taken time out from being a doctor, looking after the British rowing team, bringing up our children, keeping the house straight, feeding the parrot and looking after me, to put on a few dances?

Actually, it was my family (led by my parents) who did something very much along these lines to get me to the 1988 Olympics. They started a fund-raising campaign called 'Scull for Gold'. The only trouble with the title was I then gave up sculling and moved into a rowing boat. In Lord Glentoran's case, the fund-raising worked impressively enough to buy the sleighs and also a Land Rover to transport them, but the real turning point came when, in 1963, they were invited to join training with the Italian team, who were revelling in a brand new government-funded bob run in Cervinia.

The Italians had taken to the gregarious, friendly British underdogs. A friend was in need; they offered their help. It was an act of trans-continental generosity, something that became a rarity in late twentieth century sport as professionalism, ruthlessness and a certain hard-headedness would predominate. In other words, no one from abroad ever offered me free use of their boats or oars, but then I probably didn't qualify as friendly, gregarious or an underdog.

'From that point on, we effectively became the Italian number three team,' said Glentoran. Even so, they were hardly favourites for Innsbruck in 1964 and two Italian teams and the hosts Austria were considered prime candidates for the gold medal.

The Games began with difficulty and soon escalated to tragedy. There was an inconvenient non-appearance of snow, the Austrian military were dispatched to carve out 20,000 ice blocks for the bob run and luge, and tons of Alpine snow was excavated and packed on the ski runs. Such were the perilous conditions that two athletes were killed in training before the Games started: an Australian skier, Ross Milne, and a Polish-born member of the British luge team, Kazimierz Kay-Skrzypeski. It was not an auspicious beginning and even today, whenever Lord Glentoran is invited to reminisce, he always begins with remembrance of those two athletes who lost their lives.

More in hope than confident expectation, the British began their campaign. It went surprisingly well. Nash and Dixon were leading after the first run. It was Dixon's job to check over the vehicle afterwards, in preparation for the second run, and it was during the routine examination that he found the rear axle bolt of the sleigh had been broken. They had many spare parts with them, just not a rear back axle bolt. It looked as though their Olympics was over.

In the course of his depressed discussions, Dixon was interrupted by the Italian competitior, Eugenio Monti, known as 'The Flying Redhead' and one of the most successful bobsleighers of all time (ten World Championship medals, of which nine were gold, and six Olympic medals). Monti, on his way to the start for the Italian run, had noticed his friends in difficulty and inquired as to the problem. 'The back axle bolt's broken and we don't have another one,' Dixon told him. 'Don't worry,' Monti replied, 'just send over an English mechanic after we finish our run and you can have our bolt.' He was true to his word. 'He came down the run, told the press to go to hell and get out of the way, our mechanic got to work and we duly received our bolt,' remembers Glentoran.

The next day's competition – two more runs each – would decide the placement of the medals. Nash and Dixon made a small mistake on their last run and concluded that they had done pretty well to finish in – they reckoned – bronze medal position. As befitted amateur sportsman of the time, they repaired to the nearest bar to enjoy a coffee and schnapps while their rivals finished the competition.

Within fifteen minutes a member of their team barged through the doors, shouting excitedly 'What are you doing in here? You've won the medal. You've won the gold!' The weather conditions had suddenly deteriorated and the course had slowed dramatically. The remaining bobsleighers could not compete with the earlier time posted by the Britons and Monti, for his act of selfless sportsmanship, finished with a bronze medal. He was also awarded the first ever Pierre de Coubertin Medal for sportsmanship.

It was to Glentoran's inexpressible relief that the Italian came back four years later in Grenoble and won gold in both the two-man and the four-man. Monti never regretted his generosity. Even when the Italian press gave him serious grief over the matter, he flatly refused to accept wrong-doing. 'Nash and Dixon didn't win because I gave them the bolt. They won because they had the fastest run.' But you could say that they also won because they had a little luck in the weather and a lot of luck in the kind friendship of Eugenio Monti.

If you ask Lord Glentoran today if pure luck played a part in his triumph, he is the first to agree. 'God, yes, fortune has changed my life not infrequently down my seventy-odd years. It was chance that led me to that Olympic gold and that, as you know Steve, can change the course of your life for ever. It opens many doors and that's a wonderful thing. It also, I have found, puts a responsibility on you to forever live up to your achievement.'

There are two postscripts to this story. The first is that in 1976, in Innsbruck, Lord Glentoran was made President of the Olympic Jury. He met up again with an old bobsleighing friend, now working for ABC TV, the Canadian Victor Emery. They hailed one another and then a thought sprang to mind. 'Why don't we . . .' mused Emery, ' . . . go down the bob run one last time before the Games start.' 'We'll have to get official clearance,' said Glentoran. 'What are you talking about? You're President. You run the thing,' reminded Emery. Glentoran conceded this was true. They commandeered a four-man bob, filled the middle places with two stray Englishmen and set off for one last adrenaline-rush on ice. 'Unfortunately,' said Glentoran, 'one of the new chaps sat in my seat so that I had to give him a good kicking after the start to make him move up. I went round the first bend standing up.'

And the second postscript? Inevitably in life luck deserts you just as swiftly and randomly as it arrives. Suffering from Parkinson's disease, Eugenio Monti committed suicide with a self-inflicted gunshot wound to the head in 2003. The bobsleigh track where Nash and Dixon trained with him was renamed in his honour.

*

There are reasons why I relish this story. I have to admit a special interest. I am an amateur(ish) brakeman myself, one whose sprint was more powerful than his sense, I admit, though I have every reason to intimately understand how many things can go wrong on any bobsleigh run. That is why the Nash and Dixon story is so compelling. This is the Olympic story, almost a fairytale, where for once it all went right.

I once had a dream of competing – or was it winning? – at both the Summer and Winter Olympics. It wasn't an entirely groundless dream either, because from 1985 to 1989 I was (sort of and accidentally) a member of the British bobsleigh team. I have my friend Larry Tracey, a man who epitomised the spirit of *Cool Runnings*, the film about the Jamaican bobsleigh team that competed at the 1988 Calgary Olympics, to thank for this. They crashed and failed, but everyone loved them. I watched with interest, secretly thinking, 'That could've been me.'

It began with my utter disillusion with rowing. Post-Los Angeles I was single sculling again, although I can't say it was going very well. In fact, I can say it was pretty terrible. The scull was challenge enough, but I was also at loggerheads with the woman that led the sport, Penny Chuter. I started to think, 'Who needs this? What's the point? I've got my Olympic gold medal. Maybe that's all I can hope for. Perhaps it's time to walk away from the sport.' So I did – I walked away from sculling and into bobsleighing.

It happened by accident, as these things so often do. Larry, mad keen on the sport, was going over to Winterberg in Germany, where the British held their national championships. He knew I was fed up. 'Try it out,' he said. I tried it out. It was completely insane, so naturally I thought I'd do some more of it, and we decided to compete together in a two-man bobsleigh.

We had a few runs and I was installed as the brakeman, the lead sprinter on the team, who basically gives the sleigh a mammoth great push at the start. It went relatively well until a crash, when we finished the course with the sleigh on top of us. Larry was yelling, 'My head's bleeding,' because he could feel something seeping out of his helmet. In fact, he'd been scooping ice into his helmet as he slid down the track and then it melted against the warmth of his head and poured out round his ears when he stood up.

It seemed like a good sport to me, but probably the best thing about it was the discovery that the internal politics of bobsleigh were even worse than rowing, and gradually the truth began to dawn on me that it didn't matter which sport you entered, diplomatic struggles always ensued – or in my case undiplomatic struggles.

I came back to rowing, fully reinvigorated, vowing never to set foot in a bobsleigh again and I never gave it another thought . . . until two years later. Larry's fault again. This time he had set up the Irish bobsleigh team and was trying to win selection to the Winter Olympics. Would I, he asked, just help teach them the rudiments of being the brakeman? A sane man chasing his second gold medal in the rowing event in Seoul a year later would have said, 'No.' I said, 'Yes.'

That was how I found myself pushing a cart on wheels up and down Larry's driveway as part of the Irish training regime. Then we went out to take part in the British Championships again and in the two-man with Peter Brugnani I came second, just missing my chance to qualify for the Calgary Olympics. Would I have gone? I'd have been tempted and that might have altered the direction of my life completely.

My last flirt with the sport was at the British Championships two years later. The Olympian Tom de la Hunty asked me to push him in the four-man and we won a gold medal. It's around the house here somewhere, but the whole construction of the team

213

altered after that. The British Bobsleigh Association employed a former East German coach to run things and the selection criteria changed. Tom's face suddenly didn't fit – and I was asked to push the former Army corporal Mark Tout on the World Cup series. My last race was Sarajevo. We finished eleventh.

I called it a day after that last run in 1989. It is a completely crazy sport, but I did enjoy it. I think everybody should have a go once in their life, because it's exhilarating. In what other sport, as a novice, can you complete a course just two seconds outside the Olympic record? It was mad, it was wonderful and, who knows, perhaps it was just the distraction I needed at a time when I was so close to walking away from rowing.

Tony McCoy

What do some people tell you in sport? That you make your own luck. To an extent it's true. If you put in the work, determination, sacrifice and have all the other attributes a champion needs, you will have a higher chance of succeeding, but it isn't guaranteed and sometimes wonderful, random, pure luck drops a gift into your lap. Even then, you might need to be smart enough to take it, though.

Tony McCoy may be obsessed with his sport, but, like most successful athletes, he also knows that you need to take your opportunities when they arise. In 2001–02 he was chasing down Sir Gordon Richards's record of riding 269 winners in a season. It was a record that had been set in 1947 (on the flat) and many in the sport believed it to be unassailable, but they had reckoned

John Naber, making the impossible possible in the 100 metres backstroke at the Montreal Olympics in 1976.

If Tiger won the US Open in 2008, with a serious injury in his left knee, it may have been because his dad had prepared him years ago for the task.

The one-man revolution, Dick Fosbury, flopping over the bar to win gold at the 1968 Olympic Games.

Lewis Hamilton's preparation for world domination is a textbook case of getting all the ducks in a row.

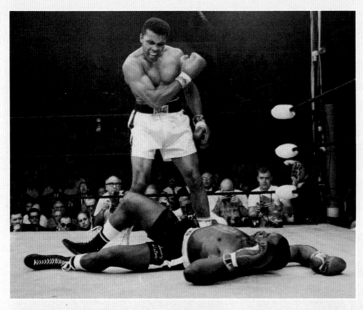

No one embodies the invisible power of self-belief more than Muhammad Ali.

Only belief could have carried Nottingham Forest to successive European Cup wins and that belief was all the doing of Brian Clough.

Cathy Freeman's belief in her ability kept her focused to win the 400 metres in Sydney, despite immense pressure.

Daley Thompson became the first athlete to hold Olympic, Commonwealth, European, and World titles at the same time. Why shouldn't he whistle on the Olympic podium if he wanted to?

Oscar Pistorius is the living example of someone whose apparent disability has been turned into something entirely positive.

Lance Armstrong's fight against cancer remains one of the landmarks of human, let alone sporting, comebacks.

Matt Hampson's refusal to surrender to bitterness following his rugby accident is the greatest heroism I can imagine.

Franz Klammer's fight back to form was as treacherous as any of his downhill races.

Tony McCoy is an extraordinary sportsman, one who defies medical advice and disbelief to pursue his over-riding goal in life – the next winner.

We forget the million stubborn, dogged, obsessive, committed and determined moments of practice that had gone before Jonny Wilkinson's famous kick.

Nicole Cooke is a genuinely tough athlete, a mixture of mind and muscle.

Tanni Grey-Thompson – one of the most competitive athletes on the planet.

Emil Zatopek, the greatest long-distance runner of the twentieth century – to achieve that he trained and trained like a demon.

Teamwork played a huge part in Sir Roger Bannister breaking the four-minute mile. Here, he congratulates his friends and pacemakers, Chris Brasher and Chris Chataway, after the race.

'The Concession' underlined Jack Nicklaus's belief that good sportsmanship should be as much a part of the game as good competition.

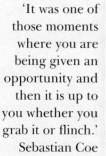

Tony Nash and
Robin Dixon won
gold with some
Italian generosity
and a bit of luck
with the weather.

'It was one of
those moments
where you are
being given an
opportunity and
then it is up to
you whether you
grab it or flinch.'
Sebastian Coe

Bobby Charlton
ascribes much of
his success to the
'luck' of being born
into a family with
a brilliant football
gene pool.

Jesse Owens had star quality because he symbolized the power of truth over propaganda.

Sportsmen like Ronnie O'Sullivan are dazzling technicians, but they have something that's harder to explain, and so we term it 'genius'.

There was something special about Ayrton Senna, even before the triple world champion was immortalised after his fatal injury at Imola on 1 May 1994.

The flamboyant image is an expression of Shane Warne's personality, but the statistics of his fifteen-year Test history are the expression of his graft.

Few people can truly be both a sports star and a celebrity. David Beckham is one of those few.

Three Olympics, three silver medals – but Katherine Grainger wasn't satisfied.
That is what separates elite athletes from sensible people.

Winning Wimbledon seven times
in eight years and then retiring –
now that's what I call perseverance.

Carl Lewis winning his fourth
consecutive long jump gold.
He had every quality you need
to become a champion.

without the grim determination of National Hunt's greatest jockey, A. P. McCoy.

Over the darkest days of that particular winter the winners for McCoy had been harder to come by, but on the morning of 23 January 2002 his tally stood at 209. Every victory from now to the end of the season would count towards his quest. He set off to a race meeting at Southwell, in the East Midlands, a venue not necessarily synonymous with the glamour of the Cheltenham Festival or the Grand National meeting at Aintree. The race, an unremarkable three mile novice chase, wasn't attracting the glitterati either, but a few punters placed their bets, lifted their binoculars and then watched as an absolutely farcical event unfolded.

It was an ordinary race (to begin with) on an ordinary horse by the name of Family Business. They loped along, just off the pace, until, at the tenth fence, the horse made a successful bid for independence. He stopped with dramatic suddenness, jinked to the left and McCoy fell off. The jockey was sickened, annoyed with himself and flung his skull cap to the ground in disgust. The horse was retrieved and led back in disgrace towards the unsaddling box. Tony hitched a lift in the Land Rover following the field back towards the weighing room.

However, on the way back he looked absently out at the course and noticed that only three of the seven starters were still in the race. A little light bulb switched on in McCoy's calculating brain. He spied his trainer's head lad and called to him, 'Bob, get the girl to come back here with that horse, just in case.' The stable girl complied. McCoy looked at the course again and there were still three horses labouring round on the extremely holding ground. 'Listen,' he said, 'I'm going back to pop this one round – you never know what might happen.'

Family Business was taken back to the fence of his previous misdeed, McCoy remounted and re-entered the race. Two of the three horses in front had fallen. Both had been remounted, but McCoy still had an instinct that something usefully unusual might happen. Sure enough, What a Wander was leading, but suddenly downed tools and refused. McCoy was now third. Eaux Les Coeurs then took up the front running, before throwing off his rider in a similar state of revolt. McCoy was now second. The only horse in front of him was Red Radish, who, caught up in the revolutionary fervour of the day, joined the strike force by whipping round at a fence and unseating his rider. McCoy won the race because he was on the only horse still in it.

He didn't know it for a while, because he was so far behind he couldn't see clearly what was happening. He simply crossed the line and only then received the news that he was in receipt of his 210th victory of the season. It is said McCoy rarely smiles. It is probable that he managed one at that moment. It had taken ten and a half minutes to complete a course which would normally take just six. McCoy was ridiculed mercilessly by his fellow jockeys and classified 'a jammy git'. He went on to break Sir Gordon Richards record with 270 wins that season. He certainly enjoyed a ridiculous run of luck that say at Southwell, but I can't help thinking a lesser champion would never have seen the opportunity.

LORD COE

Seb says entirely the same of the race that significantly kick-started his international career. Luck may be blind, but the recipient can't afford to be. 'It was one of those moments where you are being given an opportunity and then it is up to you whether you grab it or flinch. Sometimes you have to be brave.'

I agree with him. When the Australian short track speed skater, Steven Bradbury, won gold at the 2002 Winter Olympics it was due to a pile-up of the four skaters in front of him at the last turn. 'Obviously, it was pretty freaky,' he had the decency to admit. It remains one of those remarkable coincidences that the American favourite for the race was called Apolo Anton Ohno.

Seb's story is subtly different. It was a bank holiday weekend in 1977 and he was running in a 400 metres at the Herringthorpe Track in Rotherham, a low-key, South Yorkshire meeting. He duly won and motored down to Crystal Palace with his trainer father, Peter, to run an 800 metres at Crystal Palace in a GB versus West Germany fixture. He won that as well and could consider the weekend a success.

Then he was stopped in his tracks by an unexpected invitation. One of the leading contenders in the Emsley Carr Mile the following day had pulled out through injury. The BBC, due to televise the event, were sweating on a suitable replacement. The star of the show would be world mile and 1,500 metres record holder, Filbert Bayi of Tanzania, but the BBC were anxious to avoid a procession. 'Would you run?' Seb was asked by the selectors, since he was in the right place at the right time, uninjured and available. Essentially they needed somebody to make up the numbers. A twenty-year-old Briton with potential would do.

He, his father and the selectors had a conversation. The officials noted that he had already run on two successive days, Filbert was unbeatable and that the mile was a rare distance for this relative novice, as Seb had run a mile only once or twice in the previous twelve months. They were concerned not to put pressure on a flowering talent by asking too much too soon. But Seb's father knew it was too good an offer to turn down. 'My old man said, "What have we got to lose? Let's go." I'd already done the maximum I had set out to do that weekend. This was a fantastic bonus and an opportunity to race the world's best miler.'

History records that the Emsley Carr Mile (named after an athletics-loving sports editor of the *News of the World*) was won by one Sebastian Coe, who beat the world mile record holder, Filbert Bayi, on the line. 'Bold King Coe' was hailed by the headline writers and one of Britain's greatest ever distance runners was off the blocks.

BOBBY CHARLTON

Of all the sportsmen I have met in my life, Sir Bobby Charlton stands out as one of the nicest. There is not a hint of arrogance in him, despite the fact that he is one of the finest footballers this country has ever produced. Even as a Chelsea supporter it causes me no pain to celebrate one of Manchester United's greatest and it is always a pleasure to come across him. There is a straightforwardness and decency about him, not something you always find in football, and it is typical of his modesty that Bobby ascribes so much of his success to the 'luck' of being born in the right place at the right time.

That place was the North East, specifically the town of Ashington, where he was brought up among a family – on his mother's side at least – that was both gifted and passionate when it came to football. All four of her brothers, the Milburns, played professional football. George played for Chesterfield, Jack for Leeds United, Jimmy for Leeds and Bradford, and Stan for Chesterfield and Leicester. Second cousin Jackie became a Newcastle United legend.

Young Bobby was steeped in the lore of the game long before he was considered old enough to go with brother Jackie to watch Stanley Matthews play for Blackpool against Newcastle at St James' Park. His childhood sounds like one long outdoor football match, with coaching lessons from any and every uncle who happened to be about at the time. However, it was his grandfather, his mother's father, who made the earliest and deepest impression. A trainer of professional sprinters, Tanner Milburn's whole life revolved around sport and it was almost certainly due to his encouragement and efforts that all four of his sons enjoyed footballing careers, in contrast to so many young men of the time, whose only hope of employment was the coal mine.

Tanner kept a close watch on the progress of Bobby. Often, when the boy was playing for the school football team, he would find his grandfather watching him intently through the perimeter railings and he took no offence when the older man later analysed his performance. He was modest even then, a listener, willing to improve, and when he felt the attention of his grandfather fully on him it only drove him to a greater commitment. He wasn't just playing for himself, he was playing for his grandfather's approval, which meant so much to him.

Bobby learned an early lesson at his grandfather's knee: that with talent anything is possible, provided that talent is allied to sensible living and unstinting hard work. That is pretty much the life of a rower laid bare. Talent is nothing without the graft which underpins it.

In the case of the two young Charlton brothers, the work couldn't be separated from pure fun. They played because they loved playing, sometimes for six or seven hours in the local park. Boys would come and go, but Bobby Charlton would be a fixture, kicking the ball until it was dark, playing by the light of the streetlamps with the last few stragglers until the local policemen told them off and sent them home. This was the North East's version of Brazil, where playing football came as naturally as breathing to boys whose only ambition was to be a footballer and who thought of very little else from dawn to dusk.

Other lessons were also being absorbed, though. Bobby had a hard upbringing – 'Life could be as hard as nails,' he has said. Their father was a miner, his income was meagre and there were many times when the family went hungry. Meals were boosted by produce from the local allotment and the occasional killing of a communal pig. The family whippet might rouse itself into action and triumphantly return with a rabbit from time to time, but this was rare enough to be memorable.

Perhaps part of Bobby's commitment to football stemmed from the lesson of his father and the driving desire of the son to escape the confinement of the pit. He saw first hand the strain, dirt and danger that life down a coal mine forced on its workers. His father was stoic throughout, though, only ever missing one day of work and that was because an accident had severely injured his face so that half of it was inflamed and twice its normal size. Such visual demonstrations of the toughness of the job would have made quite an impression on a growing boy.

Not that Bobby remembers his childhood as totally grim. In fact, it was filled with a cast of hilarious, loving and diverse characters. His Uncle Buck was one of the few Milburns who were not attracted to football. Instead he became a poacher of considerable local renown. So prolific were his hauls that he developed a reputation for using dynamite to catch his prey. The older Bobby now thinks this unlikely; but his younger self had glorious pictures in his head of 'the river exploding with beautiful salmon'.

On his father's side was Uncle Tommy, a kind and gentle man, who bought Bobby his first football boots, a pair of Playfair Pigskins. It is entirely typical of Bobby that the name of those boots is deeply embedded in his memory and he felt that day would be the best of his life.

Bobby himself has no doubt where his 'luck' lay. 'From our mother we received the benefit of a brilliant football gene pool – and her passionate insistence that neither of us [Jackie and I] neglected any talent we'd been given. From our father I like to think we learned to be steadfast in what we did and proud of it.'

I know exactly what he means. From my family I inherited a physique that was apparently well adapted for rowing, but there are countless big blokes out there who can, with a bit of training, gulp up sufficient oxygen to row a boat. It's a convergence of characteristics that makes you or breaks you and so much is dependent on life's little accidents of place and time.

If I hadn't been born by the river, if I hadn't been to one of the very few secondary modern schools in the country vaguely interested in rowing, if I hadn't had parents who let me leave school without a 'proper job' and explore the possibilities in a sport that traditionally provided no income at all, there would have been no career, no Olympic medals and no part of the story would have been the same. There would have been no meeting with Ann, no children, no friendships with Matt or James or Tim or any other of the countless mates I have in rowing, no sponsorships, no speaking engagements, but perhaps no illnesses, no diabetes, no body ravaged by the effects of twenty-four years of intense training as well. It is impossible to know how different my life would have been.

I might still be working on a building site, having gone into business with my dad. But I don't need to dwell on the what ifs. My family had the great good sense to settle in Marlow and then supported me unstintingly in my ambition. When our school desperately needed to raise funds to buy a boat, it was my parents and those of the other boys who clubbed together and found a hundred different ways to raise the necessary money.

At first, of course, my parents were a huge embarrassment. No teenage boy wants his mum and dad to tag along when he's competing, but as time went by, as they continued to follow my competitions all over the world – they came to every single World Championships except the one in Tasmania in 1990 – I began to see the benefits. It was comforting to turn up at a major event and find their camper van on site, so that I could shut the door, have a cup of tea and return to normality just for a few minutes. Plus there were always biscuits.

As Ann and I produced a family of our own, Mum and Dad used to come not just to support me, but to babysit the children. I took them completely for granted in my younger days, just like my children take me completely for granted now. That is just as it should be, but I can look back and see just how much I owe my parents for their support and – let's face it – blind faith that somehow rowing might pay off.

Bobby tells me his father was a quietly courageous man. He must have been to survive a working life down a coal mine. My dad, Geoff, was similarly reticent. He was, and is, a loner, which must be where I get it from. I remember once when he was working on the construction of Ann's clinic he decided to sleep nights in the half-built shell, open to the night sky, rather than stay with us in the house.

My mother, Sheila, is the more gregarious one. For about ten years Mum ran the youth club in Marlow Bottom, held at the Village Hall once a week. For years and years she was also secretary of the Barn Club, essentially a pub/club in the village with which we had a strong family connection. My grandfather on my mum's side built the original building and my dad added the extension. My sister, Jane (both my sisters are considerably older than me, so that growing up I was more of a project than a pain), worked there and even I, when I gave up hard labour in the fruit shop, used to work there on Saturday night/Sunday morning, tidying up the empties and sometimes helping to drain them. Mum taught all three of us kids to drive, and then trained as an official driving instructor to earn extra money to help me with rowing. Talk about commitment to the cause.

Mum was also unofficial landlady to several rowing strays, including my old rowing pal, Adam Clift and our crew-mate, Julian Scrivener. We were living in the flat over the garden centre at the time; the boys slept in the old office and a box room next door.

She and I don't have similar temperaments – I am much more like Dad – but I definitely get my temper from her. It doesn't go very often, but when it does, the sound and fury are pretty spectacular.

I think perhaps my interest in charity work stems largely from her as well. When I retired I set out to raise £5 million in five years for a group of different children's charities through my charitable trust. I am keenly aware I've lived a privileged life and it seemed only right to do something which gave back to those who haven't been so lucky. I knew that after 2000 my name would have a certain shelf-life and I wanted to capitalise on that. In the event, we managed to raise the target amount and now it has shaded up to £6 million, supporting about 400 different projects in five or six years. I very much wanted the emphasis to be on children. If you give something to young people, there is more chance to change the course of their lives and perhaps they in turn will mature into people who want to help others. I know from experience that we all need help on the way.

I mention my family, because I have in common with Bobby Charlton a sense of gratitude that genetics and events so conspired to present me with not just a career, but a life. He feels most profoundly the 'luck' of his early years and to this day is modestly grateful for the life that seemed to fall into his lap. I perceive it in a slightly different way, in that plenty of sportsmen and women squander the early advantages they are given, but in Bobby I see a hugely skilful individual, devoted to his sport and determined to make the most of himself. The fact that he has remained a humble man despite two glorious careers, for Manchester United and England, is his own unassuming doing.

Like Tony McCoy, in a different way, he had the will and common sense to make the most of his so-called fortune. Luck is winning the lottery. Earning 106 caps for England and scoring 199 league goals for Manchester United is class.

8

STAR QUALITY

I HAVE A WELL-DESERVED reputation for being a misery guts. This is a fact I have just conclusively proved on live TV. First, I used a four-letter word in my post-race BBC interview (although it was actually seven letters in its context, if you're being pedantic) and then I asked Dan Topolski, the interviewer, to shoot me.

It's Atlanta, it's 1996 and I have just shown that I am not at my most charismatic after a race. Nor before a race, come to that, when I'm extremely introverted and moody. I don't think charisma is one of my chief qualities. My family would probably agree. I wouldn't say Ann thinks I'm boring, she just thinks I'm miserable. I have not run to meet fame with my arms outstretched. I have ambled along and bumped into it, inadvertently.

This – my fourth Olympics – has not been a joyful occasion. I have never been so stressed, so annoyed, so disgusted with myself. I have never felt the strain of an Olympiad cycle so acutely. What should have been a glorious achievement has become somehow shrouded in gloom and despondency. What makes it worse is that I know it's my fault.

Remember the old days, back in 1984, when rowing was a little backwater of British Olympic sport? Back when it was just the guys and me in our allsorts coxed four? Back when nobody cared? 'And now we're going over to Lake Casitas for the final of the coxed four,' said Des Lynam to his BBC audience seconds before the race started. There was no preamble and virtually no media interest in the build up. With victory came a little more attention on the road to Seoul, followed by another surge in interest towards Barcelona. But Atlanta was different altogether. Suddenly there was this huge glare of self-inflicted, on-going attention and I had made the matter much, much worse by opening my big mouth and telling everyone within hearing that on 27 July we were going to win.

Why didn't I keep my lips sealed? I know why. Because I believed it and because our sponsors expected us to turn up at events and be positive. I had to say something. I couldn't stand there, when asked, and mumble something about 'may the best men win'. We were the best men. I said so and at the time I was happy to say so, but as the event got nearer and nearer I began to see that I had made a bloody great target of myself. What started as a means of motivation had turned into something else altogether, something scary, and I was afraid of letting people down.

Meanwhile, a media frenzy was developing and my emotions when I arrived in Atlanta after our various training camps were really quite traumatic. I felt – for the first time in my career – that I couldn't cope. The boundaries had changed. Suddenly I felt the burn of the media spotlight. Some athletes yearn for fame as well as glory. I didn't want any part of that. I accept that I am recognised, I know it comes with the territory of winning, but I infinitely prefer to occupy the space in the background.

However, there is no background to be had in Atlanta. It is up front all the way. I have always tried to play my part with the media. I think that's only right and I was brought up to be polite and courteous by my parents, although Matt may laugh hollowly at that. But the older I become, the lower my tolerance seems to be. I react by stifling my feelings. I'm a bottler-up, not a spiller. So here in Atlanta I've been entirely unable to offload the dark emotions I have been feeling, especially on Matt. I don't know if he has sensed something is wrong with me, but he always seems to say the right things – just something light or businesslike or inconsequential. I feel bad for Matt because I am supposed to be the senior partner.

As far as I was concerned it all came to a head after our first heat. We were the first race of the day and off we trundled to the lake, rowed, won and then came into the press marquee to meet the press. It was our first press conference there of any note and the place was packed with media representatives. I had never seen anything like it. For years I'd been facing benign little press chats, maybe with a handful of ex-rowers. It was a comfortable zone. We knew virtually everyone we talked to by name.

Suddenly I was hit by the impact of what we were trying to do – a fourth medal in a fourth Games. I wasn't prepared for this level of interest. It was a surprise – and you know I hate surprises. Cameras lenses, notebooks, recorders, faces, mouths asking questions in stifling heat, pressing me further and further back into the corner of the tent. I started to feel claustrophobic. I felt enclosed, cramped, trapped.

'I've got to get out of here,' I said to Matthew. It was the first time I had seen my children in ten days – they were staying with their grandparents off site to try and introduce a note of normality – so I made them my excuse. I just held on to Natalie and Sophie like shields, brushed past everyone and fled.

That was the moment that I realised my sport had changed for good. For years, for a century, rowing, apart from the University Boat Race, was on nobody's radar. Until the Atlanta Games, rowing was a backwater sport, but now it has come of age. I might be proud of that one day when I'm boring the grandchildren, but here, this week, it's been a totally unsettling experience.

I had no idea. I was in this bubble of self-absorption, messing about on the river. I had no concept that suddenly the world's media would descend en masse to examine my private dream. I didn't like the exposure. I hated the pressure. I was worried for Matt and my family, and, as it turned out, I also needed to be concerned about my dad, of all people.

He's like me. He's a very quiet person by nature and wouldn't normally say boo to a goose, but now it is affecting him badly. He and Mum are staying with a family somewhere on the outskirts of Atlanta and I've been told that they were invited to a village hall to meet the locals and Dad was asked to say a few words as the father of the 'famous Steve Redgrave'. He stood up, but he couldn't control his emotions and started to cry. I have never ever seen my father cry.

Can you imagine how that made me feel? He was enduring that kind of stress because of something his son was trying to do. I was horrified. We were getting to the sharp end of the racing and my mind, instead of being focussed, was reeling round all over the place, churning with thoughts over which I had no control.

It was awful. The time waiting around between races was sheer hell. 'If the process of being an Olympic rower is this bad, why the hell am I doing it?' I asked myself. I couldn't make it shut up. It was undermining me, interrupting me, sabotaging me. I was completely disgusted with myself. I was sleepless too.

And then the bomb went off. It had to be the night before our final. I put on the TV on the morning of our race and there was the news flash: 'A bomb has detonated in a park in Atlanta. Nobody knows how many have been killed. An IOC spokesman says the Games will carry on.'

'Yes, but they might carry on without me.' That was my immediate thought. I didn't know if I wanted to be part of something that meant fellow humans being carted off in ambulances. If lives were in danger or, worse, destroyed, what was I doing climbing into a boat?' I was stunned. I'd focussed four years of my life on this day and now I didn't even know if I wanted to race. I didn't know what to do.

Well, what you do is put one foot in front of the other. You go on. That's what I did. In that lull you get before a big race I was lying in the athletes' marquee looking at some unseen corner of the roof and listening to the tannoy system telling the assembling crowd that there would be one minute's silence before the race in commemoration of those injured in the bomb attack. This truly was a private hell. I just hoped Matt wasn't picking up my feelings.

That's when I sat up and talked to myself: 'Just think how much effort and work you've put into this. You have nerves, but you know where the knife edge lies after all these years of competition. Control the nerves, harness them. Remember the sacrifice, your own and those around you. Don't waste it. Give it your best shot. Win, lose or draw, do your finest. This day, if there is going to be a new Olympic champion, why should it not be you?'

We went out, climbed into the boat and warmed up on the water, just a gentle low intensity paddle, followed by short bursts of power. I tried to disguise my feelings. I hoped Matt would assume I was on automatic pilot. As we paddled back past the grandstand I could see that a vast crowd had already gathered. The noise sent a shiver down my spine. Then I heard it: 'Come on, Dad!' It should have been impossible to pick out any voice in the crowd, but I am convinced I heard Natalie calling to me. Tears welled up in my eyes. That wasn't like me. Where was my control? Just minutes to go before the race and I still wasn't myself, but this was Matt's future, too. I couldn't let him down. We'd been through so much together already. Training, eating, sleeping, living for this one moment when so much could go – and it seemed was going – wrong.

I didn't tell him any of this. The start gun fired and we just reverted to what we knew best. We powered off and suddenly we were a length in the lead. We held it and we held it, but with 350 metres to go the Aussies and the French started to close the gap. I didn't want to respond too soon and have nothing left for the sprint to the line – 'Just maintain,' I continued to say. Matt maintained.

At 300 metres, 'Go now!' I commanded. We made our move. It was enough. We crossed the line first and physically I think we both had a little bit left, but mentally I just felt this huge moment of release. It was over. Thank God, it was over. It was not the competition I had dreaded so much, it had been the torment of everything surrounding it. The raw emotion of it all made me a maniac in the aftermath.

Dan Topolski: 'Fantastic row. Great achievement. How did you see the race unfold?' Me: 'Matt f**king took it out at the start like he's never done before.' I heard myself saying it. The four/seven letter word was out of my mouth before I could stop it. Well, it was too late to do anything about it now. Just go with the flow, I said to myself. Just pretend it didn't happen. Then I came out with my other masterpiece about shooting me. As interviews go, it was my all-time most disastrous.

I met a few of the BBC guys in the production unit afterwards and thought I would be in for it, but do you know what happened? They apologised. They apologised for putting my profanity on air, as though it was their fault not mine, and they carefully explained that the offending word had been cut from all the subsequent transmissions. There you have it – the power of an Olympic gold medal.

It's later now and I'm wondering whether I meant it? Am I going to give up rowing? Right now, packing up all my things, it feels like it. I don't want to go through that torment and torture ever again. What for? Shouldn't four gold medals satisfy anyone's hunger for competitive vindication. I'll be thirty-eight next time and I'm ill. Don't be crazy, everyone tells me. Retire at the top. Surely, surely, this time, this medal, feels like closure on an amazing sixteen-year Olympic career? Surely my wife and children deserve a little bit more of my attention? Surely I can't go messing about on a river for ever?

SPYRIDON LOUIS

I sometimes wonder idly how many times the Olympic movement nearly collapsed in the effort of its establishment. Many times probably, so often surviving by some quirk of fate or political expediency long lost in the mists of time. By all accounts the first revival of the modern Olympics, in Greece in 1896, was a slightly disappointing occasion, lacking vast crowds and genuine home-grown heroes until the day of the marathon.

Perhaps the outcome of that marathon altered the flow of history as an event which was viewed with a studied yawn suddenly became the cause of national celebration The nineteenth century marketing men had done their job. The marathon began at Marathon, just as it would in Athens 2004, but there were notable differences. The 1896 athletes had rather more trouble actually getting to Marathon than was the case for Paula Radcliffe and her competitors over a century later. The method of transportation was a decrepit old horse and cart, which took a plodding five hours through cold wind and rain to get there. When the competitors finally arrived they were freezing, so much so that the hospitable people of Marathon lent them their jackets and hosted a knees-up party. Wine flowed. The runners were asked if there was anything else required before the race the next day. 'Yes, more wine please!' they said, now thoroughly warmed up.

Half the runners were probably still hungover the following day, which would have made the eggs and milk, three hours before the start of the race, something of an ordeal. Among the favourites were the four foreigners in the ranks: Edwin Flack, a London-based Australian accountant, an American, a French-man and a Hungarian. Also in the line-up was a young Greek villager from Amarousion. Spyridon Louis was unknown on the international stage, but had friends in the crowd, including his father-in-law who stood by the side of the road and offered him a beaker of wine and an Easter Egg. Inspired, perhaps by the crowd, perhaps by the egg, Louis set off in pursuit of the leaders. Soon he overtook the American, the Frenchman obligingly collapsed, and eventually he found himself running behind the only man left to beat, Flack, who had previously won the Olympic

800 metres. Louis finally caught up with the Australian and an army officer, excited by the turn of events, fired a pistol shot into the air and everybody cheered. A hundred years later and he would have been arrested by the riot squad.

Towards the end of the race (he had never run further than ten miles in his life), Flack started to weave and sway in distress. A friend asked a Greek spectator to save him from falling while he rushed off to get some kind of blanket. The by-now-delirious Flack misunderstood the nature of the approach and, thinking he was under assault, whacked the kindly Greek on the chin with his fist.

Spyridon Louis was the ultimate victor and he became an instant folk hero in Greece. History is unclear about whether he was a poor shepherd, a rich farmer or a post office messenger, but he didn't really need to be more than the Olympic marathon champion to satisfy every desire of his compatriots. He was showered with free gifts in an ecstasy of patriotic celebration. Among other things, he received watches, jewellery, wine, free haircuts, free clothing for life, free meals, free coffee, a shot gun and a Singer sewing machine.

I can't say I resent Spyridon's good fortune. I have never quite seen the need for a sewing machine, especially as for twenty years of my life I dressed in lycra and flip flops, and I don't envy his moment of glory either, even though it seems to have been a great deal more romantic than some of mine. 'That hour was something unimaginable,' he apparently said. 'It still appears to me in my memory like a dream. Twigs and flowers were raining down on me. Everyone was calling out my name and throwing their hats in the air.' None of the above happened when I brought back my first gold medal. No twigs, no flowers and the only people calling out my name were at the check-in desk at Los Angeles Airport.

I would remain anonymous for a few years yet, but I admit that if Matt and I had wanted to be superstars we didn't help our own cause much, because after our triumph in Barcelona we could both be found in the Athlete's Village launderette, solemnly doing our washing.

JESSE OWENS

It has to be the greatest story in twentieth century sport, but not just because Jesse Owens won four gold medals at the 1936 Berlin Olympics, and not even because Owens goes down in history, in my view, as the greatest Olympic athlete of all time. Owens's story simply sends shivers down your spine. If it had happened 2,000 years ago we would have called it a parable. To me, he had star quality not because he was marketed or hyped by an outside agency, not because of a quick bit of trick photography and a lightning storm of flash bulbs, but because he symbolised the power of truth over propaganda – a black man turning Hitler's monstrous racism into a visible lie. The Nazi ideology proclaimed Aryan racial supremacy. One lone black man, the grandson of slaves, made a mockery of that twisted belief, under the very gaze of Hitler.

Every part of his tale seems to offer a lesson. The seventh child of a large family, he was born in Alabama in 1913 and named James Cleveland Owens, but, if you believe the romantic stories, James became 'Jesse' when a teacher misheard the little boy's pronunciation of his initials, 'JC'. When he was seven he was expected to pick a hundred pounds of cotton a day. At nine, the family moved to Cleveland, Ohio, and he worked pumping petrol and delivering groceries. At running, he was a natural. A prodigy. A phenomenon. When it was time to graduate from high school, so widely had his fame as an athlete spread that twenty-eight American colleges tried to recruit him. In 1935, the year before Berlin, he astounded the sporting world by breaking three world records and equalling a fourth in less than an hour at a college event. The long jump record he established that day (with one jump) would survive for the next twenty-five years.

He had issues, though. If we are going to laud him for his humanity, it is reasonable to note that humans come by a fair amount of trouble. This same year, 1935, he was threatened with exposure as the father of an illegitimate daughter and he hastily married the mother, a high-school sweetheart. Then he was revealed as the recipient of money – $159 – for a company job as a 'page' that didn't actually oblige him to work. This was considered a scandal for an amateur athlete and he was forced to pay the money back.

It is a peculiar fact that for much of the twentieth century – and I would have cause to know this more than most – the authorities preferred the concept of 'amateurism' to 'professionalism'. Athletes of all kinds were expected to take part in sport, whatever the cost, strain or injury to themselves, living in a hovel, stewing old bones by a campfire if necessary, for the greater glory of pure competition.

But I had a mortgage to pay. Not that being a professional rower did pay the mortgage. In 1984, the year I went to Los Angeles, my annual grant from the Sports Aid Foundation totalled £300. I am not implying ingratitude. Every penny was welcomed, but, fortunately, I was competing at the time when professionalism – and therefore payment – became acceptable, whereas Owens was to be plagued by financial problems most of his adult life.

There were more issues, too. The effects of racism on his reputation and career were enormous. In 1935 when he set those world records, the Sullivan Award, presented annually to the best amateur athlete in the United States, was given to a golfer named William Lawson Little, who was white. The following year, when Owens triumphantly returned as quadruple Olympic medallist, the award was given to Glenn Morris, the Olympic decathlon champion, who was not only white, but was considered sufficiently wholesome to play the title role in *Tarzan's Revenge* for 20th Century Fox in 1938.

Ironically, the German people, as opposed to the Nazi hierarchy, had heard of the exploits of Jesse Owens and were hugely excited by his arrival in Berlin. They were enraptured by the stories that preceded him and spent the duration of the Olympics mobbing him for autographs, even thrusting paper through his hotel room windows for him to sign.

When the Games began on the track, he lived up to his extraordinary reputation. His victory in the 100 yards was by a full yard, having led all the way against his fellow countryman, Ralph Metcalfe. The German, Erich Borchmeyer, upon whom the Nazi hopes were pinned, trailed in fifth place. The fascist propaganda that portrayed 'negroes' as inferior was exposed as a lie.

Owens's next event would be the long jump, where he found himself embroiled in competition with Carl Ludwig 'Luz' Long, literally the blue-eyed boy of the Nazi leaders. With his blond hair, Long was the physical embodiment of everything a fine Aryan should be in Hitler's warped ideology – except a loyal member of the party. He was charming, friendly and sympathetic – a flagrant breach of unofficial party rules. Then he increased his offence, by offering the American smart advice, which almost certainly led to his own relegation to the position of silver medallist.

Owens was having trouble with his run-up. His first practice run, though, had been misinterpreted by the officials as a genuine first attempt and they refused to change their designation. His 'second' attempt was a no jump. There was only a third and final assault on the qualifying standard. It was then that Long introduced himself. They chatted and, in the course of their conversation, Long advised the American star to start his take-off further back from the board. It was a self-destructive piece of sportsmanship as far as Long was concerned, as Owens broke the Olympic record to win the event with the leap of twenty-six feet and five and a half inches, but a friendship had been established and history was made.

It is a poignant footnote to the story that Long, such a

resonant symbol of human decency, was killed fighting for Germany eight years later. He and Owens had corresponded after their meeting in Berlin, but suddenly the German's letters stopped coming. Owens probably guessed the reason long before official confirmation arrived, but he continued to stay in touch with Long's family all his life.

The 200 yards provided Owens with his third Berlin gold medal, with no trouble at all. He won by four yards in a time of 20.7 seconds, a new Olympic record. Interestingly, as a sign of the slowly expanding progress of black American athletes, the silver medal was won by fellow countryman, Mack Robinson, whose younger brother Jackie joined the Brooklyn Dodgers and became the first black major baseball player of the modern era.

Owens's fourth and final gold was provided by the sprint relay, an event in which he was not even expecting to take part. He had already been told by the relay coach that he had had 'enough glory already', but, in the period leading up to the race, two of the American sprinters were mysteriously asked to stand down from the squad. Their names were Stoller and Glickman, Jewish names, and although it will remain forever unproven, there were reasonable suspicions that the only two Jews on the US track squad were being quietly dropped to spare the embarrassment of the German hosts.

They say that sport and politics should never mix. I have never known a time when politics could be relied upon to stay out of sport – not in Owens's lifetime and not in mine. It is such an easy wagon to hitch to when politicians want to make a powerful point and it doesn't cost them anything except an athlete's wellbeing. Owens would go back to tickertape parades in New York and Cleveland, but then what? To racial discrimination and rank disrespect. The President himself, Franklin D. Roosevelt, never even sent a letter of congratulations, let alone invited him to the White House. Attitudes have changed significantly in the past seventy-plus years of course. It was good to see the American athletics team at the World Championships in Berlin in 2009 all had 'J.O.' embroidered on their racing kit as a mark of respect to this wonderful athlete.

We take it for granted these days that a successful sporting performance, be it at the Olympics, in the Ashes or winning the Rugby World Cup, acts as an invitation to visit some of the finest pieces of real estate in the land. I have met the Queen, most of the royal family, all the recent prime ministers and fellow bobsleigher, the late Prince Rainier of Monaco.

The Queen gave me my MBE and Prince Charles my CBE, but the meeting with the Queen that naturally stands out in my mind is my knighthood in 2001. There were over hundred people there at Buckingham Palace to receive an honour and yet she had two questions – and a very firm handshake – for every one of them. I don't know how she did it. I can't believe she was wearing an ear piece, but it was really very impressive.

I had to stand with one knee on a stool, then she whipped out a sword and touched both shoulders. There was no 'Arise, Sir Steve.' She didn't say anything at that point, which quite surprised me. Once the 'knighting' was complete, I had to walk backwards a couple of steps and make a bow. There was ample room for mishap. Luckily, none took place.

For poor Jesse Owens none of the perks of sporting prowess were available. It makes me very sad that, in his later years, he had to race against dogs, horses and trains just to make enough money to live. At least the story has a happier ending, though. As race relations improved, America began to appreciate its famous sporting son and he eventually developed a repertoire as a corporate speaker. He had five basic speeches, including one on religion, one on patriotism and one – slightly more practical – on marketing for salesmen. Owens became 'a professional good example', in the words of a contemporary writer, William Oscar Johnson. His public image was carefully tended and no mention was made of his mistresses nor his 1966 conviction for non-payment of taxes.

This idea of the 'good example' interests me. It is such a double-edged sword. So many times in modern sport, and life come to that, an individual is raised to heights too exalted to maintain and then torn to pieces for failing. I have always been aware that I am in the public eye and, to a great extent, I separate that Sir Steve from the one who is really me. Sir Steve, I would say, performs his duty, gives his speeches and enjoys giving back to the sport that helped create him. I, on the other hand, am quite happy pottering about the house, admiring the garden and eating cake. I think sometimes the problems begin when you believe your own publicity – good or bad.

I have seen excerpts of Owens's speeches and they sound almost too perfect, too scripted, to be true. I suppose they were polished many times in the writing and telling, but I can identify with the core of what he said: 'I owe everything to the Olympics, which I see as the greatest movement in the world. I never fail to be moved by the sight of 10,000 men and women singing, living and playing together. Where else can you see so much discipline, so much determination? Every night they come back to the Village as individuals, yet as the flame dies on the final day you'll see them all looking around for the friends they have made.'

Owens had some tremendous speechwriters, but he deserved them. His feats robbed a psychopath of his propaganda triumph and the colour of his skin was the most formidable reproach to the racists. One statement he made really strikes a chord with me. It may be something that no scheming politician will understand, but ask an athlete – he or she will. He said, 'The road to the Olympics does not lead to any particular country or city. It goes far beyond Moscow or Ancient Greece or Nazi Germany. The road to the Olympics leads, in the end, to the best within us.'

Ronnie O'Sullivan

Sportsmen like Ronnie O'Sullivan, Shane Warne and the late Ayrton Senna are dazzling technicians, but that isn't the end of the story. They have something more, something that's harder to define, and so we term it 'genius'. I am not sure whether genius is entirely the right word, but it does cover the idea that these talents are massively out of the ordinary. Is that the definition of 'star quality'? Perhaps, but how would I know for sure? Rowers rarely need to be geniuses – just masochists. However, for the purposes of this discussion, I am happy to accept that O'Sullivan is a genius on the snooker table and I have powerful witnesses – no less than half the Rolling Stones. It is no surprise, Ronnie being Ronnie, that he has made friends among the rich and famous, and he recounts a story of once hooking up with Rolling Stone Ronnie Wood, who is a big snooker fan, and my favourite snooker player, Jimmy White, and going back to Wood's house.

White and O'Sullivan were persuaded by Wood and Keith Richards to play an impromptu exhibition game in Ronnie Wood's palatial snooker room, while they were plied with jugfuls of vodka and orange. They played eleven frames. By the end, White had six centuries and O'Sullivan had five. 'This is like Mozart,' Richards said. From a musician of such fame, this was serious praise. O'Sullivan was suitably flattered. 'I've watched *Amadeus* and to me that was a massive compliment. After every frame, Jimmy and I couldn't wait to set up the balls for the next one. Eleven frames, eleven centuries.' The vodka and the inspiration combined to produce a glorious demonstration.

There are some sports, like snooker, which are heavily dependent on touch and mood, while rowing is always, at heart, fiercely dependent on work ethic. There is little room to be mercurial on a rowing lake and I have to admit I'm pretty poor at snooker. My highest break is seven. I usually play pool in the local pub with a few mates, but once I played with Dad on holiday on a full-size table and both of us were missing pockets, not by inches, but by feet. We were awful.

Jimmy White, as I say, is my favourite player of all time, although you always felt that if he just gave a little more time and thought to a shot maybe he would have won at least one of those six World Championship finals he contested. At least he was fun to watch.

As a character, O'Sullivan is in the Jimmy White mould, but he seems to have more composure. Which is surprising since you would have to say O'Sullivan had more difficulties to absorb as a teenager than most people encounter in a lifetime. At one stage, his parents were both in prison, his father serving eighteen years for murder and his mother a short sentence for VAT evasion.

He was in Thailand, competing as a teenager when his mum called to tell him that his father was being held by the police after a fight in a bar which culminated in a man being stabbed to death. He flew home, with his chaperone, and was collected from the airport by his mum. There cannot have been many times when a chauffeured stretch limo arrived outside Brixton Prison. O'Sullivan tried to look after his little sister and maintain his fledgling professional snooker career, but his way of dealing with the situation was not always entirely conventional. On one occasion he threw a two-day party, which probably wasn't ideal on the domestic front, but was a brilliant method of distraction.

He may not have had too much guidance at that stage, but his gift as a snooker player was beyond doubt. He had made his first century break at the age of ten and when he was fifteen he became the youngest player in the history of the game to score 147, at the English Amateur Championships.

But beyond the statistics – three times winner of the World Championship at the Crucible, five times world number one – is the manner of those victories. Ronnie, nicknamed 'the Rocket' for his super-fast playing style, is an instinctive, attacking, natural player. He reminds me, in many ways, of a sportsman from another field, John McEnroe. They share many traits, a flair for rampant controversy being one of them, but, more to the point, both are raging perfectionists, subject to torment and frustration.

A spell in the Priory, the addiction clinic, helped to resolve some of Ronnie's more debilitating problems, but some of the things he talked about subsequently rang bells for me. He said, 'Part of my addictive personality is striving for perfection and, because I never achieved it, I constantly felt a sense of failure. It had been the pattern of my life for six or seven years: strive for perfection, fail to achieve it, despair. The strange thing was that I was comfortable being miserable.'

I understand that sense of striving. My original ambition was to succeed as a single sculler. It may surprise a few people to know that in some ways I felt I'd failed at the end of my career. I never did win that gold medal in single sculling, but then again maybe that's just being ridiculously greedy.

Ronnie concluded, 'Wanting to be the best, wanting to win, is an asset, but you can make yourself very unhappy when you don't reach the standards you set for yourself.' I think I am a little kinder on myself than Ronnie. I didn't achieve my ultimate ambition, but I'm pretty satisfied with what I got instead.

ARYTON SENNA

I remember the accident. Most people do. There was something special about Senna, even before the triple world champion from

Brazil crashed his Williams into a wall at Imola on 1 May 1994. He was fatally injured. He was thirty-four.

I think it was partly because he died young that a legend grew up so quickly around him. The crash was inexplicable and remained so even after an exhaustive inquiry, but these are the facts. He was leading the race, on course for his forty-second Grand Prix victory, when unaccountably his car appeared to understeer off the track. It hit the concrete wall at the high-speed Tamburello corner, tearing off the right front wheel and nose-cone before spinning to a halt. The impact was so great that Senna sustained three serious brain injuries. The arguments still rage about whether he died on the track or later in hospital. I don't suppose, in the scheme of things, it matters. He died, he was an extraordinary man, and the myth began.

'He looked serene. I raised his eyelids and it was clear from his pupils that he had a massive brain injury. We lifted him from the cockpit and laid him on the ground. As we did, he sighed and, although I am totally agnostic, I felt his soul depart at that moment.' That was the testimony of Professor Sidney Watkins, the neurosurgeon who was head of the F1 on-track medical team.

It is significant that even a self-respecting agnostic should identify the existence of Senna's soul, because there was a spiritual aspect to Brazil's F1 hero. Whether it was true or not, there were certainly other drivers, notably team-mate and on-going rival, Alain Prost, who believed he had a dangerously close relationship with his God. Following one of their stupendous crashes, at Suzuka in 1990, for which Senna was unarguably at fault, Prost said ominously that to Senna death is a game.

It may be that Senna was deeply religious and believed he had the protection of his deity, but how can we know now? I appreciate that there are many athletes whose confidence is advanced or whose nerves are stilled through faith in a higher enterprise, but I didn't follow F1 closely enough to discover whether Senna's intense and supreme confidence drew its force from his own skill or something less tangible. I do know that on his grave are carved the words, 'Nothing can separate me from the love of God.'

Most people – religious or not – do at some stage invoke God. You have to be a pretty tough character not to look for some external aid in a crisis, even if it's just, 'Oh my God, help me out here.' However, I don't see myself as being at all religious. To be absolutely honest, being a rationalist I find the whole idea pretty odd. I'm a realistic, pragmatic person and if you really sit down and think about it, the existence of an all-knowing, all-seeing deity doesn't make sense to me. How would this being allow so many terrible things to happen in the world?

Yet you do tend to find that quite a few sportsmen and women, especially in individual sports, are devout believers. I have my own theory about this. It seems reasonable to me that they would search for outside help and inspiration when they are so much on their own. At times of nerves, trauma and isolation it is only human to seek some comfort and sporting life can be pretty lonely. I never asked 'God' to help me beat another crew. I couldn't see why He would have anything against a crew of Italians or Croatians or Australians.

Clearly, Senna thought differently, and in some ways that informed the reaction to his death. The outpouring of grief was extraordinary. When his body was brought home for his funeral in São Paolo, the government of Brazil declared three days of mourning. An estimated three million people lined the streets. Three of his motor racing colleagues – Damon Hill, Emerson Fittipaldi and Prost – were among the pall-bearers, all enmity forgotten.

Ten years later, Damon Hill, his Williams team-mate on that day at Imola, spoke about the circumstances of the crash, saying, 'I am convinced he made a mistake, but many people will never believe that he could. Why not? He made many mistakes in his career. I have listened to and read endless theories about why, or how, he could have crashed on such a "simple" corner at Tamburello. No one other than Aryton and me know what it was like to drive that car, through that corner, in that race, on that day, on cold tyres. He was identified with pushing to the limit and beyond. It was not the fault of anyone else that he kept his foot flat when he could have lifted it.'

Whether right or wrong, it was a courageous thing to say. Those guarding the legend of Senna were unwilling to hear one whisper of 'error', and certainly we will never know for sure. Senna did have a reputation for wilful non-application of his brakes, but so supreme were his driving skills, so perfect his attention to detail, so acute some sixth, maybe seventh, sense of survival that the main response to the announcement of his death was disbelief. He was a winner, not a loser. In the ten years he raced in F1 he competed in 161 Grand Prix, won forty-one and established sixty-five pole positions. He was a risk-taker, but a survivor. As a boy he had once come home to his mother clutching one set of car radio speakers and an ignition key. 'What's that?' she asked. 'It's all that's left of the car,' he replied. 'The rest wasn't worth bringing.' I'm not trying to imply recklessness, but only a sportsman intent on finding his limits would dare behave like that. And he was an expert, an expert in anything that boasted an engine, long before he reached F1.

A Lotus engineer remembers there was much speculation that Senna was cheating because his car often, and inexplicably, out-performed his rivals. Finally, the engineer lost patience with the questioners. 'I said, "Don't lose any time any more checking the bloody car just after we've been making pole position. If you want to disqualify something, disqualify the bloody driver, because he's just too fast."'

My favourite story, the one which I think really explains Senna, goes right back to his F3 days. He was on a flight to Japan when he recognised an acquaintance, a fellow driver, sitting further back in the cabin. Senna came along to chat – on one particular subject, his own shocking defeat by a driver called Calvin Fish in a Formula Ford 2000 in 1982. Senna offered an explanation that took somewhere between seven or eight hours. 'His intensity was nearly pathological in the sense that he was more than just describing that he had had a difficulty and lost a race. It was more like a personal slight that he could actually lose a race,' said the recipient of the deluge. I can't imagine a mind that could function like that. If I ever talked to Ann about rowing for seven or eight minutes I'm pretty sure she would just hand me a bin liner full of rubbish and say, 'Put that in the dustbin on your way out, would you?'

Senna demonstrated the completeness of his passion. He remembered everything: exhaust pressure, water temperature, oil pressure. He remembered them for every lap. Senna didn't make small talk and wasn't into exploiting his worldwide fame. He wanted to drive his car fast and gave the appearance of bending every waking thought to that process. His knowledge was encyclopaedic, but that alone would not have been enough. He seemed to feel his way round a car, experience it in a way that went far beyond sitting in a driver's seat pushing pedals.

Is that star quality? He was certainly not the possessor of a flamboyant, extrovert, jack-the-lad personality. Quite the opposite. He was intense, quiet, focussed, and yet all across the world there was a sense of loss and real mourning when he died. I think some people transcend their sport. They have a gift, a talent, a presence that takes them to a different realm. We, who are so plainly mortal, can only watch them and admire.

DAVID BECKHAM

I was watching a TV quiz show one day when they asked a question about me. It surprised me. It was this: 'Out of these three athletes, who earned the most money in 2000? Was it David Beckham, Lennox Lewis or Steve Redgrave?' I didn't know whether to laugh or cry.

At the time, David Beckham was playing for Manchester United and on a contract that made him one of the highest paid footballers in Britain, not to mention just about the most famous clothes horse in the world. Lennox Lewis had just fought

Evander Holyfield for the heavyweight title of the world in Vegas and had already entered the realm of a multi-millionaire. I wasn't remotely in the same league. I was stunned when one of the contestants chose me. I'm not pleading poverty, but it wasn't until after Sydney that I broke even in terms of my domestic finances. I spent twenty years in the red, sometimes deeply.

The amount of money that Premiership footballers get paid is ridiculous, but I understand the power of market forces. I don't even think it's good for all of them in the long run. Money can make you comfortable, but comfort is no environment for a winner. It can make you a celebrity, but not a winner. Few people can be both. I would say, though, that David Beckham is one of those few. I like David. I met him properly at the presentation in Singapore to decide the host city for the 2012 Olympics. It was 2005 and the London bid team had come mob-handed with VIPs to try and persuade the IOC to choose London over the well-documented merits of Paris, Madrid, Moscow and New York.

I was there in my capacity as chairman of the Athletes' Advisory Group. There was quite a roll call: Lord Coe, of course, Tony Blair, Jonathan Edwards, Denise Lewis, Tanni Grey-Thompson and Beckham. Some people minded that a footballer was included, but I thought it was great that this calibre of star was showing such support for the bid.

He seemed a really nice guy and there was a moment during our time together when I really thought we clicked. We were at a video presentation – one he was in himself (doing a crossword to humorously dispel the rumours that all footballers are thick)

– but neither of us could see the screen properly. We both had to move into the audience, so I walked alongside him, shielding him from his many fans (not having quite so many – or any! – there myself). This is where being 6' 4" and wearing the scars of too many jammy dodgers comes in handy. Basically I ended up being his bodyguard. I pointed that out to him. 'Actually, we're looking for a bodyguard,' he mused with a grin. 'Oh, I'd be interested in that,' I told him. I would have been, too, but he never came back to me.

SHANE WARNE

Much as I admire him, I can't claim to be the soul-brother of Shane Warne, the greatest leg spinner in the history of cricket. Take our differing reactions to coming across John McEnroe. In my case, we were both at the BBC Sports Personality of the Year awards at the same time, in 2000, but I felt it would be intrusive to go up and say hello. When Warne met McEnroe for the first time, he was – you might say – entirely uninhibited.

It was at Jimmy'z, the most expensive nightclub in Monte Carlo (and, no, I've never been there), where Shane had ordered the first round of drinks with a bunch of friends and was presented with a bill for $350. 'Jeez, mate,' he called to the barman. 'I said a round of drinks not the whole bloody bar.' After a few more rounds he spied McEnroe, peaceably sitting with friends of his own at a glass topped table near the dance floor. As with many occasions in Warne World, it was too good an opportunity to miss.

Warne sank to his knees, crawled along the floor and wedged himself underneath the glass table. Once in position, he turned himself to face the most irascible tennis player of all time through the glass and shouted, 'You Cannot Be Serious!' How did McEnroe take it? 'I don't think he was too happy about it. I was a bit pissed.' I'll be honest. I have never had the urge to do anything like that. Whatever X-Factor, star quality or charisma Shane Warne possesses, I definitely don't share it. If Warne is a box of fireworks, I am an infinitely less combustible entity.

However, don't let that fool you into thinking we don't have a lot in common. We do. I had no idea, but Shane Warne has quite a history with rowing boats. He proposed to his ex-wife in one for a start. It should have been a romantic moment, rowing on a beautiful stretch of water in the Lake District, except a huge pleasure boat was bearing down on them at the time and the novice Aussie oarsman was going round in circles, only escaping into a thicket of bank-side bushes at the last available moment. He also remembers rowing as part of the Victoria Sport Institute's idea of a gainful experience. 'It was a freezing cold winter's morning and I thought, "Arrrgh, this is bloody hard."' Welcome to my world, Shane.

In his world I would have to admit to being highly average. At school I regarded cricket as a skive, a reason for being on the school field all day instead of in the classroom. In those days I thought of myself as more of a batsman than a bowler, but when recruited to play for the Lord's Taverners in more recent times I've told them I'm more of a bowler than a batsman. This was purely a ploy to avoid the fast bowlers on the other team. I'm not saying I've faced Curtly Ambrose, but David Seaman, the former Arsenal goalkeeper, had a wicked fast ball and I've even been on the field at the same time as Sir Gary Sobers. Shane Warne is a fantastic sportsman, if incredibly annoying whenever England played Australia, but I have never received a ball bowled by him and it is my fervent hope I never do.

If anything, I'm foremost a fielder. In my heyday as a rower I was so fit that compared to some of the others in the field I could run around and look remarkably busy. Mind you, as these 'others' might include people like Nicholas Parsons, the actor, TV and radio presenter, who was born in 1923, this is nothing to boast about.

At first sight, you could scarcely find a character more opposite to mine than Shane Warne's. I have never been tempted to bleach my hair blond (. . . well, maybe once). I have never, even for one single millisecond, thought about getting my ears pierced. I have never been caught in the tabloids smoking a sly fag when I was being sponsored by a nicotine patch company. They call him 'Hollywood', I'm stolid 'Marlow Bottom', but when you scratch beneath the surface of personality, when it comes to our sport, I think Shane and I share deeply held philosophies.

We both know it doesn't come easily. He talks about the passion, desire, will to win, discipline and sacrifices that an elite athlete must contribute to make any assault at all on the pinnacle of sport. He might have looked as though he just turned up at a cricket ground after a crate of beer and a night on the tiles, but he worked at his game all right. The flamboyant image is an expression of his personality, but the statistics of his fifteen-year

Test history are the expression of his graft. Totals: 145 Tests, 3,154 runs scored, 708 wickets taken, over a thousand wickets in all international competitions.

In his prime Warne played with a bamboozling wickedness and absolute authority that would reduce grown men in helmets to quivering wrecks. He didn't just bowl his opponents, he bedevilled them. One South African cricketer admitted to seeking psychological help to face Warne and he probably wasn't the only one.

'We wish you were English . . .' the spectators sang at the Oval on his last visit, when England won the Ashes in 2005. It made a significant change from 'He's blond, he's bent, His . . .' (never mind) – another Warne song favoured by the Barmy Army – but I didn't realise how deeply England was implicated in creating the phenomenon of Warne.

His dream was to be an Aussie Rules player, but like me in my desire to be a single sculler, he was thwarted. He played in the St Kilda reserves, their Under-19s, and he even trained in the first team. He was close but never quite made it. 'In 1989 they gave me the flick. Sent me a letter. Basically saying, no thanks and good luck. I thought, "Now what am I going to do for the rest of my life?"

'It was pure luck. A mate of mine was going to England to play cricket and he said, "Why don't you come too?" I thought about it. For about one minute. Then I said, "Count me in" and about a month later I was there in Bristol, the proud owner of half a £40 Ford Cortina, playing cricket for the Imperial Rugby Club.'

Growing up, Warne hadn't really cared about cricket. It was

the summer game, at a time when all his mates would be down on the beach, having fun, playing in the surf, eating fish and chips, and there he would be, in the middle of a field playing cricket for five hours. Why would that appeal to him as a career?

So it was by accident that Warne found himself at nineteen years of age, playing cricket three, four, maybe five games a week, and all the time adding to his ball skills and life skills while he was doing it. He probably played about a hundred games in six months.

It wasn't all work. There was a nightclub called Busby's where the pints cost 20p and Shane started to think that maybe he could live this life after all. He lived in a room over the bar of the rugby club, and he'd cut the grass or paint fences to make extra money and all the time he was learning and practising spin bowling. It was a crash course in taking wickets.

'Anyone can have a skill,' he says, 'but you have to learn how that skill works. In bowling, you have to do so many things. Outsmart a batsman, get a plan, set him up, drag him across their crease . . . these things only come with experience. The more you play, the more you understand. That's the theory anyway. I have seen cricketers who make the same mistakes over and over again. "How can they do that?" people say. "They've played fifty games." But they haven't. They've played the same game fifty times.

'No one ever masters a game. Not even Tiger Woods gets a hole in one on every short hole he plays. That's where the madness lies. You're driven as a sportsman to better yourself all the time. It can cause all kinds of grief and frustration, but it is the only way to improve. Whatever else I did, I always tried to get better.

'Yeah, I always had an extrovert personality and I know how it developed, too. I had no choice. As a kid, we'd be out in some park in Melbourne playing cricket, me and my mates. I'd be experimenting with my bowling and one of my friends would whack the ball so hard it would disappear over the fence. They'd all laugh at me, give me huge abuse and I'd think to myself, "Oh, righty-ho mate, very funny. I'll get you out next ball then." I laughed it off. I developed a thick skin. I didn't really care what people said. It just made me more and more determined. My mentality always was, "I'm going to get you."

'A lot of people throw in the towel. I get more determined. When something bad happens, that's when I try even harder. I've always wanted to foster the reputation that I'm laid back, that I didn't give a rat's arse, but it's not true of me at all. I never let anyone know if I was struggling with injuries or any other kind of problem. And at times, it was bloody tough, but I did give a rat's arse actually. I was very focussed. The image was just a front.

'The bling and blond streaks, that was just me. What you see is what you get. I played like my personality. I just go out and give it my best every single time. If someone's too good for me on the day, I shake their hand, share a beer and say, 'Well played." When Kevin Pietersen scored the century against us at the Oval in 2005, I ran out to meet him and said, "Well played. Well done. Soak it up. Enjoy it. Never take it for granted.'"

I don't think Shane ever did take it for granted. He remembers with absolute clarity how it all began. New Year's Eve,

1991. He'd been selected for the first time to play for Australia. David Boon and Geoff Marsh, two of Australia's great players, took him out to an old Sydney hotel and they sat there with an eski full of beer watching the fireworks explode over the city. They wanted to impress something on him.

These were the days of the old school rules. You didn't speak unless spoken to, and what they said has stayed with Shane all this time. 'Remember, always, that playing for Australia is something special. You're very lucky to have the privilege and honour. Not many people have done it before you.'

Shane made his debut against India two days later and there on the scoreboard in giant flashing letters it said, 'Congratulations Shane Warne – you are the 350th Test cricketer to play for Australia.' And he thought, 'Jeez, this game's been going for over a hundred years in Australia and I'm still only the 350th man to be picked to play for this country. That's got to be pretty special.' It still ranks up there as one of the most special moments of his career.

'One of my other special moments was against England, funnily enough. It was near the end of my career, my second last Test, at the Melbourne Cricket Ground, before I retired in 2007. I remember coming into the bowl and this huge roar going up among 91,000 people. I really wanted to do something special and I managed it. Five for thirty-odd and I knocked over Andrew Strauss for my 700th wicket. Whoever's been writing my script deserves a big thank you.'

I know what he means. 'The Ball of the Century' is a case in point. We don't have this option in rowing, to be immortalised for one brilliant stroke. Who would know? Who could see? It has to be enough that the crew can feel when they're cutting through the water almost perfectly, but thanks to cameras and TV replays we can watch 'Gatting's Ball' forever. Poor old Gatt. Has there ever been a look of greater astonishment on the face of a sportsman?

It was day two of the First Test in the 1993 Ashes series at Old Trafford. The pitch favoured spin bowling and Warne came in with the leg break to Gatting after his usual short run-up. The ball bounced a few inches outside the leg stump, Gatting came forward to meet it with bat and pad in time-honoured fashion, but the ball turned sharp left and clipped his off stump, bails flying. He just couldn't believe he was out.

The memory of his expression still makes me laugh. 'He looked as though someone had nicked his lunch,' said Graham Gooch, the England captain, of his well-upholstered team-mate. Martin Johnson, the cricket journalist, aptly observed, 'How anyone can spin a ball the width of Gatting boggles the mind.'

It was a great moment in sport, when the laws of physics seemed to surrender to the great spinner. Even the perpetrator admits it. 'When I see it on TV from time to time, I think, "Bloody hell, that was pretty special."'

It is so hard to walk away from moments like that and Warne flirted with a comeback. In his case it was for the Ashes series in 2009. He played it down at the time, but such was his self-belief and continuing love of performance that he did give it serious consideration. 'The adrenaline, the adulation, it's hard to let go,' he said. 'And all the time there's these questions rolling round in your head. Are you still good enough? Do you still think you can do it? Jeez, I miss that. The competition. Where are the substitutes for that? You can play golf for a sandwich and a beer, but it's not quite the same thing.'

One more Ashes, one special trip. Warne made a deal with himself – if Australia started to play badly in the lead up to the tour, if they didn't discover a new spinner, he'd do it. Then they lost in India, lost in South Africa, they tried three or four spinners and none of them seemed to be quite right.

'When people asked me I denied it. "Nah. Look, I'm not interested," but deep down I was definitely contemplating it. But in the end I had to accept it was unworkable. You can't just rock up and bowl. If you could, I'd never have retired at all.

'And then I also realised I had had twenty years on the road. My kids are twelve, ten and eight, and I missed a lot of things when they were growing up. That was part of my sacrifice. I missed the "Cool Kid of the Week" certificates they won at school, or their dancing, or their football, or their netball. Now I have the opportunity to try and make up for some of that. I'm a taxi service at weekends and I love it. I love kids. I might not have been a good husband, but I think I've been a good parent. So I wasn't prepared to go away for another three or four months for the Ashes.' He couldn't stay away completely, however. Commentating on the Tests was a nice compromise.

It's very hard to pin down what exactly makes a star and Shane doesn't know any more than I do but you recognise one when you see one. He knows he put bums on seats at cricket matches and he knows that when some people walk into a room there's just this breathless hush that seems to fall like a veil. 'Some have it, some don't, some try and never get it. Muhammad Ali is the sportsman I most admire. He has it. I've never met him, but the most intimidating person I've ever met in the flesh is – no doubt about it – Bruce Springsteen. It took me quite a bit of courage to ask him to have his photo taken with me. I did, of course. Being shy isn't really part of my character.'

In 2000 Shane Warne was selected by a panel of cricket experts as one of five Wisden Cricketers of the Century, the only specialist bowler amongst them. 'There was Sir Donald Bradman, Sir Jack Hobbs, Sir Garfield Sobers, Sir Vivian Richards and Shane Warne . . . I think my knighthood got lost in the post somewhere,' he said ruefully.

9

PERSEVERANCE

IT'S A BLOODY GOOD JOB I don't get hangovers. I might have expected one this morning. The morning after my first ever drugs test. It seemed rather like adding insult to injury: I'm seventeen years old and in my first World Championship race in Moscow; I'm eliminated in the single sculls, and then I'm called in for a drug's test. I couldn't pee to save my life. Fortunately, there a crate of Polish beer on hand for just such an emergency.

It helped that the British team doctor liked a bit of a tipple himself. I reckon we were there a couple of hours, knocking back the beers while I decided whether I could produce a specimen or not, and by the time we came out the whole place was deserted. Everyone had packed up and gone. God knows how we got back to the hotel. I was drunk. All I can remember is going to the doctor's room in this massive hotel near Red Square to carry on drinking.

Fortunately, it doesn't hurt as much as it should, not physically, but not every pain is physical, as I have not long ago discovered. When your best friend dies in front of you, just collapses and ceases to live with no warning, it jars you in ways I can't describe. No day goes by when I don't think of Bill, with that mischievous grin spread across his face. My larger-than-life best mate, closer than a brother, dead at seventeen.

He wasn't 'Bill' when we met. He was Robert Hayley, but we renamed him at school in honour of Bill Haley and the Comets, and it stuck. Thanks to rowing, we became virtually inseparable. I knew of him before that, but we weren't really close friends. Then our English teacher, Francis Smith, invited us to try out for the rowing team – in other words, get into an old boat he'd borrowed – and before we knew it, Bill and I were best buddies. He was either in my house or I was in his, both sets of parents treating the visitor as a second son. We lived in the same village, walked to school together, rowed together, went on holiday together, watched comedy films together. I had no reason – why would you as a teenager? – to think the friendship would ever end.

Bill thought like I did about the rowing. 'Going out on the river in school time? What a skive! What a no brainer!' There were twelve of us to start with. Within two or three weeks, four were left. Me, Bill, Clive Pope and Stuart Painter. The following year Stuart left and a boy called Peter McConnell, a year younger than us, joined.

Bill wasn't big, but he was very strong and very competitive.

I think he would have made a brilliant lightweight if he'd lived. He was also a talented artist. For some reason the four of us just clicked as a team. We had our ups and downs, like our first race at the Bedford Regatta in the hot summer of 1976, when we capsized like idiots as we climbed out of the boat, but mainly we knew nothing but success.

The coaches of other schools, like Radley, Shrewsbury and Eton, used to laugh at us, because we rowed so badly, or at least not prettily, but there was obviously huge leverage and power there because for four solid years we beat almost everyone we rowed against. We were four lads from a secondary modern school up against the public school system, and yet we had tremendous success.

It was partly because Francis made it so much fun. I remember after school we'd all pile into his yellow Morris Minor Estate and drive to the river to train. It never seemed a burden. We'd train five or six days a week and often compete on the off day, the Saturday. When Francis suggested we enter our first competition, it didn't frighten us. We thought, 'Oh, what a laugh.' We never dreamed about winning and yet that is exactly what we did.

It was the Avon County Schools event just outside Bristol and, of course, we had no idea what to expect. We were there to have fun. I presume we were as excited about the journey as anything. I know it was FA Cup final day – Southampton versus Manchester United – and the underdogs won with a goal by Bobby Stokes late in the game. Our story was a similar 'tale of the unexpected'. There we were on the water in Bristol, complete competitive novices, beating everyone we rowed against, including Monkton

Combe School (twice) and then, I think, Reading School in the final. Whoever they were they wore blue and white striped vests. They were dressed a good deal more smartly than we were, the motley crew from the secondary modern in our invisible string vests and knotted handkerchiefs, but we still won.

We went from strength to strength. We were very, very successful in the Junior 16s, winning a bronze medal in the National Championships. In the land trials held around the same time I was setting new levels. This brought me unwanted attention. There were people involved in British rowing who wanted to break up our school four and parachute me into one of the GB squad boats, but I wouldn't do it.

Loyalty matters to me hugely. It's the sort of person I am. If you come to me and discuss a situation openly round a table, there's a good chance of something happening. But if you do what they did, splitting up the squad eight to row in two fours against us, to try and prove we weren't fast enough, then it just puts my back up and makes me want to prove you wrong. I flatly refused to leave our boat. I was stubborn about it. I also think I was right. Our ambition became to race in the 1979 World Championships in Moscow. The ambition of British rowing seemed to be to stop us.

Eventually it came down to the National Championships in Nottingham, when we were due to race the GB squad four. If we won, we should have gone straight to the World Championships, but they changed the rules, so that if we won we would still have to hang around until the Monday and race the same crew again in a best-of-three competition. It wouldn't work the other way, of course, and if we lost that was it – we would be out. It was totally unjust, but we still reckoned we would beat them.

It's funny what you remember. We were staying in the halls of residence at Nottingham University and one night we went to the bar. There was a jukebox there and we put on a Sex Pistols' B side, 'Who Killed Bambi', over and over again, until someone was so sick of hearing it they went and pulled out the plug. Bill, as usual, had been the ring leader.

On the day of the race we were confident. We carried the boat down to the course, attached the seats and prepared as usual for the start. For some reason, just as a joke to settle us, before we clipped our seats in Francis said to Clive, 'OK, you might not have seen one of these before. This is your rowing seat and this is how it works.' As we had done this about 300 times before, he wasn't serious, but, although I say I don't believe in fate, sometimes you wonder. Halfway through the race, Clive's seat either broke completely or the runners jammed. Whatever the cause, our race and our dream were over. We wouldn't be going to the World Championships after all. Bill was too old to race in the Juniors next season and the Great Marlow School four was finished.

I was in tears, but I had another event, the single scull, to compete in. It was all a mad rush, but someone had time to tell me before the race began that if I did well I could still be going to the World Championships on my own. I didn't care. I couldn't be arsed. I was in no frame of mind to compete at all – but I won by 17 seconds. It's funny the way things turn out. I was going to Moscow after all. It didn't depress me, but I wouldn't have been human if I hadn't felt a pang of regret that the four of us hadn't qualified together. We got over it, though, as few things put a damper on the fun for long when Bill was around.

Maybe a couple of weeks later, Bill was at my house as usual. We were watching a comedy film, Tony Hancock in *The Rebel* I think it was, about a sculptor whose efforts at art keep going disastrously wrong. I think we were laughing. I can't remember clearly. It was all wiped out by what happened next. Suddenly Bill stood up and said, 'Can I have an apple?' I thought that was odd, because normally he wouldn't ask, he'd just help himself. As he picked up the apple from the fruit bowl in the lounge, he collapsed on the floor. That was it. I think I knew from that moment he was dead.

Things happened very quickly. My sister was there in seconds giving him mouth-to-mouth resuscitation. An ambulance was called. A doctor arrived. I had to phone his parents at Henley Golf Club and tell them, as calmly as I could, that their son had been taken ill and was being ferried by ambulance to High Wycombe Hospital. His mother, Joan, said she would meet me on the way.

I remember my thoughts so clearly as I waited for her. 'We're going to remember this day, Bill and I. We'll have such a laugh about this when he's better.' But deep down I knew it wasn't true. I knew before Joan came out to tell me in Accident and Emergency that he was dead.

I walked out of the building in floods of tears. I didn't know where I was going. I found myself walking along a path that led to the nurses' accommodation. By freak coincidence, Bill's girlfriend, who was a nurse, was walking down the other way, a silver bowl filled with instruments in her hand. 'Steve, what on earth's the matter,' she said, seeing me so distraught. 'It's Bill. He's dead,' I told her. Neither of us knew what we were doing. She simply handed me the stuff in her hand and fled in panic towards A & E, and I just stood there, bizarrely holding this silver bowl, tears running down my face. I was thinking how miserable I'd been when we hadn't qualified for the World Championships, but what was that compared to this? We wouldn't have gone to the World Championships anyway because my crew-mate, my best friend, was dead.

I found out later he died of a heart condition, but what difference does it make how it happened? It happened. My only consolation is that he crammed a whole lifetime into his seventeen and three quarter years, no question about that. It helps a little, that thought, but not much. Many people counselled me and they all said the same thing: 'It's a terrible tragedy, but you have to go on. He would want you to go on.'

Now, after all that Polish beer, my head does pound a bit. I wonder how the doc feels this morning. Worse than me I bet. Not getting bad hangovers was a useful quality when you went out with Bill. You know, no matter what we did, I think he and I would have been friends for life, so I have done what I thought he would have done and carried on rowing. I found his Great Marlow School sweatshirt mixed up with my stuff the other day. I probably ought to give it to his mum.

*

Marlow Bottom, 2009, home. I persevered. By the time I retired after Sydney, I'd been rowing for twenty-four years. Maybe it was testimony to how much fun it was in those early days that I contrived to keep going so long. It was probably the greatest skive of all time.

I had the chance to persevere, Bill didn't, but I owe my school crew-mates and Francis Smith a great debt of gratitude. I kept going way, way beyond the dictates of common sense because, essentially, I loved it. If the hard work in the early days had been miserable, if our coach had been a humourless taskmaster, if my best mate hadn't been there, perhaps everything would have been different.

It's been thirty years since Bill died and for years and years not a day went by when I didn't think of him. I'd often talk to him in my head before races. 'If there is such a thing as an external power. If you're up there watching over me . . . this is going to be a tough race. This is going to be a difficult situation and I could do with all the help I can get.' Funny, but I never got any answers.

As I've made clear, I don't believe in fate. I don't believe I won five gold medals because Bill died, but I do believe in sliding doors. One opportunity closes, another opens. It is how you take your opportunities that matters. I suppose I took my opportunities. I learned young that life can be very haphazard, seemingly cruel and certainly random.

I have never had a friendship as close as the one I had with Bill. I was closer to Matthew than anyone else, partly because we spent so much time together, and it may not be a coincidence that the deepest and most meaningful conversation we ever had was at the World Championships in Tasmania, on our way to the cinema, when I talked about Bill for the first time and he talked to me about his elder brother who died.

To a greater or lesser extent I suppressed the grief I felt, but as I've aged I've become more emotional. I pretend I haven't but I have. Quite a few years after Bill died, I went to see the film *Top Gun*, with Tom Cruise as a fighter pilot. Essentially it is the story of two guys whose lives are totally intertwined and one dies. I couldn't believe the effect it had on me. I had to walk out. I was in tears, distraught. It still gets to me now when I watch it. It turned out that suppression, distraction and maturity all work up to a point, but there are still moments when it comes flooding back.

I'm a very matter-of-fact bloke. I think I've rationalised things. Bill and I had great days together, just not many of them. He was a huge part of the beginning of my career, but not around for the middle or the end. That's just the way it was. I can accept the facts. But I never did give his sweatshirt back.

FRANCIS SMITH

It's quite simple. Without Francis Smith it would never have happened. Without enthusiasts like Francis Smith many sporting achievements would never happen – records would go unattained, talents would remain undiscovered, gold medals would stay uncollected and knighthoods would be unbestowed. Unsung and unremembered, except by the lucky sportsmen and women they inspired, those enthusiasts nevertheless hold a vital place in the history of British sport.

Francis was an English teacher at Great Marlow School, the learning establishment he had joined in 1957, a long time before the name 'S Redgrave' appeared in the register. In practice, my dyslexic brain was never going to absorb much English and so, looking at the size of my feet, he said to me one day when I was nearly fourteen, 'Fancy coming down the river to do a bit of rowing?'

He took a keen interest in sport and knew me already as a runner, a swimmer and an occasional rugby player, not because I wouldn't have liked to play rugby more often, but because Great Marlow was a footballing school, although we did supply a few county rugby players and I seem to remember being in a team that beat its rivals 50–0.

If my career is considered a great example of persistence, then Francis far surpasses me. He taught at the school for thirty-eight years and for the vast majority of that period he gave up all his spare time, for no reward, except the pleasure of watching generations of pupils improve at their sporting endeavours. Rowing was a particular favourite of his. He had rowed himself as a boy and man, to no great Olympic standard he admits. He was probably a little on the small side, but his switch to coaching was an inspired move.

He made the sport fun for his crews, he introduced them to hard work, he entered them in regattas, he taught them to win. He is a wonderful man and it strikes me as a sporting calamity of the modern age that such passion and commitment has virtually disappeared from our schools altogether. How much potential are we wiping out with our pretence of playing high-quality sport in schools when in reality some pupils are lucky to receive two hours in a gym?

We trained five or six days a week, squeezing into his little car – Bill, Clive, Peter, Nicky the cox and I – for the daily dose of training on the river. He had other things to do. He had a wife and family for a start and he was captain of Marlow Rowing Club, but he never failed in this commitment to his motley teenage crews. As things developed, it was arranged that pupils should become members of Marlow Rowing Club, so that they were able to use the club's equipment. By the time I arrived, there had been one or two crews in each year, including girls, and a four had won the National Schools Regatta. His only reward was the frequent successes, often over public school teams vastly better equipped than we were. I was lucky to have him, but whether he was lucky to have me in those days is another matter altogether.

Francis Smith: This lad appeared, and he was large compared to the others, but by way of his general construction and lack of development, he was all arms and legs. It's true, by the way. I did look at his hands and feet, and concluded, as you do with puppies, that he was going to grow to quite a size. He had a reputation already as a good swimmer, athlete and rugby player but my instinct was that rowing might suit him even better.

You could see at once Steve had the potential to be good. How shall I describe him? He was very strong obviously, but it was more than that. He became a leader somehow or another. He seemed to have the power beyond pure strength. Confidence, authority perhaps, I don't know. But the others thought he was the bee's knees. That feeling was not necessarily replicated elsewhere, certainly not on the bank at his very first regatta – the Avon County Schools in Bristol – where he fell off his seat and treated the audience to a loud barrage of old English words.

My view was always that if I enjoyed it, they would enjoy it. So while we trained hard it never seemed dull and it culminated in that four winning several things. They won two events at the Marlow Regatta. In 1975 they won the National Schools Regatta, that my previous four had won, and then the following year they won the National Championships Under-16s. That was the season they were virtually unbeatable.

I hesitate to say we did it properly, but we did try to take it seriously. We did land-training, long-distance rowing, short-burst rowing, all the facets of training that older club rowers might attempt. The results spoke for themselves.

Then we came to the attention of the selectors and Steve was under some pressure to leave the boat and take occupation of a GB squad seat. But loyalty was a huge word in his vocabulary. When he was told that he should comply with the instruction to leave his old school friends, he did precisely the opposite. He stayed with them. His character as we came to know it as an Olympian was already formed as a schoolboy.

Eventually Steve was siphoned off to the GB rowing team

and five years later he won his first Olympic gold medal. Was I surprised by that? No. Because if that's what he wanted to do, that's what he would do.

I still live in Marlow, not far from the school, and a typical route home will often find me driving past Redgrave Place, a relatively new road named in honour of our famous son. He is a bit of a celebrity round here, but he doesn't, and never did, behave like it. He wasn't even properly naughty as a teenager. They would occasionally disappear up the river for longer than I deemed entirely necessary, but they were a good collection of boys at heart. I am only glad they enjoyed it. I know I did. And the fact that Steve went on to five Olympic gold medals has never amazed me at all. I would say it was fairly typical.

Francis Smith may say that my persistence, which led me to eventually winning five gold medals, was always there. But without his own perseverance with a bunch of Secondary Modern kids I would have never stepped into a boat at all. And for that I will always be very grateful.

KATHERINE GRAINGER

Three Olympics, three silver medals – what a fantastic achievement you would say unless you'd actually seen Katherine and her crew-mates after the race in Beijing. I was there and it was devastating. They sobbed uncontrollably. They wept in interviews, on the phone, on the shoulders of friends and family.

It was almost agony to watch. The British team had achieved some magnificent victories on Shunyi Lake: the men's coxless four (my old boat), and Mark Hunter and Zac Purchase in the double, but when Katherine's boat, the women's quadruple sculls, were overhauled by the rampant Chinese for the line there was a general air of desolation about the place.

Katherine and her crew, Annabel Vernon, Debbie Flood and Frances Houghton, went into the race as three times world champions. They had lost once to the Chinese at a World Cup race in Lucerne, but were still considered right up there as joint favourites. I'd spoken to them a couple of days before the final. It wasn't a speech, as such, but I'd reassured them that, hard though it would be and nerve-racking as it was, they were here for a reason – they were good enough. We go through years of getting up in the dark, in the rain, in the cold, scraping ice off the windscreen and our faces, to go through endless, boring routines of training and preparation and this was why we did it – for a shot at an Olympic gold medal.

Katherine told me later that my words had made her cry. She had never been so emotional. 'Where did that come from?' she wondered. It reminded me of myself at Atlanta and the almost-crushing pressure I had felt. Katherine, at thirty-two and the most successful British female rower in history, would have felt huge responsibility for the others. She would have been desperately keen not to let anyone down. I am sure her outpouring of grief in defeat was as much for the others as for herself. It was an additional irony that of the Chinese crews in Beijing, all but one failed to achieve their potential. That one was the women's quad.

Many expected Katherine to retire after that. 'Oh yeah?' I thought, being something of an expert in this field. Sure enough, after a holiday in Africa, she came back to announce that she was carrying on to London, when she will be thirty-six. 'Beijing just didn't feel like closure,' she said, which much echoed my feelings after Atlanta.

Katherine and I are quite close. Our paths have crossed many times and we have the Sydney Olympics in common. That's where she won her first Olympic medal and I won my last. I keep an eye on what she is doing. I remember being very emotional the year before Beijing, when a back injury had robbed her of a great deal of time, and yet she climbed back in the four and they rowed brilliantly to win the World Championships in Munich in 2007. I hugged her when she came off the water and, honestly, I was almost in tears.

So now she's going for gold in London. It's a risk. 'What if it's another silver or worse' is the unspoken thought hanging in the air. And that is what separates elite athletes from sensible people. 'Hedge your bets, play safe, be content' – those concepts are entirely alien to us. 'Go for it, sacrifice for it, do your utmost for it' – these are the fundamentals that drive us. I understand completely why Katherine must go on. I support her decision. It is now one of the things I most want to see in my lifetime: Katherine Grainger smiling through an Olympic medal ceremony, a gold disc hanging round her neck. If she wins it will be fantastic. If she doesn't, it won't be a disaster. It won't change my view of her. It's the act of going for it that matters.

Of course, there are a few things I don't have in common with

Katherine, like her degree in law from Edinburgh University, her masters in medical law from Glasgow University and her on-going PhD in homicide at King's College in London. I won't bring up my famous CSE in woodwork again, but, suffice to say, we have achieved different standards of formal education.

It may help – it may not – that Katherine is studying psychopaths. I've asked her if she finds any similarities between mass murderers and elite athletes and, somewhat disturbingly, she says they're similar in a lot of ways. 'They're often ruthless, driven and incredibly successful in their chosen field,' she said. 'They have levels of obsessive intensity and determination. They're willing to trample on people in their quest. There are similar human traits put to different use: either for good or for evil.'

I'm pretty sure Katherine is not saying that all top athletes are psychopaths, but clearly we are at the extreme on the spectrum of human behaviour. In Katherine's case, the story begins with extreme competitiveness. 'I had a big sister and very early on it was ingrained in my psyche that I was in competition with her. Anything she did, I would also try to do and I would do my utmost not to be second best.' As in the family life of Andy Murray or Tanni Grey-Thompson, the level achieved by an older sibling was just something to shoot for and surpass. 'I was incredibly competitive, really determined to win, whereas my sister would be torn between winning and protectiveness. I was happily oblivious to any kind of handbrake.'

Katherine had a really happy childhood in Bearsden, Glasgow, an outlying suburb where you could play out in fields with other children late in the Scottish summer evenings, when it was still light at 11 p.m. It's probably the kind of childhood that no longer exists.

Rowing didn't remotely occur to her in the beginning. Her school didn't row and her only experience of it came via next door neighbours. They were very keen rowers on the River Clyde and their son would chat to her on the doorstep, showing her his blisters and callouses, which was hardly conducive to making the sport seem attractive. In the end, she did go out in a four with them. It was quite fun, but there was no moment of epiphany. Years and years later, Katherine's mum admitted that their neighbour had come round and excitedly told her that one of her daughters had real potential as a rower. History should record that the promising Grainger was . . . Katherine's sister.

'Getting into rowing at Edinburgh University was just a huge matter of chance. I wasn't looking for it. I wasn't keen. It was a complete accident. I'd actually been far more interested in joining the martial arts club. I was a black belt already, but this did not seem to go down too well with the other members, so at the freshers' fair I looked into other exotic sports, like skiing and sailing, and it was only when I was leaving that I noticed another girl I knew from my hall of residence. I offered to walk back with her. "Oh hang on," she said, "I just want to hear about the rowing club. Are you interested?" "No, no, no," I said, with some vehemence, remembering those neighbourly blisters.'

But the girl behind the desk was very persuasive and very persistent, and before Katherine knew where she was she had become one of eighty female novices standing by a river to try out for sixteen places. It was that horrible competitive instinct kicking in again. The odds were compelling. Only sixteen from eighty . . . hmmmm. She made the sixteen.

'Even then, it was so much work and rowing seemed to overtake everything else. I'd joined the sailing club and never been sailing. I'd joined the juggling club and never juggled. I kept saying to myself, "I'll just give it to Christmas and then I'll really have to think about giving up." Christmas came and went. Looking back, what kept me there was the people. These friends just became so special to me that I went on to be their bridesmaid, their children's godmother. I know we'll be friends all our life. It seems to be a speciality of the sport.'

The following year they were assigned into fours. Katherine wasn't in the first four, which slightly disappointed her. She wasn't in the second four, which she still understood. She wasn't in the third four, so she thought, 'OK, I'll be in fourth four,' except she wasn't in the fourth four either. 'I was in the remedial four,' she remembers. 'That was a bracing dose of reality.'

But she persevered and then something wonderful happened. 'The first female captain of the boat club, an amazing athlete, took an interest in us. We blossomed. "Oh my God, someone believes in me," I remember thinking. By the time I reached the fourth year of university I was rowing for Great Britain. How much we all owe to chance and chance meetings we have along the way.'

Katherine went to her first Olympics at the age of twenty-four. It was Sydney. And somewhere, on the same rowing lake that I raced on, she was celebrating madly with her crew-mates in the quad scull, because they'd achieved the first GB women's Olympic rowing medal. Silver.

'Perspective is everything. That silver was fantastic. I was over the moon with joy. It was honestly one of the happiest days of my life. It was like Christmas. I was the youngest, most inexperienced oarswoman in the boat and I had been so keen to live up to the others: Gillian Lindsay, Guin and Miriam Batten. An Olympic medal of any colour was just a magical moment.'

In Athens four years later Katherine was in the pair with Cath Bishop. The Romanians were favourite, unbeaten leading up to the Games, except when Katherine and Cath had won the World Championships in 2003. It had been a tougher campaign and a more intimate relationship. 'On the day, I have to accept we really under-performed. Silver that time was shaded with knowing disappointment.

'In Beijing we were just heartbroken. There were no shades of anything. It was pure, unadulterated grief. This time I wasn't the youngest and least experienced. I was the eldest and most experienced. I felt I'd let people down at my third Olympics in front of billions of people. I was inconsolable for a while. It took me months to even watch the race on DVD. It sounds ridiculous – at the end of the day, it's just a race – but I felt a terrible sense of loss, not of the race but of something dear to me. It was as though I had lost something of myself.

'I basically needed to get perspective. I went away to South Africa and Namibia for a holiday and I eventually came round to the idea that the result did not define me. The result didn't change me and I still had the opportunity, if I wanted it, to go on and row in London. I wanted it. I want it very much.

'It could be the most perfect ending for my rowing career. Or not. Things don't happen just because you want them to. I know I have to do things differently this time. That's why I have taken up the challenge of the single scull – Steve's old favourite – for a while. I want to freshen things up, stay positive, enjoy myself throughout the whole three years of training, but I know it will all come down to one moment in the end.

'I know the stress will be great and there are no guarantees, but if I look no further than Steve, what an inspiration. He was just so solid. Where other people would have given up, he persisted. Through illness and injury, he persisted. It is not a very glamorous quality – persistence – but it was the cornerstone of his enduring success. He's not a bad role model and, anyway, I'll be two years younger in London 2012 than he was when he won in Sydney. I just have this sense, this instinct, that I'm not done.'

Three years out from London 2012 Katherine has come back from the World Championships in Poznan with another silver, this time in a single scull. An amazing performance. Nobody in the world of rowing really expected her to achieve a medal of any colour. A single scull normally takes years to master. I don't think she has particularly enjoyed all-year training and racing on her own, but to come out the other end, to have done something different, to have changed the routine, that has to have given a great boost to her confidence and self-belief that in London she can achieve her dream.

CARL LEWIS

Frederick Carlton Lewis and I were fellow athletes at four successive Olympics: Los Angles, Seoul, Barcelona, Atlanta. As I've said, I was in the stadium in Seoul when he came second to Ben Johnson and I was also there in Atlanta when the crowd was going wild as he had one last attempt to qualify for the long jump showdown. I'm pretty sure he never came by the rowing lake, though. I'd have remembered – he is a distinctly unforgettable person.

Carl Lewis is one of those athletes who has just every quality you need to become a champion. Preparation? He was born in Alabama, the state that produced Jesse Owens, and his parents were packed with good athletic DNA. His father, Bill, was an American footballer and track athlete, while his mother, Evelyn, was considered one of the top US basketball players. By way of icing on the cake, they set up their own track club when Carl was seven.

Belief? Small for his age, he seemed the least talented of all his siblings, but as he developed, so did his confidence. Aged eighteen he told his college coach, at their first meeting, 'I want to be a millionaire and I don't ever want a real job.' I can identify with that, by the way. The trouble is, only one of them came true for me.

Overcoming adversity? Five weeks before the Barcelona Olympics he ran an abysmal 100 metres in the Olympic trials and finished fourth in the 200 metres final. It was the end of his Olympic track career, or so they thought, but following his third successive gold in the Olympic long jump in 1992, the US four by 100 metres relay team had a crisis. The American sprinter Mark Witherspoon had suffered a severely pulled tendon in the back of his foot. Carl joined the relay team of Mike Marsh, Leroy Burrell and Dennis Mitchell. Result: 'Record del mundo' flashed on the Olympic screen. The US won gold in a new world record time of 37.40 seconds. Carl ran the anchor leg.

Obsession? His quest to match Jesse Owens's record and win four gold medals in one Olympics was satisfied at the first attempt in Los Angeles 1984.

Competitiveness? I would say you'd have to be pretty competitive to spend twelve years winning gold at the Olympics.

Teamwork? It is significant that Carl had one coach, Tom Tellez of the University of Houston, throughout his entire career.

Luck? See Witherspoon's tendon (above).

Star quality? There have been few more successful, controversial, highly visible characters in the history of track and field. To win nine gold medals in four successive Olympics is unprecedented in the world of athletics. However, like my bronze in Seoul, everyone forgets the other one. He also won silver in 1988, losing out to his training partner Joe DeLoach by four one hundredths of a second in the 200 metres.

Perseverance? It's so unglamorous, persistence, so lacking in X-factor. Instead it implies a dogged refusal to give up, a stubborn relentlessness that supersedes all other qualities. But Carl had it in bucket loads.

I have to admit, Carl was not a universally popular figure. He was occasionally considered cold, aloof and arrogant. It is also true that subsequent exposures revealed a purported cover-up over allegations of inadvertent drug use. Both Lewis and DeLoach had been cleared to compete just before Seoul, having tested positive for low levels of three banned stimulants. The United States Olympic Committee accepted their claim of inadvertent use in over-the-counter cold remedies. The positive tests were not made public knowledge until 2003. Perhaps the time lapse of fifteen years owed something to the immensity of Lewis's reputation – not popularity but reputation.

However, he did earn respect for his behaviour at the Seoul Olympics in 1988. Lewis's father, Bill, had died in 1987. Not long before, in a symbolic act, his son had placed his LA Olympics 100 metres gold medal in his father's hands. 'I want you to have this, because it was your favourite event,' he is reputed to have explained. When his mother expressed her surprise, he added, 'Don't worry I'll get another one.'

The following year, Johnson denied him his wish. 'I didn't have the medal to replace the one I had given [my father] and that hurt,' said Lewis, 'but I could still give something to my father by acting the way he had always wanted me to act, with class and dignity.' He shook Johnson's hand and then walked away, ignoring the barracking of a group of Canadian fans. He wasn't to know he would soon be receiving that gold medal.

If I'm absolutely honest I had mixed feelings in Atlanta, watching him go for his fourth consecutive victory in the long jump. Going, in other words, to match my record, since I'd just won my fourth gold on the rowing lake with Matt. What was Carl Lewis even doing as an athlete in Atlanta? After Barcelona, everyone assumed his Hollywood acting career would now take precedence, but it didn't happen. He was thirty-five now, positively creaking with old age in sprint terms, but summoning a great effort he had qualified for Atlanta in the long jump in the US trials, coming third, ahead of Mike Conley by just one inch, but significantly behind Mike Powell, who had won thirty-four straight long jump competitions after the Barcelona Olympics.

Lewis, the three-times defending Olympic long jump champion would be there in Atlanta, but it was largely expected to be an honorary role. He would arrive, take the applause, then leave the stage to a younger, further, faster field. It was twelve years since Los Angeles or as Lewis preferred to call it, 'fourteen hairstyles later'. But resilient champions seldom conform to scripts. Inspired perhaps by the home crowd, usefully aided by one of the favourites, Cuba's Ivan Pedroso, suffering a hamstring tear, and thoroughly roused by the intensity of the competition, he moved through the field.

After two of the three qualifying rounds, he was in fifteenth place, with only the top twelve going through to the final. He had one jump to save his Olympian dream. I wonder if his thoughts mirrored mine whenever I felt under particular duress. It's the dialogue of the champion. The one that reminds you it's been done before. 'I can do this. I have done this before. I know this gold medal is within my capability. Someone has to win it. Why shouldn't it be me?'

He flew down the runway, leaped and landed 8.39 metres away from his take-off point, not merely qualifying but doing so in first place. You can just imagine the eyes, the microphones, the cameras, the flash bulbs suddenly turning his way as one. Hollywood could wait.

There I was with Ann, watching all this unfold. Emmanuel Bangue of France took an early lead in the final. Powell was second. Lewis ran through his first try and fell short in his second. It was now his third jump. Inspired by the limelight, driven by a champion's need to reassert himself and spurred on by the support of 82,000 spectators, he tore through the air to make a huge leap of 8.5 metres. His rivals submitted. Powell strained a groin muscle in pursuit of the distance and in attempting one last assault on the leader finished face down in the sand.

How did I feel sitting there watching all this? Actually, I was pleased for him. I know what it takes and if you've got it, you deserve it. It is a pretty good effort – four straight Olympic golds in the same (in my case, nearly the same) event. It takes some doing. It reminds me of something a rival once said of Al Oerter, the American discus thrower who won four Olympic golds from Melbourne in 1956 to Mexico in 1968. It was after that final Mexican gold, but when no one could entirely believe the legend was leaving the stage. 'If Al turns up in four years time in his coffin,' said the East German, 'it might be close.' Now that is star quality, as well as serious perseverance.

That is pretty much how America viewed Carl, too, in Atlanta. 'Lewis beat age, gravity, history, logic and the world at a rocking Olympic Stadium in Atlanta to win the Olympic gold medal in the long jump,' wrote a correspondent of *Sports Illustrated*. 'It was quite possibly his most impossible moment in an impossibly brilliant career.'

Before leaving the scene of his triumph, Carl remembered to bend down and scoop a few grains from the sandpit into a bag, in remembrance of the impossible dream. Martina Navratilova did the same at Wimbledon once, picking a few tufts of grass and storing them as a keepsake following her ninth and last singles title. Needless to say, there is no record of me collecting a little vial of Sydney lake water when I won my fifth gold medal. I was too busy trying to breathe.

Pete Sampras

Pete Sampras was supposed to be 'boring'. No wonder I like him. What public opinion really meant by this was, first, he kept winning Wimbledon, which seriously annoyed British fans of Tim Henman and, second, he didn't shout, scream, swear, reduce rackets to splinters of hypercarbon or, like Andre Agassi, wear nail varnish. He was a straightforward, clean-living, fame-scorning athlete whose tennis game, particularly on grass, was smoothly irresistible.

Yet it didn't seem to matter that he won fourteen Grand Slams, a record which stood until Roger Federer surpassed it at Wimbledon in 2009. It didn't seem to impress that he became Wimbledon champion seven times in eight years, from 1993 to 2000, defeating in the finals a long cast list of much more charismatic characters – Courier, Ivanisevic, Becker, Pioline, Ivanisevic again, Agassi and Rafter.

He never deviated from his own quiet way. 'There are some players who add a bit to get more PR. I wasn't about that. My major goal was to hold up that trophy at the end and I didn't want anything to get in the way of that. I kept it pretty quiet. I kept it simple.' The more I know about him, the more I like him.

If Agassi arrived in the sport like a cannonball, with his paint-splashed clothes and long frosted hair, Sampras was the antithesis, with his short-back-and-sides. It was a slower introduction. By the time we had come to appreciate his whiplash serve and ruthless dispatch at the net, he was already holding a fistful of championships. In his prime, opponents weren't opponents, they were prey.

It was a curious quirk of history that three great American tennis players arrived on the scene simultaneously, all roughly the same age, but vastly different in temperament. Sampras was one. Jim Courier, who won four majors in three years with a brutal baseline game, another. And Agassi, who played for twenty years, won eight major titles and married Steffi Graf to ensure the line of good tennis players coming out of Vegas continued. Talk about perseverance!

In their contrasting ways they were all primed for stardom, but Sampras began the gold rush. He won his first major, the US Open title, when he was nineteen in 1990 and, curiously enough, told the world's press the 'monkey is off my back'. Rather than feeling elation, he felt relief. Chronologically, he was a follower of the successes of John McEnroe and Jimmy Connors. Temperamentally, he could hardly have been more different.

For a couple of years, Sampras was overhauled by his rivals. Courier was an unstoppable beast, especially on clay, where his warring, aggressive, relentless battling simply wore his opponents down. Unfortunately, in the long run, it seemed to have had the same effect on Courier. By 1994 it was over. He was reading books at change-overs and would never win another major again. He finally retired in 2000.

Agassi, meanwhile, was a player of infinite variety, who would win majors on every surface, and his lone victory at Wimbledon in 1992, over the storm-serving Goran Ivanisevic, propelled him from brat to beloved as far as the London audience were concerned.

Sampras could not have presented a greater contrast. His grass game improved to the point of impregnability, but his character remained unmoved. He persevered with himself, in a sense. He certainly persevered with Wimbledon. I believe to win those seven men's singles titles in eight years was an act of almost impossible dominance.

The only anomaly was 1996, when he was beaten in the quarter-finals by Richard Krajicek. Something was inspiring the towering Dutchman that year, as he went on to win the tournament, beating MaliVai Washington in a final remarkable for the interruption of a female streaker in a waitressing pinny. Incidentally, for whatever reason, rowing has never attracted a streaker as far as I know. I'm told that certain ladies on motor launches at Henley sometimes display their wares, but I've been too busy rowing to pay any attention.

Only once did Sampras slip out of character at his 'second home', as he called Wimbledon, and that was after his last victory there in 2000. He still didn't rave or scream, but he did, at last, let his emotions overwhelm his tendency towards undemonstrative control. Having lost the first set to Patrick Rafter of Australia and been thoroughly inconvenienced by typical London summer weather (rain), he prevailed in four sets, won his thirteenth grand slam and, at the moment of victory, in the gathering dusk, he bent over, put his hands to his eyes and cried.

He then embraced his tearful father and mother in the crowd. It was the first time they had ever seen him play at Wimbledon, which tells you much about the non-extrovert nature of the entire Sampras clan. Many tennis players travelled with an entourage, including the memorable occasion when Agassi arrived in London with Barbra Streisand in tow.

The following year, ominously, Sampras lost in the fourth round to a nineteen-year-old Swiss lad in five sets. He read the signs correctly. Roger Federer would go on to surpass his record of major titles and install himself as one of the greatest players in tennis history. A year later, Sampras retired. Gloriously. He won the US Open one last time. He was thirty-one.

What interests me is what happened next. He played golf. He played the infuriating game so well, his handicap came down to two at the Bel-Air Country Club. He didn't bother to play tennis, watch tennis or follow tennis. He became a father of two little boys. He had a house built in a secluded spot in Southern California. 'I like my privacy,' he said. 'I don't want any neighbours to see me and I don't want to see any neighbours.' He didn't have to exploit his image, fortunately. He had won $43 million in prize money alone, so he could relax. Except he couldn't.

'After two and a half years it starts wearing thin. You're playing golf every day. You've put on some weight. You wake up in the morning and you feel unfulfilled. I talked to my wife about it. She could see I was restless. I said to her, "I just feel a little bit empty. I need more than this."

'I thought, "This is what people do when they are sixty. I'm thirty-three! Can I spend the next twenty-five years doing this?" It's tricky. The life I had was so focussed and scheduled and disciplined . . . and then, cold turkey, you're done. At first you like it, but after a while you feel restless. "What's next with my life? What am I going to do next?" That's hard. I can understand why athletes come back. It was very clear to me. Some miss the limelight, but for me it was the focus. I miss having a schedule, I miss being in shape.'

Oh, I hear him, but surely, surely, I wouldn't have been so stupid as to want to mount a comeback. Would I?

*

It was an accident waiting to happen. You retire. You're not bored. You don't miss it. The relief of not training every day in all weathers is intense. Then something triggers a set of thought processes that are borderline insane – only you don't know it at the time. I know where it began. I can pinpoint the exact moment. I was standing in my bathroom on the morning of the first World Cup event of the season in Milan, where the World Championships would be taking place later in the summer of 2003. Matt and James would be racing in the coxless pair. I was rehearsing in the mirror what I would tell the BBC later that day about my expectations of the race.

'Matt and James smashed the world record last year. They're faster than any other pair on the water. I can't see them being beaten from now until they win the Olympics in Athens.' That's what I thought. That's what I was going to tell Steve Rider.

By a quirk of TV scheduling, by the time I was in front of the microphone with Steve, ready to do my bit, the result was already known. We were pretending this was a pre-race conversation, but in fact the race had already taken place. 'Well, Steve, how do you think it will go?' asked Steve Rider, and since Matt and James had been beaten into third place by the Croatians and the Italians – a horrendous result by their own and British standards – he was obviously expecting me to say . . . 'Oh, I think it could be a tough race for them today . . .'

Here is the thing about being utterly obstinate. I didn't think it was right to retract my real opinion. I didn't want to be a smug git and hedge my bets just because I knew the result. If I believed Matt and James would win when I talked to my bathroom mirror that morning, it was proper that I should say so now. I said so, finishing with my classic – and now entirely disproved – statement: 'I can't see them being beaten from now until they win the gold medal in Athens.' Steve Rider's face was a picture. He widened his eyes – because he knew I knew the result – and said with a ghost of a smile, 'That's a bold statement, Steve.'

After that first disappointment, Matt and James seemed to get their season back on track by winning the next World Cup race and so I was optimistic that the first Milan result was a blip. Soon enough the World Championships came round and I confidently expected to be right in my initial prediction.

Steve Rider and myself were in Milan at the rowing venue, hosting *Grandstand Live*. We all knew it was going to be a tough race between the powerful Australian pair and our guys, but what happened was absolutely stunning – and not in a good way. The Australians took an early lead and dominated the race to win gold. Matt and James were not even second. They were not even third. Instead, they trailed in fourth. It was the first time in his career that Matt had not finished on the podium of a World Championship or Olympic event. It was that much of a seismic shock.

Our presenting position was well away from the boating area, and because Matt and James did not win a medal we didn't have a chance to interview them straightaway. It was only after they had packed up their boat that they came over to speak to us. James arrived first. I only had a couple of private seconds with him before the cameras rolled, but the first thing he said to me – less than thirty minutes from the race finishing – was that they were going to quit the pair and do a four next year instead. I couldn't believe my ears.

I knew by now that James, in particular, didn't think he could row in a pair any more. He had decided that almost before they came off the water in Milan. He was consumed by the belief that he could not row on bowside (he'd switched from stroke since Sydney) and therefore the pair could not continue. I thought he was wrong. I still think he was wrong. I'd switched from stroke to bow in my career. It's do-able and, once something's do-able, you do it. Matt, I knew, would just go with the flow. If James was deeply unhappy, then he wouldn't put up any strong arguments.

'Hmmmm, I could get in that new Olympic four,' I thought to myself. 'And if I can't get in that I might get in a pair. And if I can't get in that I might get in the eight. They're reigning Olympic champions after all. Surely, even after a three year lay-off I'm in the top fourteen of male British rowing athletes?'

So that is where it began. I found myself with a head-full of 'What ifs . . .' What if there is a newly constructed pair? What if they need some extra bodies in the boat? What if there's a seat in another Olympic boat? What if I root out my old Lycra shorts? And so forth. All retired athletes are like Horatio Nelson. They hold the telescope up to the wrong eye. I still saw myself as the athlete I once was, not the slightly tubbier, more mellow, less fit, more Jammy Dodgers-addicted human I'd become.

Mildly delusional, I was convincing myself it would be possible, training for the Olympics for just twelve intense months, instead of the long, hard four-year slog. I neglected to consider that it was only because of the long, hard, four-year slog that five gold medals were nestling in a drawer somewhere.

There was only one thing to do about my imaginary comeback. I phoned Jurgen and asked him to come round to the house for a chat. He thought I wanted to give him the benefit of my opinion about James and Matt, so he came over, we sat in the dining room and I said, 'I'm thinking about making a comeback.' He almost fell off his chair. He was stunned, but he was a good enough man, friend and coach to say he would give it some thought. I told him it was totally his decision, but if he thought it was right I'd be willing to give it a go.

A couple of days later we were both at the Leander Club for

some function or other. We didn't speak to each other, but he caught my eye and he just gently shook his head.

I have been retired for nearly ten years now. I was really looking forward to stopping so that I could escape the boring routine of training. Now what do I miss most? Routine. I do appreciate the irony.

In my new life, post-Sydney, post-athlete, post-active Olympian, every day is different. I can be in London at a business meeting, half way down a mountain on a skiing holiday, at a conference as a speaker, on a pontoon reporting for the BBC, in a crowd watching Natalie play netball, on a golf course willing the ball to fly straight, in the kitchen at home wondering who's eaten all the biscuits ... No day is ever the same.

I thought I would love this new life. No schedule, no pressure, no pain. But there's not much passion or desire or many challenges either. I hate to say it, but everything feels like a hobby. It is now that I find one particular quality is needed most. Retirement takes a lot of perseverance when your whole adult life has revolved around competition.

I think I can see myself coaching one day. That would give me a new challenge – trying to help other people – and an outlet for all those attributes that helped me to achieve in my career: preparation, belief, a sense of teamwork, competitiveness – these never truly disappear in the mind of an athlete. Ask any of the people I've written about in this book. But then I'm held up by the thought that I spent nearly twenty-five years flogging mind and body in a rowing boat for little or no money. Do I really want to work six or seven days a week at that intensity again?

Sometimes I wish I'd been a golfer instead. Look at Tom Watson, still with a passion for the game, still able to play at the highest level amongst men thirty or even forty years younger than himself. Rowing isn't like that. The physicality involved makes it a young person's sport. In 2007, I agreed to row in a veterans' race at Henley. The chap organising it said airily, 'Oh, we'll have a handful of practice sessions before hand.' I was aghast. 'I can't do that,' I said. 'I'll need at least ten sessions to get anywhere near to some sort of fitness.' It took me three outings to stop my hips seizing up. We did, however, win on the day.

The following year when I rowed in a veteran's eight I could feel the old competitiveness creeping back. I was starting to get annoyed with my team-mates for not taking it seriously enough. It was crazy of me. I resolved to stop. Then I broke my foot at the European Tour Pro-Am event at the London Golf Club in the spring of 2009 and the decision was made for me. Strictly speaking I should have been appalled at such a stupid accident – I just slipped over when walking back to the car. In fact, I was still in a pretty good mood – I had won the prize for the longest drive.

So where am I these days? Pretty contented. I was sitting in my garden the other day, with Ann and the kids around, enjoying the sunshine and the relaxation, thinking, 'Isn't this nice.' But I do wish my health was better. I don't sleep particularly well with all the beeping and entanglements of my diabetic equipment. My colitis is still there but rarely flares up. I could lose a few pounds.

But if you were to ask me if I'd do it all over again, with all the good and bad that came with it, the answer is, 'Yes, I would.' Ask me if I would do it again, even if the results weren't guaranteed, the answer is still yes. 'Yes, I think so.'

It was a privilege. It was a quest. It was a challenge. And I've always been inspired by a challenge.

INDEX

Note: 'SR' denotes Steve Redgrave.

disease *see* illness and disease
Dixon, Robin (*later* Lord Glentoran) 205–11
drugs, performance-enhancing 145–50,
    265, 286
Dunwoody, Richard 112, 117, 118–19

East Germany 149–50, 162, 179–80
Eaux Les Coeurs (horse) 216
Edwards, Eddie 'the Eagle' 155–6
Edwards, Jonathan 253
Elizabeth II, Queen 242
Emery, Victor 210–11
Emsley Carr Mile 217–18
England (cricket team) 257, 259–62
England (rugby team) 125–8
'Eric the Eel' (Eric Moussambani) 156–8
European Cup (football) 64–5

Family Business (horse) 215–16
Federer, Roger 290, 293
Ferguson, Sir Alex 116–17
Fish, Calvin 251
Fittipaldi, Emerson 250
Five Gold (horse) 111
Flack, Edwin 235–6
Flood, Debbie 278
Flood, Toby 94
Fogle, Ben 119
football
    Beckham, David 252–4
    Charlton, Sir Bobby 218–22, 225
    Clough, Brian 62–7
Foreman, George 49–51
form, loss of 98–100, 285
Fosbury, Dick 25–7
'Fosbury flop' 25–7
Foster, Mark 131
Foster, Tim 96, 118
    Atlanta Olympics 161, 169
    character and qualities 164, 168–9,
        170–71, 175, 183
    injuries 171, 181
    jokes and banter 177–8
    Sydney Olympics 160–61, 168–70
    training 10–16, 73
Fraser, Donna 60
Frazier, Joe 49, 50, 130
Frédy, Pierre de *see* Coubertin
Freeman, Cathy 55–62

Gallen, Ian 197, 199–200, 202–3

gamesmanship 41–3, 69, 136
Gatting, Mike 261
GDR (German Democratic Republic)
    149–50, 162, 179–80
German Democratic Republic (GDR)
    149–50, 162, 179–80
Glentoran, Lord *see* Dixon, Robin
Glickman, Marty 241
goals 17–19, 53–4, 99, 124, 189
golf
    Nicklaus, Jack 152–3
    Pinsent, Matthew 20–21, 154, 177–8
    Redgrave, Sir Steve 20–21, 24, 154,
        177–8
    Ryder Cup 152–4
    Woods, Tiger 4, 20–25
Gooch, Graham 261
Gorno, Reinaldo 143
Graf, Steffi 291
Grainger, Katherine 6, 277–84
Gray, Eddie 62–3
Great Marlow School 266–9, 274
Grey-Thompson, Carys 135
Grey-Thompson, Tanni 134–9, 253
Grobler, Jurgen 3, 63, 174
    Barcelona Olympics 43–5, 76
    character and qualities 44–5, 115, 160,
        167, 176, 180
    and East German doping regime 149–50,
        162
    move to Great Britain 162–3, 179–80
    Olympic gold medals 162
    and SR's illnesses 76, 115, 167, 180–81,
        183–4
    and SR's possible comeback 297
    Sydney Olympics 161–2, 183–4
    on team members 180–84
    training 10–16, 75
Guderza, Tatiana 122

Hamilton, Anthony 34–7
Hamilton, Lewis 31–7
Hamilton, Linda 35
Hamilton, Nicholas 35
Hammond, Richard 31
Hampson, Anne 91–2
Hampson, Matt 90–95
Hancock, Tony 270
Haskell, James 94
Hatton, Ricky 113
Hayley, Joan 270

PICTURE CREDITS

Credits are listed according to the order the pictures appear on each page, left to right, top to bottom. 'SSR' denotes photographs that are courtesy of Sir Steve Redgrave.

Section 1

Page 1: SSR, SSR, SSR; Page 2: SSR, Colorsport, Colorsport; Page 3: SSR, Offside, Action Images; Page 4: Getty Images, Getty Images, Mirrorpix; Page 5: Topfoto, Colorsport, Colorsport; Page 6: Getty Images, PA Images, Colorsport; Page 7: Corbis, PA Images, Colorsport, Colorsport; Page 8: SSR, SSR, Topfoto.

Section 2

Page 1: PA Images, Getty Images, PA Images, PA Images; Page 2: PA Images, Getty Images, Colorsport, Colorsport; Page 3: PA Images, PA Images, Richard Stanton, PA Images; Page 4: Colorsport, Colorsport, PA Images; Page 5: PA Images, PA Images, PA Images, PA Images; Page 6: PA Images, PA Images, PA Images; Page 7: PA Images, PA Images, Colorsport, Colorsport, Getty Images; Page 8: Colorsport, Colorsport, Colorsport.